Patriarchy and Gender in Africa

Patriarchy and Gender in Africa

Edited by
Veronica Fynn Bruey

LEXINGTON BOOKS
Lanham • Boulder • New York • London

Published by Lexington Books
An imprint of The Rowman & Littlefield Publishing Group, Inc.
4501 Forbes Boulevard, Suite 200, Lanham, Maryland 20706
www.rowman.com

6 Tinworth Street, London SE11 5AL, United Kingdom

British Library Cataloguing in Publication Information Available

Library of Congress Cataloging-in-Publication Data

Library of Congress Control Number: 2021931413

ISBN 978-1-7936-3856-4 (cloth)
ISBN 978-1-7936-3858-8 (pbk)
ISBN 978-1-7936-3857-1 (electronic)

Contents

Acknowledgments

There are so many memories of my childhood where gender stereotypes were shattered. As a single parent, my mother was everything. Mama was the boss of our home. She took on the fatherly role and responsibility. She extended her caregiving role by fostering many homeless children and other family members. My deepest admiration for Mama's house was her penchant for equality and justice. There were no boys or girls chores in Mama's house. Everyone learned how to cook, clean, wash, fetch water, and manage the family business. The only reason to be excused from doing chores was if you had to do schoolwork. Guess who got away with not cooking? I hated it. Well, fast forward to the period I survived the civil war in Liberia (1989–1992) and later, my experience with the outside world has been anything but fairness and equality. Although I suffered male violence and abuse, I also defied it. This book is clear evidence of my continuous struggle for gender justice.

This book would not be possible but for many special individuals in my life, some of whom I may inadvertently omit to mention. First and foremost, thank you Mama for giving birth to me and instilling values that have shaped me into what I am today. Professors George Kieh and Samuel Zalanga, thank you for coming up with the book title and granting me the opportunity to run with it. Trevor F. Cowell, Joseph Parry, and Shelby Russell, your professionalism and on-going support at Lexington Books is unparalleled. Also, thanks to the copyediting team at Deanta Global and Jayanthi Chander for her excellent project management and communication skills in dealing with the production of the book. Thank you all for guiding me gradually through the conception of the idea to the final release of this book. To my fellow authors, you rock! We have been on this journey for two years. Whether it was me changing jobs or COVID-19, through thick and thin, you threaded the paths with me. I cannot thank you enough for trusting me to be your leader.

Finally, there are two very important males in my life who give me hope to believe the possibility of gender equality. They are the reason I wake each day with optimism and a reason to live. First to my husband, Douglas Christopher Bruey, you are the best man I have ever known. Thank you for accepting me for who I am, believing in my ability to control my destiny, and trusting that we are in this fight for gender justice together. To our Petit Prince, there is no limit to the joy in my bosom knowing that I am raising a feminist in you. You will always be my pride, joy, and honor.

Introduction

Veronica Fynn Bruey

OVERVIEW

The primacy of patriarchy and discrimination against women in Africa requires a comprehensive and holistic approach that meticulously examines why girls and women struggle to rise above entrenched misogyny and how they can flip their socio-economic status and leadership role in society. *Patriarchy and Gender in Africa* is long overdue, considering the autocratic and violent rogue regime of governance of men in the public and private sectors within and across nations of Africa for centuries. Even in the modern colonial and post-colonial eras, both White men and Black men have controlled the masses in Africa without including women in leadership.

Patriarchy and Gender in Africa comes on the heels of increasing global awareness about gender inequality with the #MeToo movement and anti-racist explosion of Black Lives Matter across the globe. The #MeToo movement has seen several high-profile prosecutions of sexual abuse, harassment, and bullying perpetrated against women in the workplace, in big corporate bodies, in public institutions, and in the academy. The Black Lives Matter movement has expanded beyond police brutality in the United States, moving toward diverse expressions of collective lament regarding institutional racism, colonial violence, White supremacy, and male dominance against Indigenous lands, Black women, migrants from the Global South, and LGBTQI communities. Whether these historical events in the Global North will translate to any amount of change in Africa is yet to be assessed. Notwithstanding, patriarchy and its effect on gender roles persists, and therefore it is uniquely contextualized and examined here.

It is no secret that men hold dominant leadership roles at a disproportionate rate or that they exert power and wield control over women in diverse forms of social systems and institutions globally. Patriarchy or androcentrism, the supremacy of fatherhood whereby women, children, and other men rely totally on the rule of the father, is entrenched in many societies, cultures, systems, and institutions around the world. There are few significant exceptions to this dynamic, and they are not seen in Africa. In every facet of the continent, male dominance is fierce, violent, aggressive, and unrelenting. Interspersed within this colossal fortress of patriarchy in Africa is the injection of equal but opposite resistance by women. Recognizing the leadership trails African women have blazed for centuries is a testament to the timely arrival of *Patriarchy and Gender in Africa*.

Before we highlight the matriarchs of Africa, let us consider the following. In 2005, Liberia's Ellen Johnson Sirleaf was the first female president to be democratically elected on the continent of Africa (Fynn Bruey 2018, 1–4). Despite a gradual increase in women's participation (Coulter, Persson, and Utas 2008, 8–16), war and conflict have mostly remained the domain of men in Africa (Stapleton 2018; Fynn 2011, 33, 192; Haas, Schäfer, and Scholte 2009, 1–12). Between 1955 and 2014, 40 percent of all political instability globally took place in Africa (Williams 2016, 17). War and conflict are only one aspect of the myriad forms of violence girls and women face on the continent.

Apart from being the "spoils of war," African girls and women experience relatively higher levels of domestic, sexual, physical, and intimate partner violence than do their male counterparts (Fynn Bruey 2016, 12). For example, ~1.69.1.80 million women in the Democratic Republic of Congo, ages 15–49, reported being raped in their lifetime, while 3.07–3.36 million have experienced intimate partner abuse—the rates are significantly higher for all types of sexual violence in Sud-Kivu and Nord-Kivu (Peterman, Palermo, and Bredenkamp 2011, 1060, 1063). An estimated 76 percent of girls in Niger are forced into marriage before they turn 18 and 28 percent before they are 15 years old (Smaak and Odhiambo 2015, 2).

The correlation between child marriage, female genital cutting (FGC), and polygyny (a type of polygamy) is undeniable, as girls as young as two years old are deemed pure and ready for marriage by twelve years (Moody 2020, 1). Somalia has the highest number of FGC cases in Africa: 98 percent of girls are subjected to door-to-door performance of the practice even amid the COVID-19 pandemic (Kuma and Wambui 2020). Polygamy is generally accepted or formally legalized in thirty-three countries around the world, twenty-five of which are in Africa (Muhumuza 2018; Olasore 2016, 7; Department of Economic and Social Affairs 2011, 4; BBC News 2014).

African leaders, including Jomo Kenyatta of Kenya, Idi Amin of Uganda, Jean-Bedel Bokassa of the Central African Republic, Mobuto Sese Seko of DRC, Gnassingbe Eyadema of Togo, Jacob Zuma of South Africa, and

Omar Hassan al-Bashir of Sudan, have all blatantly displayed the polygynous status of their countries (Onyango-Obbo 2010). Flaunting the legalizing of polygyny is one thing and its impact on an African girl or woman is another (Yerges et al. 2017; Olasore 2016, 9). When Irene Atenyo, a fruit vendor, confronted her husband about taking a third wife, he beat her "like an animal"; he was able to do so with impunity, because judges in Uganda refused a petition to declare polygamy unconstitutional (Muhumuza 2018; Ugandan Radio Network 2018).

In addition to suffering from domestic violence, Atenyo has low educational and unemployment status, compounded by her reasonable fear of having to raise her children on her own and of having pregnant teenage daughters, all of which will contribute to diminished health (Arthi and Fenske 2018; Institute of Development Studies 2016, 38). In a research study in Ghana, a male respondent said, "I think that since women are not regarded in the society, that's why they're not allowed to make decisions; we count them as part of our cooking utensils and other things" (Sikweyiya et al. 2020, 5). Another expressed the belief that "[a]s Christ is the head of the church, so is a man to the house" (Sikweyiya et al. 2020, 5). There is no convincing evidence whatsoever to prove that men's incessant desire for power, control, and abuse of women is ordained by God, given that the religious book by which this Supreme Being is established was written by men.

A number of conceptual frameworks are used to rationalize men's gravitation toward power and control over women. Yet the persistence of patriarchy and gender inequality remains perplexing. Three notions help to explain this persistence. They are (1) the perception of acceptable/inclusive/healthy masculinity, which refers to allowable doses of male behavior that are internalized, maintained, and acquiesced to, by all, especially women (Ward 2018; Talbot and Quayle 2010; McCormack and Anderson 2010); (2) benevolent sexism/feminism—the belief of those, mainly women, who hold "'positive' views of women but they do so as part of a broader worldview that obligates men to protect 'traditional' women" (Radke et al. 2018, 158); and (3) patriarchal women: females who gradually process, embody, nurture, display, and value masculinity while at the same time denigrating all things feminine (Jackson 2010; DellaRovere 2018).

A combination of these three ideas is overtly or covertly exemplified in the herstories offered below.

HERSTORY: RESPECTING OUR TRAILBLAZERS

Indeed, male efforts to keep women from realizing their full potential persist—but certainly not without resistance and resilience. For instance, despite having the third-largest gender gap (an average of 33.7%) among the eight regions of the world in 2018 (World Economic Forum 2018, 26), African women make up approximately 65–70 percent of the agriculture labor force, producing 80 percent of the continent's food (Global Fund For Women 2015; African Development Bank 2015, 11). They own a third of all businesses across Africa, yet only 15 percent of African women are managing directors in the formal employment industry (African Development Bank 2015, 11).

The recognition and contribution of African women to gender equality, whether as a collective socio-political movement or a single act of courage, is crucial (Kent Law School 2019). Now is a unique opportunity to at least acknowledge, celebrate, and document some African women herstory as all the authors in this book are united in one front. That is, African women have not only resisted male oppression in the centuries past but have continued to do so, demonstrating stellar leadership characterized by equality, justice, and fairness. Nefertiti, one of the most powerful women of ancient Egypt, ruled alongside Pharaoh Akhenaten (1353–1336 BC). She is best known for her painted sandstone bust, rediscovered in 1913, and is a global icon of feminine beauty and power (Editors 2019a). Queen Cleopatra of Egypt (c 69–31 BC), well educated, clever, and multilingual, ruled ancient Egypt for 30 years with her father, brother, and son. Her liaisons with Roman leaders earned her a lasting recognition in history (Editors 2019b).

Kandake Amanirenas (?–10 BC), a queen mother of the Meroitic Kingdom of Kush (Sudan), led her troops in the sacking of the Roman fort in Aswan, Egypt, and destroyed the statues of Augustus Caesar in Elephantine in 24 BC (Fikes 2019). Makeda (Ethiopia), Queen of Sheba (c 10 BC), famous for her biblical encounter with King Solomon of Israel, defeated the serpent king and became the queen of Axum (Matshego 2019). Queen Amina of Zaria (1533–1610), the first woman to become a Sarauniya (queen) in a male-dominated society, expanded the territory of the Hausa people of north Africa, accumulating great wealth and military accolades (African Feminist Forum 2016). Queen Nzinga Mbande (c. 1583–1663) of the Ndongo and Matamba Kingdoms (Angola) fought for the freedom of her kingdoms against the Portuguese colonizers (SABC News 2020; Editors 2020a).

Dahomey Amazons, Ahosi (King's wives), or Mino (our mothers) (c 1700–1900), the all-female military regiment of the Fon People of Dahomey (Benin), fought in 1889 against the French, who are already taken hold of Porto-Novo (Dash 2011). Queen Nandi of the Zulu Kingdom (c 1760–1827), the mother of Shaka Zulu—one of the greatest kings of Africa—was instrumental in shaping her son's heroic acts and hence the entire Zulu kingdom (SABC News 2018). Queen Ranavalona the First of Madagascar (c 1778–1861), characterized as a bloodthirsty despot or an anti-imperialist heroine, is known for prosecuting Christians in Malagasy, depriving Europeans of trading privileges, and expelling all Europeans from Madagascar (Editors 2020b). Yaa Asanteewa (c 1840–1921), the fearless and brave queen of the Ashanti Kingdom (Ghana), led her army to fight against British invasion. She said to the disheartened men, "If you, the men of Ashanti will not go forward, then we will . . . I shall call upon my fellow women . . . . We will fight till the last of us falls in the battlefields" (BBC News Africa 2018). Nyabingi Muhumusa, who died in 1945 and was the first priestess and military leader of Uganda, resisted patriarchal and colonial domination in East Africa in her fight for social justice (Sandner 2018).

The end of World War II was monumental for Africans, given that they had also endured slavery, violent colonization, and ruthless imperialism, in addition to the effects of the two world wars. On October 15–20, 1945, the Fifth Pan-African Congress (5PAC) was held in Manchester, United Kingdom. At that time, Ethiopia, Liberia, and Haiti were the only independent Black countries in the world. With the decisions made at this monumental turning point, the 5PAC began the long road of helping African countries to achieve independence (Sherwood 2013)—an ongoing process, as the Sahrawi Arab Democratic Republic is still helmed by Morocco (V. Fynn 2011). Although the actions of the 5PAC and of the previous four African Congresses eventually resulted in the decolonization of Africa, the continent "retained the patriarchal ethos of Black elite men" (Farmer 2016). It was not until 1974, when the Sixth Pan-African Congress (6PAC) was held in Tanzania, that Black women's interests started to be put front and center.

Since 1974, many African women in the twentieth-century post-colonial era of Africa have championed varying strains of African feminist thinking. Following is a list of African feminists working across a broad spectrum of theoretical concepts (e.g., women's movement, matriarchy, womanism/motherism, Black African feminism, acceptable masculinity, and patriarchal woman) and temporal periods (colonial and post-colonial), who have blazed the trails of gender justice and equality, irrespective of their geopolitical locations. They are Charlotte Manye Maxeke (South African History Online 2020), Huda Shaa'rawi (Engel 2020), Funmilayo Ransome-Kuti (UNESCO 2020), Constance Agatha Cummings-John (Fyfe 2000), Bibi Titi Mohamed (Deutsche Welle 2020), Nawal El Saadawi (Almus 2020), Wangari Muta Maathai (Maathai 2020), Obioma G. Nnaemeka (Nnaemeka 2020), Catherine Obianjuju Acholonu (Acholonu 2020), Abena Busia (Busia 2020), Filomina Steady (Filomina Steady 2020), Oyeronke Oyewumi (Oyewumi 2020), Amina Mama (Mama 2017), Aisha Fofana Ibrahim ("Aisha Fofana Ibrahim" 2020), Akosua Adomako Ampofo (Adomako Ampofo 2020), and Sylvia Tamale (Tamale 2016). Still more have led or are leading the way.

The authors of *Patriarchy and Gender in Africa* stand on the shoulders of these giants in stepping forward to tackle complex contemporary issues of male dominance, discrimination, and inequality facing women on the continent today. The obstinacy of male chauvinism in Africa extends from the minutest unit of society (i.e., the family) and transcends the inter- and intra-hierarchical ethnic boundaries of the community, state, sub-regional, and continent-wide leadership structures. Thus, *Patriarchy and Gender in Africa* dissects pre-colonial, colonial, and post-independence issues related to male dominance, power, and control over the female body in the legal, socio-cultural, and political contexts. Particular focus is placed on the historical, theoretical, and empirical content analysis, case studies, and personal narratives of intersecting perspectives of gender and patriarchy in at least ten countries across the major sub-regions of the African continent.

In assessing the state, the institution, the community, and the role and impact of patriarchy and gender inequality on African girls and women, the book advances diverse interdisciplinary perspectives concerning:

- the roots and foundations of patriarchy and gender in different societies and cultures in Africa;
- the expressions of femininities and masculinities in religion and African traditional practices;
- power relations among, between, and within the sexes, with particular focus on traditional and non-traditional gender roles;
- issues of domestic, family, and personal violence at the structural, institutional, and community levels;
- issues of gender identities, gender politics, gender expressions, gender relations, and gender roles, along with the various social factors affecting patriarchy and discrimination against women;
- interconnections between patriarchy, gender inequality, and socio-economic outcomes in Africa;
- existing gaps and opportunities for policy, law, and social reform in gender justice; and
- empirical research data, case studies, and personal accounts concerning regional and sub-regional best practices and solutions in addressing patriarchy and gender inequality.

OVERVIEW OF VOLUME CONTENTS

This edited volume is divided into twelve chapters that intersect theories and conceptual frameworks with empirical research, advocacy, and stories of lived experiences across the continent. The contributors are nationals and residents of countries within and outside of the continent. They represent diverse disciplines of both African and Africanist views in gender/feminist studies, human rights, law/policy, economics, anthropology, history, political science, sociology, and theology. In the first chapter, "The Past Before Us: Reimagining Patriarchy and Gender in Africa," L. Amede Obiora examines the relationship between patriarchy and gender in Africa by zeroing in on Liberia to situate the case for engendering power, while revisiting salient analysis of patriarchy.

Johanna Bond argues in the second chapter that both the U.N. human rights treaty bodies and the African Commission are cautiously moving toward an embrace of intersectionality as an analytical framework for consideration of human rights violations in her chapter, "Intersectionality, Women's Rights in Africa and the Maputo Protocol." In chapter 3, "Building the Patriarchy Index for sub-Saharan Africa: Perceptions and Acceptance of Violence Matter Most," Verena Tandrayen-Ragoobur's research reveals that the most important elements within the patriarchal system in the region are perceptions and acceptance of wife or partner beating followed by physical, sexual, and emotional violence.

Chapter 4, "Patriarchy and Gender Challenges in Africa: Burdens of Wedlock Children in Cameroon," by Chick Loveline Ayoh Epse Ndi, explores gender discriminatory practices that arise from traditional roles that tend to assign more responsibilities to single mothers who are victims of wedlock pregnancies. In chapter 5, "Widow Inheritance in Northern Uganda: Patriarchy or Parenting," Charles Amone examines the cultural basis for the persistence of widow inheritance among the Acholi people of northern Uganda. In chapter 6, "Patriarchal and Traditional Gender Roles in Pre- and Post-Independent Eritrea: A Sociopolitical Analysis," Valentina Fusari and S. Venkatanarayanan dissect the changes in patriarchal values over a period from the starting of the armed liberation struggle in the 1960s until today in Eritrea.

In chapter 7, "Equal Spaces or Patriarchy? Examining Women's Participation in Tax Rule-making," Bernadette Malunga contends that public participation in tax rulemaking should be deconstructed from a gender perspective by interrogating issues that prevent marginalized groups, such as women, from participating fairly. Ellah T. M. Siang'andu, in chapter 8, "Zambia's Prison Laws and Allied Legislation: The Plight of Women Prisoners Accompanied with Children," argues that the failure of the prison laws to integrate gender perspectives of women who are incarcerated with children has resulted in a narrow and inadequate protection for these women. In chapter 9, "Challenging 'Super Patriarchy' in Artisanal and Small-Scale Mining Policies and Law in Zambia from an Ecofeminist Perspective," Fatima Mandhu draws on a desk-based review of the constitution and the relevant laws and policies to identify the gender gaps and assess the experience of women with respect to artisanal and small-scale mining.

In chapter 10, "Football Stadiums as Patriarchal Spaces: Experiences from Harare, Zimbabwe," Manase Kudzai Chiweshe shows that the stadium is a space in which specific forms of sexist and misogynistic behaviors are practiced in creating the stadium as a patriarchal space and that the patriarchal nature of the stadium ultimately impacts women's access negatively while often providing cover to various forms of symbolic and physical sexual violence. Chapter 11, "Mame Diarra: A Case Study of a Senegalese Female Saint and Sufi" by Cheikh Seye, examines sainthood and Sufism by investigating the spiritual life of Mame Diarra (1833–1866). In the twelfth and final chapter, Veronica Fynn Bruey narrates a personal account of a lived experience of gender and patriarchy in an African institution for the purpose of implanting her story into the long journey of the many forerunning African women who have weathered the storm of gender discrimination, misogyny, and male dominance in the African academy.

Patriarchy and Gender in Africa contributes to a deeper understanding of men's strong need to control and disempower African women and the possibility of re-thinking, re-imagining, and re-shifting thoughts and actions to center women within the discourse on institutional framework, political-legal power, economic development, educational advancement, and social justice. The well-researched chapters and international viewpoints offer hard-won impeccable knowledge to help identify misogyny, resist male supremacy, reform discriminatory laws, embrace human-centered public policies, promote best practices, harness research rigor, and expand academic scholarship, across the African continent and beyond.

REFERENCES

Acholonu, Catherine Obianuju. 2020. "Professor Catherine Obianuju Acholonu." University of California, Riverside. About the Faculty. November 24, 2020. http://www.faculty.ucr.edu/~legneref/igbo/aboutcatherine.htm.

Adomako Ampofo, Akosua. 2020. "Professor Akosua Adomako Ampofo | Institute of African Studies | University of Ghana." Academic. Institute of African Studies, University of Ghana. 2020. https://ias.ug.edu.gh/content/professor-akosua-ado mako-ampofo.

African Development Bank. 2015. "Empowering African Women: An Agenda for Action." Abidjan, La Cote d'Ivoire: Africa Development Bank Group.

African Feminist Forum. 2016. "Queen Amina of Zaria." Private Advocacy. *African Feminist Forum.* March 14, 2016. http://www.africanfeministforum.com/queen -amina-of-zaria-nigeria/.

"Aisha Fofana Ibrahim." 2020. Academic. Institute of African Studies, Carleton University. 2020. https://carleton.ca/africanstudies/people/aisha-fofana-ibrahim/.

Almus, Sude. 2020. "Nawal El Saadawi: An Egyptian Feminist." University. *The Muse* (blog). November 26, 2020. https://sites.duke.edu/dukemuse/nawal-el-saad awi-an-egyptian-feminist/.

Arthi, Vellore, and James Fenske. 2018. "Polygamy and Child Mortality: Historical and Modern Evidence from Nigeria's Igbo." *Review of Economics of the Household* 16 (1): 97–141. https://doi.org/10.1007/s11150-016-9353-x.

BBC News. 2014. "How Kenyans Are Reacting to Legalised Polygamy." *BBC News*, June 24, 2014, sec. Africa. https://www.bbc.com/news/world-africa-27 939037.

BBC News Africa. 2018. "Yaa Asantewaa, Ghana's Warrior Queen." *Video clip.* London, UK: British Broadcasting Corporation. https://www.youtube.com/watch? v=sLtvfeYGcxk.

Busia, Abena. 2020. "Busia, Abena." Academic. Department of Women's Gender, and Sexuality Studies. https://womens-studies.rutgers.edu/faculty/core-faculty /118-abena-busia.

Coulter, Chris, Mariam Persson, and Mats Utas. 2008. "Young Female Fighters in African Wars: Conflict and Its Consequences." Private. *NAI Policy Dialogue.* Stockholm, Sweden: Nordiska Afrikainstitutet.

Dash, Mike. 2011. "Dahomey's Women Warriors." *Smithsonian Magazine*, September 23, 2011. https://www.smithsonianmag.com/history/dahomeys-women -warriors-88286072/.

DellaRovere, Tiziana. 2018. "Patriarchy and the Patriarchal Woman." Personal Blog. *The Sacred Lovers Within* (blog). October 27, 2018. https://thesacredloverswithin. com/patriarchy-patriarchal-woman/.

Department of Economic and Social Affairs. 2011. "Population Facts: World Marriage Patterns." 2011/1. New York, NY: United Nations. https://www.un.org /en/development/desa/population/publications/pdf/popfacts/PopFacts_2011-1.pdf.

Deutsche Welle. 2020. "Bibi Titi Mohamed: Tanzania's 'Mother of the Nation.'" *News*. DW.COM. April 18, 2020. https://www.dw.com/en/bibi-titi-mohamed-tanzanias-mother-of-the-nation/a-52448380.

Editors. 2019a. "Nefertiti." Private. History. June 7, 2019. https://www.history.com/ topics/ancient-history/nefertiti.

———. 2019b. "Cleopatra." Educational. History. October 22, 2019. https://www.his tory.com/topics/ancient-history/cleopatra.

———. 2020a. "Queen Amina." In *Encyclopedia.Com*. Chicago, IL: Encyclopedia .com. https://www.encyclopedia.com/history/news-wires-white-papers-and-books/ queen-amina.

———. 2020b. "Ranavalona I (1792–1861)." In *Encyclopedia.Com*. Chicago, IL: Gale. https://www.encyclopedia.com/women/encyclopedias-almanacs-transcripts-and-maps/ranavalona-i-1792-1861.

Engel, Keri. 2020. "Huda Shaarawi, Egyptian Feminist & Activist." Educational. *Amazing Women in History* (blog). 2020. https://amazingwomeninhistory.com/h uda-shaarawi-egyptian-feminist/.

Farmer, Ashley. 2016. "Black Women Organize for the Future of Pan-Africanism: The Sixth Pan-African Congress." Educational. *Black Perspectives* (blog). July

3, 2016. https://www.aaihs.org/black-women-organize-for-the-future-of-pan-afric anism-the-sixth-pan-african-congress/.

Fikes, Robert. 2019. "Kandake Amanirenas (?-10 BC)." Educational. *African History* (blog). May 22, 2019. https://www.blackpast.org/global-african-history/kandake -amanirenas-10-bc/.

Filomina Steady. 2020. "Filomina Steady." Education. Wellesley College: Africana Studies. 2020. http://www.wellesley.edu/africana/faculty/steady.

Fyfe, Christopher. 2000. "Constance Cummings-John." *The Guardian*, March 2, 2000, sec. News. http://www.theguardian.com/news/2000/mar/02/guardianobituaries3.

Fynn Bruey, Veronica. 2016. "Systematic Gender Violence and the Rule of Law: Aboriginal Communities in Australia and Post-War Liberia." PhD Thesis, Canberra, ACT: The Australian National University. https://openresearch-reposit or y.anu.edu.au/handle/1885/159520.

———. 2018. "Redefining Women's Roles in International and Regional Law: The Case of Pre- and Post-War Peacebuilding in Liberia." In *Gender, Conflict, Peace, and UNSC Resolution 1325*, edited by Seema Shekhawat, 1–21. Lanham, MD: Lexington Books.

Fynn, Veronica. 2011. "Africa's Last Colony: Sahrawi People: Refugees, IDPs and Nationals?" *Journal of Internal Displacement* 1 (2): 40–58.

Fynn, Veronica P. 2011. *Legal Discrepancies: Internal Displacement of Women and Children in Africa*. Kusterdingen, Germany: Flowers Books. https://www.amazon .com/Legal-Discrepancies-Internal-Displacement-Children/dp/1453873414.

Global Fund for Women. 2015. "Women Lead Agriculture in Africa." Private Advocacy. *Global Fund for Women* (blog). September 28, 2015. https://www.glo balfundforwomen.org/keeping-food-on-the-table-in-sub-saharan-africa/.

Haas, Jörg-Werner, Rita Schäfer, and Marianne Scholte. 2009. "Masculinity and Civil Wars in Africa: New Approaches to Overcoming Sexual Violence in War." Eschborn, Germany: Deutsche Gesellschaft für Technische Zusammenarbeit (GTZ) GmbH.

Institute of Development Studies. 2016. "Domestic Violence in Ghana: Incidence, Attitudes, Determinants and Consequences." Government. Accra, Ghana: Ministry of Gender, Children and Social Protection.

Jackson, Elizabeth. 2010. "Women's Role in Maintaining and/or Resisting Patriarchy." In *Feminism and Contemporary Indian Women's Writing*, edited by Elizabeth Jackson, 111–40. London, UK: Palgrave Macmillan UK. https://doi.org/10.1057 /9780230275096_5.

Kent Law School. 2019. "SeRGJ: An Interview with Professor Amina Mama." *Video Recording*. Chicago, IL: Centre for Sexuality, Race and Gender Justice. https://ww w.youtube.com/watch?v=0dv0q6dzJr4.

Kuma, Davinder, and Evelyn Wambui. 2020. "Girls in Somalia Subjected to Door-to-Door FGM." *NGO*. Plan International. May 18, 2020. https://plan-international .org/news/2020-05-18-girls-somalia-subjected-door-door-fgm.

Maathai, Wangari. 2020. "The Nobel Peace Prize 2004." Private. *NobelPrize.Org*. November 27, 2020. https://www.nobelprize.org/prizes/peace/2004/maathai/bi ographical/.

Mama, Amina. 2017. "Amina Mama, Ph.D." Educational. *UC Davis Cultural Studies*. August 18, 2017. https://culturalstudies.ucdavis.edu/people/amina-m ama.

Matshego, Lebo. 2019. "Ancient African Queens Who Ruled the Continent Through the Years." Educational. *Africa.Com* (blog). June 20, 2019. https://africa.com/g reat-ancient-african-queens/.

McCormack, Mark, and Eric Anderson. 2010. "'It's Just Not Acceptable Anymore': The Erosion of Homophobia and the Softening of Masculinity at an English Sixth Form." *Sociology* 44 (5): 843–59. https://doi.org/10.1177/0038038510375734.

Moody, Robyne Kim. 2020. "Women Human Rights Defender's Fight against Female Genital Mutilation and Child Marriages in Africa." *Cities & Health*, October, 1–6. https://doi.org/10.1080/23748834.2020.1833597.

Muhumuza, Rodney. 2018. "Polygamy Persists across Africa, to Activists' Dismay." *AP NEWS*, October 24, 2018, sec. Race and ethnicity. https://apnews.com/article/ dee38fc829a84359a5bee3d25938b0b2.

Nnaemeka, Obioma. 2020. "Obioma G. Nnaemeka: Faculty & Staff Directory: About: School of Liberal Arts: IUPUI." Educational. School of Liberal Arts. 2020. https://liberalarts.iupui.edu/about/directory/nnaemeka-obioma-g.html.

Olasore, Remilekun Elizabeth. 2016. "The Extent of Polygamy in Africa, Any Role for the Infomration Professionals in Curbing Further Spread?" *Information and Knowledge Management* 6 (6): 7–14.

Onyango-Obbo, Charles. 2010. "There's 'Danger' in African Leaders with Too Many Wives." *The East African*, October 17, 2010. https://www.theeastafrican.co.ke/tea /oped/comment/there-s-danger-in-african-leaders-with-too-many-wives-1300436.

Oyewumi, Oyeronke. 2020. "Oyeronke Oyewumi." Academic. Department of Sociology, Stony Brook University. 2020. http://www.stonybrook.edu/commcms/ sociology/people/faculty/oyewumi.php.

Peterman, Amber, Tia Palermo, and Caryn Bredenkamp. 2011. "Estimates and Determinants of Sexual Violence against Women in the Democratic Republic of Congo." *American Journal of Public Health* 101 (6): 1060–67. https://doi.org/10.2 105/AJPH.2010.300070.

Radke, Helena R. M., Matthew J. Hornsey, Chris G. Sibley, and Fiona Kate Barlow. 2018. "Negotiating the Hierarchy: Social Dominance Orientation among Women Is Associated with the Endorsement of Benevolent Sexism: Social Dominance Orientation and Sexism." *Australian Journal of Psychology* 70 (2): 158–66. https:// doi.org/10.1111/ajpy.12176.

SABC News. 2018. "Descendants of King Shaka's Mother Nandi Want Her Grave Uplifted." *Video clip*. Kwazulu Natal, South Africa: South Africa Broadcasting Corporation. https://www.youtube.com/watch?v=mjyMmWix-XA.

———. 2020. "Influential Africans Part II: Njinga Mbande Aka Queen Nzinga." *Video clip*. Johannesburg, South Africa: South Africa Broadcasting Corporation. https://www.youtube.com/watch?v=KOlP51y7eKc.

Sandner, Philipp. 2018. "Queen Muhumuza: Fighting Colonialism in East Africa | DW | 09.02.2018." *Video clip*. Bonn, Germany: Deutsche Welle. https://www.dw. com/en/queen-muhumuza-fighting-colonialism-in-east-africa/a-42522227.

Sherwood, Marika. 2013. "1945 Pan-African Congress in Manchester." Educational. Working Class Movement Library. October 2013. https://www.wcml.org.uk/our -collections/object-of-the-month/1945-panafrican-congress-in-manchester/.

Sikweyiya, Yandisa, Adolphina Addoley Addo-Lartey, Deda Ogum Alangea, Phyllis Dako-Gyeke, Esnat D. Chirwa, Dorcas Coker-Appiah, Richard M. K. Adanu, and Rachel Jewkes. 2020. "Patriarchy and Gender-Inequitable Attitudes as Drivers of Intimate Partner Violence against Women in the Central Region of Ghana." *BMC Public Health* 20: 1–11.

Smaak, Annerieke, and Agnes Odhiambo. 2015. "Ending Child Marriage in Africa: Opening the Door for Girls' Education, Health, and Freedom from Violence." Private. Washington, DC: Human Rights Watch.

South African History Online. 2020. "Charlotte (Née Manye) Maxeke." Educational. *History of Women's Struggle in South Africa.* October 19, 2020. https://www.sah istory.org.za/people/charlotte-nee-manye-maxeke.

Stapleton, Timothy J. 2018. *Africa: War and Conflict in the Twentieth Century.* Seminar Studies. London, UK: Routledge/Taylor & Francis Group.

Talbot, Kirsten, and Michael Quayle. 2010. "The Perils of Being a Nice Guy: Contextual Variation in Five Young Women's Constructions of Acceptable Hegemonic and Alternative Masculinities." *Men and Masculinities* 13 (2): 255–78. https://doi.org/10.1177/1097184X09350408.

Tamale, Sylvia. 2016. "Sylvia Tamale." Private Advocacy. *African Feminist Forum.* March 25, 2016. http://www.africanfeministforum.com/sylvia-tamale-2/.

Ugandan Radio Network. 2018. "Constitutional Court Dismisses Petition against Polygamy." *The Observer—Uganda*, September 25, 2018. https://observer.ug/ news/headlines/58756-constitutional-court-dismisses-petition-against-polygamy.

UNESCO. 2020. "Funmilayo Ransome-Kuti Biography | Women." United Nations. Women in African History. 2020. https://en.unesco.org/womeninafrica/funmilayo -ransome-kuti/biography.

Ward, Michael R. M. 2018. "Acceptable Masculinities: Working-Class Young Men and Vocational Education and Training Courses." *British Journal of Educational Studies* 66 (2): 225–42. https://doi.org/10.1080/00071005.2017.1337869.

Williams, Paul D. 2016. *War and Conflict in Africa.* 2nd edition. Cambridge, UK: Polity.

World Economic Forum. 2018. "The Global Gender Gap Report 2018." *Private.* Geneva, Switzerland: World Economic Forum.

Yerges, April L., Patricia E. Stevens, Lucy Mkandawire-Valhmu, Wendy Bauer, Thokozani Ng'ombe Mwenyekonde, Lance S. Weinhardt, and Loren W. Galvao. 2017. "Women's Narratives of Living in Polygamous Marriages: Rural Malawian Experience Distilled and Preserved in Poetic Constructions." *Health Care for Women International* 38 (8): 873–91. https://doi.org/10.1080/07399332.2017.13 26494.

Chapter 1

The Past Before Us

Reimagining Patriarchy and Gender in Africa

L. Amede Obiora

In October 2005, I was part of a UN Expert Group Meeting in Addis Ababa, Ethiopia on the "equal participation of women and men in decision-making processes, with particular emphasis on political participation and leadership". In material respects, the world in general has come a long way since the Expert Group Meeting, witnessing the elections of women as heads of states and governments in ordinarily inhospitable arenas where few would have readily predicted such outcomes. But what, if any, transformative impacts are attributable to such novelties in high-level decision-making? What key takeaways could be drawn from records of women in leadership hierarchies about how to substantively eradicate patriarchal conditions? It is against this backdrop that this chapter examines the relationship between patriarchy and gender in Africa. Beginning with highlights of the experts' discussions, the chapter zeroes in on a cautionary survey of Liberia to situate the case for engendering power and to revisit keystone critiques of patriarchy.

With a view to contribute to the re-imagination of the relationship between gender and patriarchy in Africa, this chapter argues the significance of learning from women's exercise of power to shape and sharpen promising paths to de-patriarchalize the technology of power. Despite laudable global progress toward achieving gender equality objectives, patriarchal discrimination remains endemic in the social fabric and at every level of the political landscape. According to the global Gender Index, no country in the world has yet achieved the promise of gender equality, nor does any one country score well consistently across all pertinent measures. Concerning the quest for gender balance in sharing power and decision-making, as of June 2019, only eleven women were recognized as Head of State, and just twelve women were serving as Head of Government out of the 193 sovereign states that are members of the United Nations (UN).[1] Just 24.3 percent of all national parliamentarians were women as of February 2019, reflecting a relatively slow rise since the proportion of women parliamentarians was already 11.3 percent at the time of the United Nations' Fourth World Conference on Women held in Beijing in 1995.[2] To further complicate these objective realities, women historically register lower electoral participation rates than men, and their voting choices reportedly tend to be influenced by powerbrokers or household heads.[3]

The commemoration of the 25th anniversary of the adoption of the 1995 Beijing Declaration and Platform for Action at the celebration of the International Women's Day on March 8, 2020, provided an opportunity to reassess pathways to drive gender equality, including equity and empowerment.[4] The definitive declaration and platform was the most comprehensive global policy framework and blueprint for action to advance the realization of gender equality and human rights for women and girls.[5] To empower women, this pivotal roadmap delineated twelve critical areas of concern along with strategic targets and urgent actions, including political participation. For many, it is inarguable that the bona fide landmark instrument deserves commemoration. At the same time, however, the implementational lag in progress gives considerable pause for thought.

The implementation of the Beijing Platform for Action to achieve women's participation in power structures (enunciated in Strategic Objective G.1) and increase women's capacity to participate in decision-making and leadership (in accordance with Strategic Objective G.2) have not kept pace with keystone aspirations. This is primarily because states have not earnestly complied with the core commitments that personify the fulfillment of their obligations. The General Assembly Resolution 58/142 adopted by the United Nations in 2003 on Women and Political Participation exemplifies further injunction on the member states to eliminate all discriminatory laws, counter negative societal attitudes about women's capacity to participate equally in the political process, and institute educational programs to advance sensitization about the equal rights of women.

The confluence of factors that culminated in the generation of the Beijing Declaration and Platform for Action, buttressed by the lackluster implementation scorecards, adds to grounds for its continuing support. Contending with the floodgate that impedes uncompromising adherence to the principle of gender equality remains decidedly necessary to optimize the vision, mission, objectives, strategies, and actions integral to offset the arduousness and tenacity of patriarchal subordination. Therefore, in celebrating the significance of women's participation, representation, and leadership, it is expedient to strive to learn from how women are coping with difficulties steeped in insidious patriarchal prejudice and appraise if women's presence in political institutions indeed enlarges the space or impetus to nullify corresponding patriarchal cultures and foster transformative priorities.

ILLUSTRATIVE GENDER AUDIT

Consistent with its work program for 2001–2006, the Commission on the Status of Women (CSW) prioritized the "equal participation of women and men in decision-making processes at all levels" as a theme for its 50th session in 2006.[6] To further relevant understanding and salient deliberations, the United Nations Division for the Advancement of Women (DAW), in collaboration with the United Nations Economic Commission for Africa (ECA) and the Inter-Parliamentary Union (IPU), organized an Expert Group Meeting (EGM) in Addis Ababa, Ethiopia, October 24–27, 2005. As one of twelve experts appointed by the secretary-general of the United Nations, I was enlisted to chair the EGM, which epitomized efforts to heighten shifts in consciousness and conditions to evenly distribute power between women and men. Based on promising practices and lessons learned, the findings and recommendations of the EGM for achieving this goal were presented by a panel discussion at the 50th session of the CSW.

The overall objective of the EGM was to analyze the situation of women in decision-making processes, with specific emphasis on political participation and leadership. The terms of reference for the meeting enjoined the experts to, *inter alia*,

- examine conditions that facilitate women's representation in decision-making processes within the context of prevailing socio-economic and political transformations;
- consider the interplay between women's presence in decision-making bodies and their impact on policy formulation and the conduct of political institutions;
- explore the extent to which women's presence in decision-making bodies facilitates mainstreaming gender perspective into policies;
- examine the conditions under which political bodies commit to gender balance and gender mainstreaming in processes and outcomes; and
- propose strategies to advance women's participation and leadership through capacity-building, coalition-building, and gender-sensitive policies, programs, and mechanisms.[7]

The experts parsed key normative theoretical and empirical concerns within the following conceptual frame:

- *Political participation*—denoting the development of political agendas by women "taking part in politics" via formal and informal discussion, lobbying, activism, and other activities.

- *Political representation*—referring to the articulation and presentation of political agendas of given groups by a range of actors in democratic decision-making arenas and social forums.
- *Political leadership*—typifying key individuals shaping political agendas, taking the lead in the articulation of policies, and participating in the policy translations.
- *Political accountability*—pertaining to the requirement for representatives and leaders to be responsible for their decisions and mandates, including listening to and responding to the criticisms and demands of the public, constituencies, or electorate.[8]

Inquiring into conditions that contribute to women's ability to be effective in decision-making processes, the expert group illuminated key roles played by the presence of individual women and men in political processes and institutions. The discussion highlighted how *critical actors* and *critical structures* enhance women's influence and how the convergence of forces at *critical junctures* provides unprecedented opportunities for women to influence the policymaking process.[9] The EGM further explored several premises to underscore the importance of equally balancing the numbers of women and men in political office. Foremost among these were:

- Justice—as half the population, women have an equal right to proportional representation.
- Experience—women's difference from men's warrants careful incorporation into discussions that result in policymaking and implementation, and these differences may have implications for how women "do politics" in contradistinction to men.
- Interest—women belong and are needed in representative institutions to articulate their interests, which may differ from and conflict with the interests of men.
- Critical Mass—women can achieve solidarity of purpose to represent women's interests when they achieve certain levels of representation.
- Symbolical—women are drawn to political arenas if relatable gender role models are there.
- Democracy—the equal representation of women and men is apt to universally enhance the democratization of governance in both established and evolving democracies.[10]

A key takeaway from the experts' discussions on relevant research-based studies was the importance of looking beyond numbers to distinguish between descriptive access and substantive representation. This stressed the need for a stronger emphasis on aligning access with the policy formulation and implementation results of women in decision-making positions.[11] Acknowledging the slow but steady gains in women's descriptive representation, the experts validated the legitimacy of concerns about women's cooptation as tokens into governance machineries without the ability to foment significant shifts in policy frameworks that address women's rights or broader changes. Reviewing assessments of the substantive outcomes and impact of women's involvement in decision-making, the EGM pointed up indicative evidence that women representatives attempt to influence the formulation and implementation of gender mainstreaming policies, that they are approached by women's groups to support their causes, and that they are often perceived as less corrupt in the eyes of the electorate. The experts affirmed findings that, despite persistent obstacles, women's political presence has downstream ripple effects on policies affecting the broader society, for example, on issues like socio-economic development, peace-building, and good governance.

LIBERIA'S EXPERIENCE: EXPOSITORY OVERVIEW

Liberia is an important case study to examine objective realities of power-sharing at a critical juncture in history to better understand how to nurture enabling conditions that challenge intractable causes and effects of patriarchal domination and subordination. Liberia offers an intriguing prism as Africa's oldest independent state, and as its first country to democratically elect a woman to serve in the capacity of a president in November 2005. From 1989 through 2003, the country was engulfed in a protracted civil war that resulted in the loss of about 250,000 lives, with thousands more mutilated and raped, often by armies of drugged child soldiers led by ruthless warlords.[12] The end of the war was followed by two years of rule by a transitional government that ushered in the 2005 democratic elections.

In the twilight of the civil war, Ellen Johnson Sirleaf helped call attention to the preponderance of gender gaps in political participation in war-torn settings, underscoring how women often disproportionately bear the scourge of conflict.[13] Subsequently, in seeming defiance of this pattern, the electorate cast the mantle of authority on Sirleaf as Africa's first female president to lead the change required to rebuild the state and recuperate the integrity of governance institutions.[14] Yet, Sirleaf's election put into clear perspective the exacting contexts within which women are thrust up to navigate and lead change. This historic opening elucidated the conundrums of safeguarding the transformative potentials of gender-inclusive power sharing as a democratic ideal in fragile settings transitioning from conflict often marked by a daunting vacuum of governance structures and processes. While discounting for post-conflict exigencies, it is worth considering the extent to which Sirleaf's landmark elevation into a critical actor as Africa's first female president translated into effective gender-sensitive and socially transformative public policy preferences or results.[15]

Electoral Statistics Snapshot

What is the proportion of seats held by women in the legislature, judiciary, and elected or appointed executive positions in Liberia? Although it is important to note that such statistics are neither an adequate indicator of the prevalence of gender-sensitive policies to redress disparities nor of gender equality in the broader society, Liberia has made notable strides in increasing women's participation in government through ministerial and key decision-making appointments. However, it is still behind in attaining the 30 percent minimum benchmark advocated for all levels.[16] Targeted mapping and analysis show that higher percentages of women hold leadership positions and more responsibility in the judiciary than in the executive and legislative arms of the government; for example, two of the five justices of the Supreme Court are women.[17]

Liberia's bicameral legislature consists of the Senate with thirty seats and the House of Representatives with seventy-three seats. In the 2005 elections, although women constituted at least half of both the population and the total number of registered voters, they accounted for only 14 percent of the 806 candidates nominated for election.[18] The process resulted in the election of five women senators for the thirty seats available, and nine women were voted in to join the sixty-four members of the House of Representatives.[19] Two women contested against twenty men in the presidential race and one woman won.

With the election of Ellen Johnson Sirleaf as the president, Liberia set a historic record as the first African country to boast a woman holding the reins of power, apparently at the helm of office as the Head of State.[20] President Sirleaf received the Nobel Peace Prize in October 2011 (jointly with Leymah Gbowee and Tawakkul Karman) for her role in bringing about the signing of a peace accord that ended more than a decade of armed conflict. Venerated by some and vilified by others, Sirleaf won a second bid for the presidency in November 2011 in a controversial election that came to a head in a runoff election boycotted by her main rival. After twelve years in office, President Johnson Sirleaf's tenure ended in 2017 because of term limits. The elections that ensued in October 2017 signaled an important milestone in the consolidation of Liberia's democracy as it marked the first peaceful democratic transition of power since the inception of universal suffrage in 1951.[21] Owing to the peaceful transfer of power, President Sirleaf was awarded the Mo Ibrahim award.[22]

Salient Country Profile

Liberia is a constitutional republic with a bicameral national assembly and a democratically elected government.[23] The Constitution of the Republic of Liberia mandates the equality of all citizens. The state is a party to the Convention on the Elimination of All Forms of Discrimination against Women (CEDAW) along with the Optional Protocol. It also ratified the Beijing Declaration and Platform for Action and several regional agreements, including the African Charter on Human and People's Rights and the Maputo Protocol on the Rights of Women in Africa. Yet, Liberia ranks low in vital global indices on data computations of the conditions that enable incubation of gender equality, which is a telling proxy for pervasive patriarchal domination.

The Human Development Index (HDI) is a summary measure for assessing long-term progress in three basic dimensions of human development: a long and healthy life, access to knowledge, and a decent standard of living. The United Nations Development Program (UNDP) justified the importance of peering through the human development lens in understanding gender disparities as a persistent form of inequality. This was corollary to delineating inequality as a defining bottleneck against rectifying political decisions to reflect the aspirations of the whole society, since the few pulling ahead flex their power to shape decisions primarily in their interests.[24] Liberia's HDI for 2018 positioned it at 176 out of 189 UN members.[25] According to the Gender Development Index, which is based on the sex-disaggregated HDI, the 0.438 female HDI value for Liberia contrasts with 0.487 for males, placing it in Group 5. The Gender Inequality Index, which reflects gender-based inequalities in three dimensions—reproductive health, empowerment, and economic activity—classifies Liberia as 155th out of 162 countries ranked in the world. Liberia ranks as #97 in the Global Gender Gap Index, placing at 141 for educational attainment and 63 for political empowerment.[26] It also placed in the bottom 10 of the 129 countries measured by the Gender Development Index and made the list of fragile states identified by the Organization for Economic Cooperation and Development in 2018.

Evaluations conducted in relation to the *Revised National Gender Policy* (2018–2022) delineated a pattern of negligible budget allocations for the national gender machinery to address gender inequality during President Sirleaf's terms. For example, in the 2012–2013 financial year, USD 1,202,013, which amounted to a paltry 0.0178 percent of the national budget, was allocated and USD 1,214,752, or a miniscule 0.23 percent, was earmarked for 2013–2014. In the aftermath of the 1995 United Nation's Women's Conference in Beijing, gender-based violence (GBV) emerged to serve as a critical measure of political will and commitment to gender equality for a society in discerning circles.[27] Nonetheless, it was not until 2017, presumptively the eleventh hour of her twelve years in office, that President Johnson Sirleaf issued an executive order valid for a duration of one year to protect women against domestic violence and to prohibit female genital mutilation (FGM) for persons younger than 18 years and non-consenting older persons. The House of Representatives adopted the Domestic Violence bill in 2017, but the stipulation against FGM was obliterated.

Longstanding deficiencies within the judicial system and security sector, along with insufficient efforts to address official corruption, continued to undermine development and human rights in Liberia during President Sirleaf's terms.[28] While she dismissed some high-ranking government officials accused of corruption, her administration failed to pursue investigations into the alleged crimes, which further undermined accountability efforts.[29] Strident complaints about nepotism were also made against the administration, with none other than the president herself coming under fire because several of her children had high-level jobs in government or state-owned enterprises.[30]

Liberia was rated poorly on the issue of denial of fair trial and respect for civil liberties.[31] The constitution provides for an independent judiciary. Nevertheless, judicial officials and prosecutors appeared subject to pressure and engaged in forms of corruption such as soliciting bribes for favorable decisions; furthermore, and the outcomes of some trials appeared to be predetermined.[32] Civil libel and slander laws limited the freedom of speech, and self-censorship was widespread. Media outlets avoided criticizing government officials because of fears of legal sanction and in order to attract advertising revenue from public coffers.[33] There was credible evidence that government officials and law enforcement officers harassed journalists and media outlets that excoriated the government or high-profile officials. For example, in August 2013, the Supreme Court upheld the sentence of a prominent journalist who was jailed for failing to pay damages to the tune of $1.5 million levied against him in a libel complaint filed by a former government minister.[34] The Court followed suit by penalizing the Minister of Justice and Attorney-General for releasing the journalist from jail for humanitarian reasons. Simultaneously instituting and sitting in judgment in a contempt proceeding, the Supreme Court suspended the minister from practicing law for six months.[35] The Minister of Justice was one of President Sirleaf's female cabinet appointees and controversies revolving around the judicial order subsequently led to her resignation.[36]

In 2010, President Johnson Sirleaf dismissed her cabinet, reportedly to start with a "clean slate."[37] Yet, ten years after the signing of the peace accord that ended more than a decade of armed conflict and civil war, Liberians and the country's key international partners increased pressure on President

Ellen Johnson Sirleaf's government to expedite reforms. Perhaps, Sirleaf was inordinately challenged to reconcile the nation after fourteen years of fighting and to rebuild the economy, particularly following the outbreak of the Ebola Virus Disease in 2014.[38] The economic impact of the Ebola epidemic was compounded by a sustained decline in global iron ore and rubber prices that adversely affected exports and investments, exacerbating the country's status as one of the poorest in the world.[39]

A core insight from a preliminary post-mortem of President Sirleaf's tenure is that not even attaining the apex of power inoculates women against the far-reaching pernicious effects of the virus of patriarchy. This reality signifies the expedience of compelling sensitivity to the gravity of context in implementing the gender equality agenda. Insofar as the promise of women's participation, representation, and leadership is to counter the multifaceted manifestations of patriarchy, the enduring challenge is not just to empower women individually. It is necessary also to target adverse institutional and systemic conditions that undermine their ability to make a qualitative difference and an impactful social change. It cannot be overstated that participation, representation, and leadership *per se* are inadequate to eliminate the predicaments of gender inequality and the repercussions of the ecosystem underpinning the persistence of patriarchy.

Owing to the historical burdens of the disparate treatment of women and the privileging of men under the system of patriarchy, the guarantee of equal rights prima facie is not enough to remedy women's comparative disadvantage. Although gender equality seeks to give women and men the same opportunities or starting points to access power and control over decision-making and resources, gender equity and empowerment are critical to meaningfully level the playing field across all sectors of the society to correct objective constraints on women's ability to finish well once they gain access to the opportunities to participate, represent, and lead. Thus, consistent with the submission of the EGM, gender equity and empowerment are critical to reform conditions that enable patriarchal mechanisms of power to perpetuate gender vulnerabilities and to achieve a pathway from participation, representation, and leadership to substantive gender equality.

ENGENDERING POWER

All told from the preceding passages, how well has gender inclusion worked? Quantitatively, efforts to balance the numbers in political arrangements have registered noticeable, albeit far from optimal, progress. For the most part, gone are the days of justifying laboriously the place of women in high-level decision-making processes; many now take that for granted, and even if progress toward achieving target outcomes has been slow, it appears to have been steady. Women's inclusion in participation, representation, and leadership demonstrate some stirring returns, which in turn add to the force of the case for greater inclusion. The numerical increase organically propagates grounds in the political climate and social fabric for qualitative productivity and creativity. This is in order to go beyond just righting the wrongs of patriarchy by equalizing the opportunity for access but by also enabling favorable conditions for gender inclusion to systematically deeply ventilate and purge the inequities and perils of patriarchy.

It is especially in this context that the ramifications of women's growing democratic participation, representation, and leadership for the relationship between gender and patriarchy in Africa cannot merely approximate business as usual in tacit ratification of the status quo. It is fitting for the gradual quantitative gains to yield qualitative returns that can be channeled to defy assumptions of power coterminous with patriarchy in ways that tackle the deficits of democracy to ameliorate corresponding dividends. Herein lies a salient inflection point for the disruptive potential of women in power to help innovate on the question of patriarchy and gender in Africa.

The bottom line that frames the present attention to the implications of women in power for the relationship between patriarchy and gender in Africa is that there is a lot more that can be said and done about advantageously negotiating and harnessing the learning curve embedded in the shifting political landscape. This is particularly in order to fit the struggle against patriarchy on a continuum with broader responses to the shortfalls in values and institutions that define the overlapping crises of the state and democracy in contemporary Africa. Accumulating data about the persistent hurdle women face in participation, representation, and leadership demonstrate that the gender constraints characteristic of the status quo remain emblematic of patriarchy.

As women endeavor to engage the technology of power, the slow pace of appropriating the relative innovation of planned systematic access to qualitatively influence governance protocols, policies, standards, and incentives complicates the urgency of bridging the gender gap. Far from correcting substantive imbalances, it is a short-range preoccupation with access that risks, stymying bolder transformative paths to squarely vindicate the social purpose and public interest of this feminist priority. Ample evidence supports the proposition that access is a necessary starting point, but an insufficient step to balance the equities in the patriarchal order to attain gender equality. Unless properly construed as a part of an integral whole, disproportionately focusing on access may compound the problem of patriarchy and gender, instead of becoming an unimpeachable part of the solution. Re-imagining the relationship of access to goals, such as improving the enabling environment to deepen the quality of democracy, promises to help redeem the vision for the struggle against patriarchal hegemony by optimizing women's roles in participation, representation, and leadership.

Substantively leveling the playing field for women in power demands learning how to celebrate and employ women's differences as strengths in recognition of Audre Lorde's imperishable observation that "the master's tools will never dismantle the master's house." Such tools, as she put it, "may allow us temporarily to beat him at his own game, but they will never enable us to bring about genuine change."[40] For Lorde, jaundiced integration into the representational practices of patriarchal power is a primary tool of oppression. A manifest danger of this tool lies in its seduction of women to dissipate valuable energy by engaging futilely in the patriarchal edifice. With regard to the matter of women in power, for example, such waste is detrimental to their autonomy to first constitute themselves as a force to bolster the evidence base to uphold arguments for the consideration of alternative directions for policy and decision-making.[41] A heuristic rule of thumb from Lorde serves as a warning to women about the exacting costs of embodying and reproducing the sins of patriarchy in the quest to share power, instead of subversively contesting the crux of such power. In this vein, being preoccupied with closing the gender gap in power through participation, representation, and leadership without addressing how to reform the critical content of power implicitly ratifies and maintains the status quo.

Feminists of various ilks contend with the conventional definition and enactment of power in ways synonymous with the tools of patriarchal oppression.[42] For instance, Luce Irigaray champions the subversion of the phallic discursive and cultural order that privileges a definition of power of the masculine type. To Irigaray, if feminists "aim simply for a change in the distribution of power, leaving intact the power structure itself, then they are re-subjecting themselves, deliberately or not, to a phallocratic order."[43] By the same token, Carole Pateman posits that the social contract which legitimates the exercise of political rights is a sexual contract with deeply entrenched patriarchal problems. Arguing that women were not so much excluded from the original social contract but rather included under terms very different from those applied to men, Pateman challenges the notion that one can strip out the earlier bias while leaving the fundamental ideas intact.[44] Questioning cardinal contract narratives, she drives home the limitations of traditionally conceived liberal democratic practices in legitimating the power of the state. Consequentially, she urges deeper thinking about what democracy ought to mean and what sort of social restructuring could overturn institutions formed during modern patriarchy's prime to categorically enable women to be self-governing.[45]

DISCOURSES OF PATRIARCHY

Popular canons of the feminist theory of patriarchy are apt to enrich criticisms of the fallacies and delusions of modeling the objective and strategy to achieve equality for women in power on the basic conceptions of the state. These works presage growing discontent and disillusion with the dominant approach to women's participation, representation, and leadership. As perceptive as some of these interventions are, though, a sweeping exploration of them is beyond the scope of the present undertaking. However, instructive insights from these works suggest the remissness of proceeding with a treatment of the issue of patriarchy in 2020 as if to merely resurrect a concept many concede began to wane in the late 1980s. This is particularly given the forcefulness in the African context of the impetus for the decline, which was ascribed to robust critiques of gender as an analytical category that challenged the idea of a common identity, experience, conscience, and action among women.[46] That said, it is crucial to articulate a broad outline of the problem of patriarchy to further ground the contemporary relevance of the challenge against gender subordination in political participation, representation, and leadership.

An important achievement of a rich body of feminist research and scholarship has been to demonstrate the oppressiveness of patriarchal power relations,[47] while animating the susceptibility of the social construct to change.[48] For the immediate purposes of the subject under consideration, *patriarchy* can be construed as a resilient hierarchical system of social organization, structures, relations, and practices imbued with a set of reproductive mechanisms, beliefs, norms, values, assumptions, and ideas that signify and legitimate gender power differentials in everyday life.[49] The system of patriarchy is characterized by the institutionalization of male power as an instrument of male domination and female subordination in society.[50] Female subordination is evident from women's exclusion from primary institutions of governance, construction of the hegemonic subjectivity as "masculinist," and women being subject to male authority as citizens.[51]

The theory of patriarchy allows a distinction between the structures of male domination, on the one hand, and individual men or women, on the other hand.[52] Patriarchal domination takes several different forms that are the product of historical situations.[53] Emphasizing the importance of historicizing the struggle against patriarchy, various writers clarify that different kinds of relationships have always existed between men and women over the course of time. Patriarchy does not imply a universal or stable system in which, as Gerda Lerner writes, "women are either totally powerless or totally deprived of rights, influence, and resources;" some societies have been relatively more woman-centered and based on varying degrees of gender equality.[54] Indeed, evidence of ubiquitous and endemic male domination and control of power in post-colonial African states does not elide historical realities that empowered women to exert influence and authority in specific social settings.[55] In this light, one does not have to subscribe to debates about the invention of tradition in Africa and the consequences for paradigmatic shifts in the social construction of gender to concede the agency of African women.[56]

The question of women's agency is integral for the rigorous understanding of patriarchy as an order which reproduces itself through relationships, and it cannot be overstated that women are not merely passive pawns in male transactions therein. Amy Allen's incisive major reference entry details the risks and complications that arise from theorizing patriarchy in a manner that conceptualizes women as passive victims rather than as co-creators of history and agents of change. This exposition is invigorated by Ann Cudd's insistence that the most difficult and interesting question that an analysis of oppression must confront is the "endurance question: how does oppression endure over time in spite of humans' rough natural equality?"[57] Assuming "that agents behave rationally in the sense that they choose actions that maximize their (induced) expected utilities," Cudd suggests that the key to answering the endurance question lies in the fact that "the oppressed are co-opted through their own short-run rational choices to reinforce the long-run oppression of their social group."[58]

Consonant with Cudd's suggestion, diverse scholars corroborate in varying terms that the male privilege inherent in patriarchal social arrangements is operationalized and sustained with the socialized acquiescence and collusion of women.[59] According to Deniz Kandiyoti, women can advantageously manipulate the system and political relationships to negotiate patriarchal bargains that allow them room to secure privileged positions within a given patriarchal order.[60] Thus, it stands to reason that not all women are oppressed and/or subjugated in the same way or to the same extent within the system of patriarchy, even within the same society at any specific moment.[61]

Exhilarating elucidations of the theory of patriarchy as essentially ahistorical and universal expose the tendency to abstract the existence of women from social context. These works provide a basis to comprehend the nuances of women's experiences and the existence of cross-cutting subjectivities which interact with gender dynamics and power relations in highly complex ways to determine pertinent outcomes and impacts.[62] The intersectionality approach, which has a rich provenance but was popularized by Kimberle Crenshaw,[63] has been in the vanguard of calling attention to the intricate intertwining of gender with reciprocal structures and processes surrounding race, class, and the like.[64]

Elaborating on the view that patriarchy is produced within the construction of gender in concrete cultural contexts, Judith Butler criticizes the universal or monolithic notion of patriarchy as a colonizing epistemological strategy that fails to account for the workings of gender oppression in the concrete cultural contexts in which it exists.[65] Others espouse concurrent sentiments, denouncing the assumption that concerns of white, middle-class Western women can be equated with experiences of all women everywhere as a form of cultural imperialism that disguises the particularity of its own worldview by using spuriously general concepts.[66] Pursuant to a panoramic review of relevant literature, Valerie Bryson excoriates "patriarchy" as a mystifying device that conceals divisions in society in much the same way as male perspectives concealed the oppression of women. She poignantly drives this point home by invoking Elizabeth Spelman's epigrammatic identification of "disquieting parallels between what feminists find disquieting in Western political thought and what many black women have found troubling in much of Western feminism."[67] Nonetheless, Bryson concludes that, forceful as these criticisms are, it is far from clear that the attributed problems are inherent in the concept of patriarchy as opposed to some of its less cautious expositions. From her perspective, there seems no reason why, in principle, the recognition of the existence of patriarchy needs to involve the denial of other forms of oppression and vast questions of interconnections and possible causal relationships between the gender, race, and class systems can be opened up for exploration.

Although it is has been indispensable for the quest for equality to underscore the tremendous obstacles that women face, a recurrent empirical lesson from growing political experiences is that although differences between men and women in the power relations that are involved are intractable, they are not necessarily insurmountable. Studiedly leveraging fertile possibilities that inhere within a conventional competitive pursuit of political power to amplify the outcomes and impacts of women's power gains entails intimate knowledge and understanding of how to better eradicate the conditions that underpin patriarchy and its resilience. To this end, it is noteworthy to acknowledge Judith Bennett's articulation of the term, *patriarchal equilibrium*, to denote the idea of patriarchy as continuous-although-changing.[68] Bennet is critical of an overall assessment of women's status as getting better or getting worse, instead of considering the possibility that, despite change, shift, and movement, the overall force of patriarchal power might have endured. Therefore, she invokes the concept of equilibrium to capture the considerable patriarchal continuity that persists in the face of dynamic changes, explicating how patriarchal ideology results in outcomes that favor men and characteristics perceived as "male" to counter women's power gains. The appeal of this context is borne out by the experience of women who gain access to power, only to experience it as a double-edged sword that reasserts gender inequality.[69]

For some exponents of gender equality, the concept of patriarchy allows scope both for conventional political struggle and for an analysis of related structures of oppression; to this cohort, although the state is seen as an arena of conflict that is systematically biased against women, important victories can be won within it.[70] For others, however, the patriarchal domination of women by men is the central defining feature of state power; from such radical feminist perspective, the state is but one manifestation of patriarchal power, reflecting other deeper structures of oppression, and women's well-documented exclusion from its formal institutions is a symptom rather than the cause of gender inequality.[71] For radical feminists, therefore, state power is not to be understood in its own terms but as part of a ubiquitous system of patriarchal power; as such, it is not a neutral tool that is evenly available for men and women, and it will not automatically respond to the dictates of reason and justice.[72] This means that its nature cannot be transformed by simply changing the incumbents of the positions of power, since political outcomes are structured by society-wide power relations and not necessarily by individual decisions.[73]

Marilyn Frye, who offers a radical feminist analysis of power, identifies access as one of the most important faces of power.[74] As Frye puts it, "total power is unconditional access; total powerlessness is being unconditionally accessible. The creation and manipulation of power is constituted of the manipulation and control of access."[75] Catherine MacKinnon expands the radical trajectory through her analysis of gender difference as simply the reified effect of domination. Stressing that "difference is the velvet glove on the iron fist of domination," MacKinnon maintains that the "problem is not that differences are not valued; the problem is that they are defined by power."[76] To MacKinnon, female power is a contradiction, if male domination is pervasive and women are powerless by definition.[77] The claim that female power is a contradiction in terms spurred some feminists to indict MacKinnon on the grounds that she denies women's agency and presents them as helpless victims.[78] On a different note, interlocutors exemplified by Judith Butler fault MacKinnon for glossing over the distinction between sex, the often presumed natural and immutable biologically rooted traits that make one male or female, and gender—the socially and culturally rooted, hence contingent and mutable, traits, characteristics, dispositions, and practices that make one a woman or a man.[79] Butler's disambiguation of gender roles as performances offers further impetus to unpack the nexus between patriarchy and heteronormativity in reimagining how to engender power meaningfully.

Butler's publication also ranks high among several feminist investigations of power that draw on Michel Foucault's account of disciplinary power to critically analyze normativity. To this end, Butler argues that "feminist critique ought also to understand how the category of 'women,' the subject of feminism, is produced and restrained by the very structures of power through which emancipation is sought."[80] Some other feminists take exception to the

Foucauldian claim that the subject is an effect of power, given the incompat-
ibility of the denial of agency they perceive as implicit in such a claim with
the demands of feminism as an emancipatory social movement.[81]

Proffering the centrality of the concept of power to critiques of women's
subordination,[82] some feminists urge the urgency of theorizing the gap in
power between men and women, not just by focusing on power as a resource
to be redistributed or as domination, but as empowerment.[83] Feminists from
a variety of theoretical backgrounds have argued for a reconceptualization
of power as a capacity or ability, specifically, the capacity to empower or
transform oneself and others.[84] Hailing the promise of women's examination of power to bring new understanding to the whole concept of power,
Jean Baker Miller rejects the definition of power as domination which she
conceives as particularly masculine; instead, she defines it as "the capacity to
produce a change."[85] Nancy Hartsock equally commends the understanding
of power "as energy and competence rather than dominance."[86] Along similar
lines, Virginia Held argues that a feminist analysis of society and politics
leads to an understanding of power as the capacity to transform and empower
oneself and others. To Mary Caputi, advocates of "power feminism" reject
not only excessive focus on women's victimization, but also the claim that
women are "sensitive creatures given more to a caring, interconnected web
of human relationships than to the rugged individualism espoused by men."[87]
In contrast, these power feminists endorse a conception of empowerment that
privileges individual choice with little concern for the contexts within which
choices are made or the options from which women can choose. Because of
its tendency to mimic an individualistic, sovereign, and masculinist conception of power feminism, according to Caputi, "does little, if anything, to
rethink our conception of power."[88]

Khader, for whom empowerment is a messy, complex, and incremental
concept, defines it as the process of overcoming one or many "inappropriately
adaptive preferences" through processes that enhance some element of a person's concept of self-entitlement and increase her capacity to pursue her own
flourishing.[89] Her analysis of empowerment attempts to reconcile the tension
that "self-subordinating choices can have selective empowering effects under
disempowering conditions," even as the normative core of her account insists
that "a situation where one cannot seek one's basic flourishing across multiple domains is a tragic one."[90]

Struggles for greater participation in decision-making bodies are critical
for women's empowerment.[91] Accordingly, effectively assessing the outcome
of equal participation of women and men in decision-making requires examining whether increased political participation enhances the political empowerment of women to take decisions that affect their lives and the lives of
others.[92] To this end, Shirin Rai, who authored the background paper for the

UN EMG, defines *empowerment* as processes by which women and men take control and ownership of their lives through an expansion of their choices.[93] Rai maintains that empowerment includes both individual conscientization (*power within*) and collective action, which can lead to politicized *power with* others *to* bring about change.[94]

Conventional emphases on increasing the number of women where power and influence are brokered and shared as a measurement index of value creation in contending with patriarchal hegemony do not necessarily address the economy, efficiency and effectiveness merits of empowerment in extracting the value constituted by women's political participation. However, continuing dilemmas that characterize efforts that prioritize bringing women into politics in the status quo "as is" to advance gender equality outcomes and the complexities of the structural impediments and cultural biases to women's path in positions of power eloquently demonstrate the limitations of formalistic conceptualization of power-sharing in repudiating patriarchy.

Mounting evidence about pertinent deficits suggests that the solution to the problem of patriarchy cannot be reduced merely to the equalization of access. This is especially true given the longstanding consensus among feminists that the system of patriarchy is enduring, subversive, and not neutrally adaptive. Furthermore, the commonplace aversion to the diminution of women's agency that is discernable from the foregoing exploration demands deference to such agency in its own right. As Sen and others have demonstrated, there is a reciprocal relation between (1) social arrangements to expand individual freedoms such as political participation, and (2) the use of such individual freedoms not only to improve respective lives but also to make social arrangements more appropriate and effective.[95] To the extent that individual freedom is quintessentially a social product, constructing political agency that favors gender to the occlusion of other competing inequities of culture and structure skews the experiences of many women.[96]

This chapter proffers an argument for learning from empirical experience to refresh understandings of gender and patriarchy in Africa. Relying on the empirical example of President Johnson Sirleaf in Liberia, it speaks to the difficulties of abstracting discussions about participation, representation, and leadership from the larger political context. The chapter situates that discussion within the framework of wider explorations about the continued impact of patriarchy on politics and the distribution of power. This is while simultaneously emphasizing the need to shift away from the silo approach to examining patriarchy and the importance of building on the momentum from the growing number of studies about the complexity of how the phenomenon interacts with history, race, and other influences.

Amid growing concerns about the shortfalls and blind spots in bridging the gap of and for women in power, it is worth consistently remembering the intrinsic, instrumental, and constructive roles of gender equality. Gender equality is of inestimable value by itself. Yet it is of tremendous value in that it is also a vector of other values. In this vein, cognizance of the contingency of patriarchy on other variables reinforces the case for measuring the productivity of the global norm for gender equality in power sharing beyond simply the quantitative register to address the prospects for qualitative progress. Insofar as gender equality can stand alone as a right by itself, there is much to commend about the stature of President Sirleaf, particularly in Liberian politics and generally in world history. However, considering the indisputatble role of feminist theory and action in creating the enabling conditions that heralded her election, it is reasonable, especially in the context of a discussion about patriarchy and gender, to ponder the implications of footprints such as hers for feminist ideation, ethics and politics as the lynchpin of the resource mobilization that spurred the creation of the enabling conditions that in turn helped herald elections such as Sirleaf's. It is not unreasonable, even if for the purposes of future research, to ponder the lessons that can be learned from the footprints of beneficiaries like her about the prospects and challenges for women's leadership to advance efforts to resist, transform, and dismantle patriarchy.

CONCLUSION

Dissonances reamain between idealizations of the promise of gender equality in power sharing and empirical outcomes of a select experience in a specific setting. It is important to learn from empirical experience to refresh understandings of patriarchy and gender in Africa against the backdrop of the global agenda for gender equality in political participation, representation, and leadership. A cornerstone of the equation to close pivotal gaps in achieving the strategic objective of increasing gender equality and to consolidate the gains made by women in the political realm is to reckon with the past by leveraging lessons learned from the experiences of women who have been thrust into standard-bearing positions. With the advantage of hindsight, it is easier to grasp and grapple with some of the pertinent gaps and to conceptualize how to better leverage past lessons to enliven a constructive path forward. Privileging an understanding of patriarchy informed by the data rooted in the outcomes and impacts of women's political life experience, this material underscore the importance of de-patriarchalizing the conceptualization and exercise of the technology of power.

The election of Ellen Johnson Sirleaf as Africa's first female president took place within less than one month of the EGM in 2005. Less than a year after the EGM, I received an unsolicited offer to serve as the Minister of Mines and Steel Development for the Federal Republic of Nigeria. The experience vividly opened my eyes to the imperative for gender equality and deepened my empathy for the challenges thereof. One thing that was crystal clear from my portfolio was the imperative to bolster the resources for development. Thus, one of my core responsibilities was to attract foreign direct investment (FDI) and resolute quest for this pointed up the absurdity of preoccupations with the aspirational returns of natural resources development while neglecting to build on potentially rich human resources that were readily on hand.[97] The emphasis on FDI signified the primacy of financial asset as a development tool to the diminution of attention to non-monetary forms of capital. The irony of my portfolio was that it entailed promoting the potentials of mining Nigeria's natural resources for a country that routinely scores poorly on mining the treasure trove constituted by its population, especially women who could be even better assets. In fact, the country had been ranked the worst place to be born a woman, and other African states were in tow under the grip of patriarchy.

NOTES

1. Taiwan, which is not a member of the UN, currently has a woman as its president. UN Women (2019) *Facts and Figures: Leadership and Political Participation.* https://www.unwomen.org/en/what-we-do/leadership-and-political-participation/facts-and-figures; Vogelstein, Rachel B. and Bro, Alexandra (2020) *Women's Power Index* (New York: Council on Foreign Relations). https://www.cfr.org/article/womens-power-index.

2. Inter-Parliamentary Union, *Women in National Parliaments* (Geneva, Switzerland: Inter-Parliamentary Union). http://archive.ipu.org/wmn-e/classif.htm (Updated May 29, 2020).

3. Tripp, Aili (2001) "Women's Movements and Challenges to Neopatrimonial Rule: Preliminary Observations from Africa," 32(1) *Development and Change*, 33–54; Gine, Xavier & Mansuri, Ghazala (2011) "Together We Will: Experimental Evidence on Female Voting Behavior in Pakistan," *Policy Research Working Paper Series 5692* (Washington, DC: The World Bank).

4. Building on the campaign theme #EachforEqual, the International Women's Day 2020 popularized the "hands out" equal pose to stress a strong call-to-action commensurate with specific missions to help challenge stereotypes, fight bias, broaden perceptions, improve situations and celebrate the diverse strengths and achievements of women, while calling out inequality. https://www.internationalwomensday.com/Theme.

5. See Obiora, L. Amede (1997) "Feminism, Globalization and Culture: After Beijing," 4 *Journal Global Legal Studies*, 355–406. Bloomington: Indiana University Press; UN Women (2015) *Beijing Declaration and Platform for Action, Beijing +5 Political Declaration and Outcome* (New York: United Nations Entity for Gender

Equality and the Empowerment of Women). https://www.unwomen.org/en/digital-library/publications/2015/01/beijing-declaration.

6. EGM Aide Memoir.

7. EGM Aide Memoir.

8. Rai, Shirin (2005) "Equal participation of women and men in decision-making processes, with particular emphasis on political participation and leadership: Background Paper," in United Nations, *Expert Group Meeting on Equal Participation of Women and Men in Decision-Making Processes, with Particular Emphasis on Political Participation and Leadership.* https://www.un.org/womenw atch/daw/egm/eql-men/docs/BP.1%20Background%20Paper.pdf. The experts agreed that women's participation and representation in decision-making bodies necessitates both enhanced presence and empowerment. Emphasizing the reciprocal relationship between political leadership and accountability, they noted that leadership allows women to set agendas and that such roles orient them to be responsive to constituencies and publics. In this vein, accountability transcends the question of enlarging women's numerical presence, encompassing need to enhance their ability to transform outcomes, contents and ways actors make policy.

9. While noting that critical junctures such as peace processes and transitions to democracy provide opportunities for women's political participation, the experts emphasized that such opportunities are not gender-neutral and that women involved in such processes need to seize them to push for gender-sensitive reforms.

10. See Dahlerup, D. and L. Freidenvall (2003) "Quotas as a 'Fast Track' to Equal Political Representation for Women," Paper presented at the IPSA World Congress, Durban, South Africa, June 29–July 4. The experts problematized the questions of experience and critical mass to warn against the tendency to treat women as a homogenous group and overate the aspiration for 30 percent representation of women as a panacea and ceiling instead of a threshold minimum.

11. Jane Mansbridge (1999); Hannah Pitkin (1967).

12. BBC (2018) *Liberia Country Profile.* https://www.bbc.com/news/world-africa -13729504.

13. Rehn, Elisabeth and Sirleaf Johnson, Ellen (2002) *Women, War and Peace: The Independent Experts' Assessment on the Impact of Armed Conflict on Women and Women's Role in Peace-Building—Progress of the World's Women 2002, Vol. 1* (New York: United Nations Entity for Gender Equality and the Empowerment of Women—UN Women).

14. Sirleaf's victory is consistent with new trends on the continent regarding women's political leadership. Adams, Melinda (2008) *Liberia's Election of Ellen Johnson-Sirleaf and Women's Executive Leadership in Africa* (Cambridge University Press). Tripp proffers several reasons for heightening interests in women's political participation in post-conflict countries. See Tripp, Aili Mari, et al. (2008) *African Women's Movements: Transforming Political Landscapes 195* (Cambridge University Press). http://ebookcentral.proquest.com/lib/uaz/detail.action?docID =412733.

15. Adams, Melinda (2008) "Liberia's Election of Ellen Johnson-Sirleaf and Women's Executive Leadership in Africa," 4(3) *Politics & Gender*, 475–484 (Women and Politics Research Section of American Political Science Association).

16. Government of Liberia (2009) *The Liberia National Gender Policy* (Monrovia: Ministry of Gender & Development).

17. Visionary Young Women in Leadership (2018) *Report on Women's Empowerment in Liberia* (Monrovia: National Democratic Institute). See also Hughes, M. et al. (2014) *Women's Leadership as a Route to Greater Empowerment: Report on the Diamond Leadership Model* (Washington, DC: USAID). https://www.usaid.gov/sites/default/files/documents/1866/Diamond%20Model%20Report.pdf; Krook, M.L. et al. (2014) *Women's Leadership as a Route to Greater Empowerment: Desktop Study* (Washington, DC: USAID). https://www.usaid.gov/sites/default/files/documents/1866/Women%27s%20Leadership%20as%20a%20Route%20to%20Greater%20Empowerment%20Desktop%20Study.pdf.

18. At least one female ran in the senatorial race in each of the 15 counties, while in the lower House of Representatives 44 women compared to 441 men contested. Government of Liberia (2009) *The Liberia National Gender Policy* (Monrovia: Ministry of Gender & Development).

19. Rwanda is another example of a post-conflict zone where women's representation in governing bodies has increased in the aftermath of civil war, although its progress is much greater than Liberia's. In fact, Rwandan women have won 61.3 percent of seats in the lower house, earning this post-conflict country in Sub-Saharan Africa the highest ranking worldwide for the number of women parliamentarians. Inter-Parliamentary Union, *Women in National Parliaments* (Geneva, Switzerland: Inter-Parliamentary Union). http://archive.ipu.org/wmn-e/classif.htm (Updated May 29, 2020). However, for a critical perspective, see Hogg, Carey Leigh (2009). "Women's Political Representation in Post-Conflict Rwanda: A Politics of Inclusion or Exclusion?" 11(3) *Journal of International Women's Studies*, 34–55.

20. L. Amede Obiora (2016) "Empirical Challenges of Deepening Democracy," Paper presented at the invite of Research Committee on the Quality of Democracy Main Theme Panel, Intl Political Science Ass. Congress, Poznan, Poland.

21. Government of Liberia (2019) Beijing+25 National Review Report: 25th Anniversary of the Fourth Conference on Women and Adoption of the Beijing Declaration and Platform for Action (1995), (Monrovia: Ministry of Gender and Development). By virtue of the 2017 elections, Liberian women hold a miniscule number of nine of the seventy-three seats in the Lower House, comprising 12.3 percent of the legislative body, which is significantly more than only one out of thirty seats that a woman occupies in the Upper Chamber which approximates merely 3.3 percent representation. See Inter-Parliamentary Union Parline, *Monthly Ranking of Women in National Parliaments* (Geneva, Switzerland: Inter-Parliamentary Union). https://data.ipu.org/women-ranking?month=6&year=2020. The voters returned a woman, Jewel Howard Taylor, as the vice-president of the Republic of Liberia. Only three of nineteen or 15.8 percent of the cabinet positions are held by women, although the percentages of women's representation are allegedly higher for "top-level technocrats" within the ministries, with women holding 25.4 percent of the deputy and assistant minister positions. See Visionary Young Women in Leadership (2018) *Report on Women's Empowerment in Liberia* (Monrovia: National Democratic Institute). See also Hughes, M. et al. (2014) *Women's Leadership as a Route to Greater Empowerment: Report on the Diamond Leadership Model* (Washington, DC:

USAID). https://www.usaid.gov/sites/default/files/documents/1866/Diamond%20Mo
del%20Report.pdf.

22. https://mo.ibrahim.foundation/news/2018/ellen-johnson-sirleaf-wins-2017-ibr
ahim-prize-achievement-african-leadership.

23. United States Department of State (2019) *LIBERIA: Country Report on
Human Rights Practices*.

24. UNDP (2019) "Briefing note for countries on the 2019 Human Development
Report—Liberia" in *Human Development Report 2019: Inequalities in Human
Development in the 21st Century*: Policies matter for inequalities. And inequalities
matter for policies. The human development lens is central to approaching inequal-
ity and asking why it matters, how it manifests itself and how best to tackle it.
Imbalances in economic power are eventually translated into political dominance.

25. 2019 Human Development Report. Liberia was not one of the countries
included in the human development aggregates in 2006 as the HDI could not be computed for it. UNDP (2006) *Human Development Report 413* (New York: Palgrave
Macmillan). However, the country has not for Liberia. Between 2000 and 2018,
Liberia's HDI value increased from 0.422 to 0.465, an increase of 10.2 percent.
Liberia's 2018 HDI of 0.465 is below the average of 0.507 for countries in the low
human development group and below the average of 0.541for countries in Sub-
Saharan Africa. From Sub-Saharan Africa, countries which are close to Liberia in
2018 HDI rank and to some extent in population size are Central African Republic
and Guinea-Bissau, which have HDIs ranked 188and 178 respectively. See 2019
Human Development Report 3 & 4.

26. World Economic Forum (2020) *Global Gender Gap Report* (Geneva,
Switzerland: WEF). The insight report positions the country at 118 in terms of the
percentage of legislators, senior officials and managers; 128 for women in parliament;
and eleven for the years with female/male head of state in the last fifty years. Just
18.5 percent of adult women reached secondary level of education compared to 39.6
percent of their male counterparts. See HDI

27. Pillay, A. (2001) "Violence against Women in the Aftermath," in S.
Meintjes, A. Pillay & M. Turshen (eds.), *The Aftermath: Women in Post-Conflict
Transformation* (London: Zed Books). Lamenting the failure to sustain the momentum built by the women's movement during the political transition and negotiations in
the post-apartheid democratic dispensation, one commentator stresses that evaluating
the element of political will requires looking beyond mere empty government rheto-
ric, symbolic ribbon-cutting ceremonies and establishment of under-resourced gender machinery to examine substantive accomplishment. See Lindiwe D. Makhunga
(2014) "South African Parliament and Blurred Lines: The ANC Women's League
and the African National Congress' Gendered Political Narrative," 28(2) *Agenda*,
33–47, doi: 10.1080/10130950.2014.931732. The author relates South Africa's ruling
ANC government's palliative care approach to the well-being of women to its hijacking of women's parliament and its monopolization by the ANC Women's League
reinforcing the party's cooptation of the state to reproduce a conservative gendered
political narrative in ways that explain the asymmetry between women's considerable

presence and lack of a substantive parliamentary politics in response to the urgent needs and interests of ordinary women, in lieu of patronage politics and party loyalty.

28. United States Department of State (2019) *LIBERIA: Country Report on Human Rights Practices*.

29. United States Department of State (2019) *LIBERIA: Country Report on Human Rights Practices*.

30. https://www.britannica.com/biography/Ellen-Johnson-Sirleaf.

31. United States Department of State (2014) *LIBERIA: Country Report on Human Rights Practices*.

32. United States Department of State (2014) *LIBERIA: Country Report on Human Rights Practices*.

33. United States Department of State (2014) *LIBERIA: Country Report on Human Rights Practices*.

34. Toe v. FrontPage Africa et al. [2013] LRSC 2 (July 15, 2013). http://liberlii .org/lr/cases/LRSC/2013/33.html.

35. Contempt Proceedings Against Hon. Tah et al. [2014] LRSC 2 (January 10, 2014) http://www.liberlii.org/cgi-bin/disp.pl/lr/cases/LRSC/2014/2.html?stem=0 &synonyms=0&query=Contempt%20Proceedings%20Against%20Hon.%20Christia na%20P.%20Tah,%20Minister%20of%20Justice%20and%20Counselor%20Beyan %20D.%20Howard. The minister petitioned for a review which the court denied. See Re: Contempt Proceedings Against Hon. Christiana P. Tah, Minister of Justice and Counselor Beyan D. Howard, in the Honorable Supreme Court of The Republic of Liberia Sitting in Its October Term, A.D. (2013) "Liberia: Justice Denied—Supreme Court Refuses to Hear Tah's Petition," *AllAfrica.com*, January 21, 2014. https://allafri ca.com/stories/201401240554.html.

36. Butty, James (2014) "Liberia's Minister Resigns," *Voice of America News*, October 7. https://www.voanews.com/africa/liberias-justice-minister-resigns.

37. BBC (2018) *Liberia Country Profile*. https://www.bbc.com/news/world-africa -13729504.

38. Central Intelligence Agency (2020) *Africa: Liberia—The World Factbook*. https://www.cia.gov/library/publications/the-world-factbook/geos/li.html.

39. Government of Liberia (2019) Beijing+25 National Review Report: 25th Anniversary of the Fourth Conference on Women and Adoption of the Beijing Declaration and Platform for Action (1995), (Monrovia: Ministry of Gender and Development).

40. Reasoning that women cannot disrupt the patriarchal agenda for their oppression using the very same logic that justifies such oppression, Lorde pondered what it means when the tools of patriarchy are used to examine the fruits of that same patriarchy, to which she responded that only the most narrow perimeters of change are possible and allowable. Lorde, Audre (1984) "The Master's Tools Will Never Dismantle the Master's House," in Lorde, Geraldine Audre, *Sister Outsider: Essays and Speeches* (Berkeley, CA: Crossing Press Feminist Series), 110–114. 2007.

41. Compare Mary Becker, 6: Women's inequality cannot be adequately addressed simply by working to get women "a bigger piece of the pie," otherwise, the women

who succeed will be those who conform to patriarchal values and who do not seriously threaten the patriarchal order.

42. "Feminist Perspectives on Power," *Stanford Encyclopedia of Philosophy.*

43. Irigaray, Luce (1985) *This Sex Which Is Not One* (Ithaca, NY: Cornell University Press), 81.

44. Pateman, Carole (1988) *The Sexual Contract* (Stanford: Stanford University Press), 182.

45. Phillips, Anne, Medearis, John and O. Neill, Daniel I. (2010) "Profile: The Political Theory of Carole Pateman," 43(4) *PS: Political Science and Politics*, 813–819. Cambridge University Press. https://doi.org/10.1017/S1049096510001629.

46. Scott, Joan (1988) "Gender: A Useful Category in Historical Analysis," in *Gender and the Politics of History* (New York: Columbia University Press).

47. See Butler, Judith (1999) *Gender Trouble: Feminism and the Subversion of Identity.* (New York; London: Routledge).

48. See Bryson, V. (2003) *Feminist Political Theory* (New York: Palgrave Macmillan), 188. Accessed August 28, 2020. https://openlibrary.org/books/OL156 05538M/Feminist_political_theory.

49. Bryson, *supra* note 48 at 184. See also See Bryson, V. (1999) "Patriarchy: A concept too useful to lose," 5 *Contemporary Politics*, 4; Hunnicutt, G. (2009). "Varieties of Patriarchy and Violence Against Women: Resurrecting 'Patriarchy' as a Theoretical Tool," 15(5) *Violence Against Women*, 553–573. doi:10.1177/1077801208331246. Compare Goldberg, Steven. 1979. *Male Dominance: The Inevitability of Patriarchy* (London: Abacus).

50. One writer asserts that it is not necessary to establish "definite evidence of the first cause to know that men have power, that they have had it for a very long time, that they seem to have had it in every known human society, and that they now use it to keep their power." See Bryson, *supra* note 48 at 187, quoting Spender, 1985b, p. 42.

51. Millet, Kate (1977) *Sexual Politics* (London: Virago Press), 30.

52. The enemy is perceived as male power in all its manifestations; however, this power is socially constructed and not necessarily embodied by all men. See Bryson, *supra* note 48 at 189; and Walby, Sylvia (1990) *Theorising Patriarchy* (London: Blackwell). Along similar lines, Sally Haslanger postulates a mixed analysis of oppression that distinguishes both agents and structures by classifying oppression into two categories. By virtues of what she calls one "agent oppression," a person or persons (the oppressor(s)) inflicts harm upon another (the oppressed) wrongfully or unjustly, regards to the other arm that she dubs "structural oppression," the oppression is not an individual wrong but a social/political wrong; that is, it is a problem lying in our collective arrangements, an injustice in our practices or institutions. See Haslanger, Sally (2012) *Resisting Reality: Social Construction and Social Critique* (New York: Oxford University Press), 314. For Haslanger gender categories are defined in terms of how one is socially positioned with respect to a broad complex of oppressive relations between groups that are distinguished from one another by means of sexual difference. *Id* at 229–230. See also Allen, Amy (2019) "Feminist

Perspectives on Power," in Edward N. Zalta (ed.), *The Stanford Encyclopedia of Philosophy*. https://plato.stanford.edu/archives/fall2016/entries/feminist-power/.

53. In this vein, it is useful to note Bryson's apt proviso that such domination must be understood in its own terms, instead of being reduced to other forms of domination; for example, it cannot be parsed as a mere derivative of economic power or class society. See Bryson, *supra* note 48 at 189.

54. Lerner, G. (1986) *The Creation of Patriarchy* (Oxford: Oxford University Press), 239.

   https://www-fulcrum-org.ezproxy1.library.arizona.edu/concern/monographs/mg74qm17c.

55. See, e.g., Okonjo, Kamene (1976) "The Dual-Sex Political System in Operation: Igbo Women and Community Politics in Midwestern Nigeria," in Hafkin, Nancy J. and Bay, Edna G. (eds.), *Women in Africa: Studies in Social and Economic Change* (Stanford, CA: Stanford University Press), 45–58. See also Obiora, L. Amede (2015) "Probing the Parameters of Gender, Power, and Democracy in Nigeria," in Vianello, Mino & Hawksworth, Mary (eds.), *Gender and Power: Towards Equality and Democratic Governance* (UK: Palgrave MacMillan), 64–81, 67.

56. See Obiora, L. Amede (Forthcoming) "Feminist Legal Theory & the Technology of Culture," in Yacob-Haliso, Ola & Falola, Toyin (eds.), *Palgrave Handbook on African Women's Studies* (New York: Palgrave MacMillan). See also Obiora, L. Amede (1995) "New Wine, Old Skin: (En)Gaging Nationalism," 28 *Indiana Law Review*, 575–599. Indianapolis: Indiana University School of Law.

57. Cudd, Ann (2006) *Analyzing Oppression* (Oxford: Oxford University Press), 25.

58. *Id* at 21–22, 45 & 46. Cudd's analysis of oppression avoids relying on assumptions about the psychology of individual agents. Unlike Cudd, Serene Khader acknowledges the psychological effects of oppression, without denying the possibility of agency on the part of the oppressed. For Khader, adaptive preferences are inconsistent with basic flourishing that people might be persuaded to transform upon normative scrutiny and exposure to conditions more conducive to flourishing." Khader proceeds to draw a distinction between merely adaptive preferences, which she unfurls as those formed through adaptation to existing social conditions and what she calls "inappropriately adaptive preferences" (IAPs)—preferences that are adaptive to oppressive social conditions and are harmful to those who adopt them. She then goes on to contend that IAPs impact individuals' sense of their own worth or entitlement to certain goods not globally but rather in particular domains and contexts and in relation to certain specific individuals or groups. See Khader, Serene J. (2011) *Adaptive Preferences and Women's Empowerment* (New York: Oxford University Press), 109, 42 & 52–53. See also "Feminist Perspectives on Power," *Stanford Encyclopedia of Philosophy*.

59. See, for example, Lerner, supra note 54. This is akin to Simone de Beauvoir's proposition that one is not born but rather becomes woman. See Beauvoir, Simone de. (2011) *The Second Sex*, translated by Constance Borde and Sheila Malovany-Chevallier (New York: Vintage). As Amy Allen explains, although Beauvoir suggests

that women are partly responsible for submitting to the status of the Other in order to avoid the anguish of authentic existence (see Beauvoir xxvii), she maintains that women are oppressed because they are compelled to assume the status of the Other, doomed to immanence (xxxv). Beauvoir's ground-breaking diagnosis of women's situation relies on the distinction between being for-itself—self-conscious subjectivity that is capable of freedom and transcendence—and being in-itself—the un-self-conscious things that are incapable of freedom and mired in immanence. Women's situation is thus marked by a basic tension between transcendence and immanence; as self-conscious human beings, they are capable of transcendence, but they are compelled into immanence by social, cultural, historical and economic conditions that define their existence and deny them transcendence (see Beauvoir, chapter 21). See "Feminist Perspectives on Power," *Stanford Encyclopedia of Philosophy*.

60. Kandiyoti, Deniz (1988) "Bargaining with Patriarchy," 2(3) *Gender and Society*, 274–290. Accessed September 27, 2020. http://www.jstor.org/stable/190357.

61. Yuval-Davis, Nira (1997) *Gender and Nation* (London: Sage), 8.

62. With the advent of this critical trend, universal meanings and master narratives capitulated to emerging interests in representation, identity construction, individual experience, and multiple subjectivities. See, for example, Amussen, Susan D. (2018) "The Contradictions of Patriarchy in Early Modern England," 30(2) *Gender and History*. doi 10.1111/1468-0424.12379; Androniki Dialeti, "From Women's Oppression to Male Anxiety: The Concept of 'Patriarchy' in the Historiography of Early Modern Europe," in Marianna Muravyeva and Raisa Tovio (eds.), *Gender in Late Medieval and Early Modern Europe* (New York: Routledge, 2013), 19–36 at 21. See also Spelman, Elizabeth V. (1988) *Inessential Woman: Problems of Exclusion in Feminist Thought*. Boston: Beacon Press.

63. Critiquing single-axis frameworks for understanding domination in the context of legal discrimination, Crenshaw explains, "the intersection of racism and sexism factors into Black women's lives in ways that cannot be captured wholly by looking at the race or gender dimensions of those experiences separately." See Kimberle Crenshaw (1991) "Mapping the Margins: Intersectionality, Identity Politics, and Violence against Women of Color," 43(6) *Stanford Law Review*, 1241–1299 at 1244. doi:10.2307/1229039; Crenshaw (2016) "The Urgency of Intersectionality," *TEDTalks*. https://www.youtube.com/watch?v=akOe5-UsQ2o&ab_channel=TED. Other proponents of intersectionality stress the need to consider intimate connections between privilege and oppression in tandem with the focus on relations and sites of oppression and subordination. See Nash, Jennifer. 2008. "Re-thinking Intersectionality," 89 *Feminist Review*, 1–15 at 12. See also "Feminist Perspectives on Power," *Stanford Encyclopedia of Philosophy*.

64. Although the contemporary discussion and use of the term *intersectionality* was sparked by Crenshaw, the concept of intersectionality has a long history and a complex genealogy with important antecedents. See Collins, Patricia Hill (2011) "Piecing Together a Genealogical Puzzle: Intersectionality and American Pragmatism," 3(2) *European Journal of Pragmatism and American Philosophy*, 88–112. See also Gines, Kathryn (2014) "Race Women, Race Men and Early Expressions of Proto-Intersectionality, 1830s–1930s," in Goswami, O'Donovan and

Yount (eds.), *Why Race and Gender Still Matter: An Intersectional Approach* (New York: Routledge), chapter 1. These range from works exemplified by Sojourner Truth, Audre Lorde, Angela Davis (1984), and bell hooks (1981) to include the Combahee River Collective's notion of "interlocking systems of oppression" (CRC 1977) and Deborah King's analysis of multiple jeopardy and multiple consciousness (King 1988). See "Feminist Perspectives on Power," *Stanford Encyclopedia of Philosophy*.

65. Butler, Judith (1990) *Gender Trouble: Feminism and the Subversion of Identity* (New York: Routledge), 5.

66. See Segal, 1987, p. xi. See also Bryson, *supra* note 48 at 191.

67. Spelman, *supra* note 62 at page 6. See Bryson, *supra* note 48 at 191 and 190 asserts that it is not necessary to believe in the immutable and biologically based 'badness' of men to agree that women in radically different societies or situations do frequently have experiences in common involving marginalization or exclusion from 'male-stream' political life; these experiences may reflect the systemic exercise of power by men over women. Nevertheless, the idea that all women are therefore united in a common sisterhood that transcends all man-made divisions can be dangerously misleading and attempts to compare the experiences of women in very different societies that are based on the premise that these are essentially "the same," conceal vast gaps in experiences.

68. Judith M. Bennett (2007) *History Matters: Patriarchy and the Challenge of Feminism* (University of Pennsylvania Press), 63.

69. An analogous illustration, albeit in a different context, can be gleaned from the longstanding experience of women who make every effort to curb the constraints of the private sphere by exiting and gaining more access to work, only to encounter familiar faces of patriarchy in the form of workplace sexism in the public sphere. See, for example, Amussen, Susan D. (2018) "The Contradictions of Patriarchy in Early Modern England," 30(2) *Gender and History*. doi 10.1111/1468-0424.12379

70. See Bryson *supra* note 48 at 194.

71. *Id.*

72. Bryson, *supra* note 48 at 194. Compare Lukes, Steven. 1986. "Introduction," in Steven Lukes (ed.), *Power* 63 (Oxford: Blackwell). Explaining that what power means is essentially contested, Lukes posits that conceptions of power are themselves shaped by power relations, suggesting that how we think about power may serve to reproduce and reinforce power structures and relations, or alternatively it may challenge and subvert them. To this extent, conceptual and methodological questions are inescapably political as they may contribute to the continued functioning of power or they may unmask the principles of operation that are of increased effectiveness if hidden from view. See also "Feminist Perspectives on Power," *Stanford Encyclopedia of Philosophy*.

73. Bryson *supra* note 48 at 194.

74. Compare Iris Young's identification of five faces of oppression, namely economic exploitation, socio-economic marginalization, lack of power or autonomy over one's work, cultural imperialism, and systematic violence (Young 1992, 183–193).

75. Frye, Marilyn (1983) *Politics of Reality: Essays in Feminist Theory* (Berkeley, CA: Crossing Press Feminist Series).

76. See MacKinnon 1989, 219. Pinpointing heterosexual intercourse as the paradigm of male domination (MacKinnon 1987, 3), Mackinnon insists that if gender difference is itself a function of domination, then the implication is that men are powerful, and women are powerless; "women/men is a distinction not just of difference, but of power and powerlessness. ... Power/powerlessness is the sex difference" (MacKinnon 1987, 123).

77. MacKinnon 1987, 53.

78. See "Feminist Perspectives on Power," *Stanford Encyclopedia of Philosophy*.

79. See Butler, *supra* note 47.

80. See "Feminist Perspectives on Power," *Stanford Encyclopedia of Philosophy*: Butler notes: "Foucault points out that juridical systems of power produce the subjects they subsequently come to represent. Juridical notions of power appear to regulate political life in purely negative terms . . . . But the subjects regulated by such structures are, by virtue of being subjected to them, formed, defined, and reproduced in accordance with the requirements of those structures" (1990, 2). This Foucauldian insight into the nature of subjection—into the ways in which becoming a subject means at the same time being subjected to power relations—thus forms the basis for Butler's trenchant critique of the category of women, and for her call for a subversive performance of the gender norms that govern the production of gender identity.

81. *Id.* Alcoff, Linda (1990) "Feminist Politics and Foucault: The Limits to a Collaboration," in Arlene Dallery and Charles Scott (eds.), *Crises in Continental Philosophy* (Albany, NY: SUNY Press), chapter 6. Benhabib, Seyla (1992) *Situating the Self: Gender, Community and Postmodernism in Contemporary Ethics* (New York: Routledge).

Benhabib, Seyla, Judith Butler, Drucilla Cornell, and Nancy Fraser (1995) *Feminist Contentions: A Philosophical Exchange* (New York: Routledge).

82. "Feminist Perspectives on Power," *Stanford Encyclopedia of Philosophy*.

83. See "Feminist Perspectives on Power," *Stanford Encyclopedia of Philosophy*. Serene Khader offers some insights to rethink the question of empowerment in feminist theory. See Khader, *supra* note 58. Susan Moller Okin's *Justice, Gender, and the Family* exemplifies liberal feminist critiques of the unjust distribution of the benefits and burdens of power which she designates as a "critical social good" to be redistributed more equitably (Okin 1989, 136). In contrast to Okin, Iris Marion Young argues against the atomistic understanding that obscure structural and institutional contexts that shape individual relations of power (a distributive model of power) and approaches it as a thing that can be possessed and distributed or redistributed, instead of as a widely dispersed and diffused social relation of domination. See Young, Iris Marion (1990) *Justice and the Politics of Difference* (Princeton, NJ: Princeton University Press), 32–33.

84. "Feminist Perspectives on Power," *Stanford Encyclopedia of Philosophy*. This feminist theory of power tends to understand power not as power-over but as power-to. Wartenberg (1990) argues that feminist understanding of power, which he calls transformative power, is a type of power-over, albeit one that is distinct from domination because it aims at empowering those over whom it is exercised.

85. Miller, Jean Baker (1992) "Women and Power," in Thomas Wartenberg (ed.), *Rethinking Power* (Albany, NY: SUNY Press), 240–248 at 241. Miller validates women's use of power in ways that simultaneously enhance, rather than diminish, the power of others. *Id* at 247–248.

86. Hartsock, Nancy (1983) *Money, Sex, and Power: Toward a Feminist Historical Materialism* (Boston: Northeastern University Press). Hartsock argues that precursors of this theory can be found in the work of some women who did not consider themselves to be feminists—most notably, Hannah Arendt, whose rejection of the command-obedience model of power and definition of 'power' as "the human ability not just to act but to act in concert" overlaps significantly with the feminist conception of power as empowerment (1970, 44).

87. Caputi, Mary (2013). *Feminism and Power: The Need for Critical Theory* (Lanham, MD: Lexington Books), 4.

88. *Id* at 89.

89. Khader *supra* note 58 at 176.

90. *Id* at 189. Khader's definition of empowerment enables her to rethink certain dilemmas of empowerment that have emerged in development theory and practices. For example, many development practitioners define empowerment in terms of choice, and then struggle to make sense of apparently self-subordinating choices. If choice equals empowerment, then does this mean that the choice to subordinate or disempower oneself is an instance of empowerment? To circumvent this dilemma, Khader emphasizes the conditions under which choices are made and the tradeoffs among different domains or aspects of flourishing that these conditions may necessitate. Discussing a case of young women in Tanzania who chose to undergo clitoridectomy *after* receiving education about the practice aimed at empowering them, Khader asks: "Are the young women who choose clitoridectomy disempowered because they have few options for unambiguously pursuing their flourishing or are they empowered because they have exercised agential capacities by making a choice?" To this hypothetical, she asserts that her analysis of IAP allows for an affirmative response to both scenarios. *Id* at 187.

91. Kabeer, Naila (1999) "Resources, Agency, Achievements: Reflections on the Measurement of Women's Empowerment," 30 *Development and Change*, 435–464. See also Parpart, Jane L., Shirin M. Rai, Kathleen Staudt (2002) *Rethinking Empowerment, Gender and Development in a Local/Global World* (London: Routledge).

92. Rai, Shirin (2005) "Equal participation of women and men in decision-making processes, with particular emphasis on political participation and leadership: Background Paper." Available at https://www.un.org/womenwatch/daw/egm/eql-men/docs/BP.1%20Background%20Paper.pdf.

93. *Id.* To Rai, empowerment can be seen both as a process, where it takes place in institutional, material and discursive contexts and as an outcome that can be measured against expected accomplishments such as a numerical representation of women in political institutions.

94. *Id.*

95. Sen explains that one of the strongest arguments for political freedom lies in the opportunities it gives citizens to discuss, debate, and participate in the selection of values and in the choice of priorities. As he put it, the capabilities and substantive freedoms of people to live the kind of lives they value and have reason to value can be enhanced by public policy, but in the same vein, the direction of public policy can also be influenced by the effective use of participatory capabilities by the public. He elaborates on this point by citing the example of how established conventions and prevailing mores which mediate social dynamics such as gender equity are in turn influenced by public discussions and social interactions which are themselves influenced by participatory freedoms.

96. Sen.

97. The incongruity reminded me of a comical but spot-on observation from a television episode of kids' letters to God in which one participant asked why God keeps making new babies while taking some lives, wondering if it was not better to keep the ones that he has already.

REFERENCES

Alcoff, Linda. 1990. "Feminist Politics and Foucault: The Limits to a Collaboration." In *Crises in Continental Philosophy*, edited by Arlene Dallery and Charles Scott. Albany, NY: SUNY Press, 6: 69–86.

Allen, Amy. 1998. "Rethinking Power." *Hypatia* 13 (1): 21–40. Accessed September 27, 2020. http://www.jstor.org/stable/3810605.

———. 1999. *The Power of Feminist Theory: Domination, Resistance, Solidarity.* Boulder, CO: Westview Press.

———. 2008a. *The Politics of Our Selves: Power, Autonomy, and Gender in Contemporary Critical Theory.* New York: Columbia University Press.

———. 2008b. "Power and the Politics of Difference: Oppression, Empowerment, and Transnational Justice." *Hypatia* 23 (3): 156–172. https://doi.org/10.1111/j.1527-2001.2008.tb01210.x.

———. 2019. "Feminist Perspectives on Power." In *The Stanford Encyclopedia of Philosophy*, edited by Edward N. Zalta. https://plato.stanford.edu/archives/fall2016/entries/feminist-power/.

Arendt, Hannah. 1970. *On Violence.* New York: Harcourt Brace & Co.

Beauvoir, Simone de. 2011. *The Second Sex*, translated by Constance Borde and Sheila Malovany-Chevallier. New York: Vintage.

Benhabib, Seyla. 1992. *Situating the Self: Gender, Community and Postmodernism in Contemporary Ethics.* New York: Routledge.

Benhabib, Seyla, Judith Butler, Drucilla Cornell, and Nancy Fraser. 1995. *Feminist Contentions: A Philosophical Exchange.* New York: Routledge.

Bryson, Valerie. 1999. "'Patriarchy': A Concept Too Useful to Lose." *Contemporary Politics* 5 (4): 311–324. https://doi.org/10.1080/13569779908450014.

———. 2003. *Feminist Political Theory.* New York: Palgrave Macmillan.

Butler, Judith. 1990. *Gender Trouble: Feminism and the Subversion of Identity.* New York: Routledge.

Caputi, Mary. 2013. *Feminism and Power: The Need for Critical Theory.* Lanham, MD: Lexington Books.

Cartwright, Nancy. 2007. *Hunting Causes and Using Them: Approaches in Philosophy and Economics.* Cambridge: Cambridge University Press.

———. 2010. "Will this Policy Work for You? Predicting Effectiveness Better: How Philosophy Helps." Speech presented at PSA Presidential Address, Montreal, Canada.

Childs, Sara, and Mona Lena Krook. 2006. "Should Feminists Give Up on Critical Mass? A Contingent Yes." *Politics and Gender* 2 (4): 522–530. https://doi.org/10.1111/j.1467-9248.2007.00712.x.

Collins, Patricia Hill. 2011. "Piecing Together a Genealogical Puzzle: Intersectionality and American Pragmatism." *European Journal of Pragmatism and American Philosophy* 3 (2): 88–112.

Combahee River Collective. 1981. "A Black Feminist Statement." In *This Bridge Called My Back: Writings by Radical Women of Color*, edited by Cherrie Moraga and Glora Anzaldua. New York: Kitchen Table/Women of Color Press, 210–218.

Crenshaw, Kimberle. 1991. "Mapping the Margins: Intersectionality, Identity Politics, and Violence against Women of Color." *Stanford Law Review* 43 (6): 1241–1299.

Cudd, Ann. 2006. *Analyzing Oppression.* Oxford: Oxford University Press.

Dahl, Robert. 1957. "The Concept of Power." *Behavioral Science* 2: 201–215.

Dahlerup, Drude (ed.). 2006. *Women, Quotas and Politics.* London: Taylor & Francis.

Day, Lynda R. 2008. "'Bottom Power': Theorizing Feminism and the Women's Movement in Sierra Leone (1981–2007)." *African and Asian Studies* 7 (4): 491–513.

Enloe, Cynthia. 2017. *The Big Push: Exposing and Challenging the Persistence of Patriarchy.* Oakland, CA: University of California Press.

Fraser, Nancy. 1989. *Unruly Practices: Power, Discourse and Gender in Contemporary Social Theory.* Minneapolis, MN: University of Minnesota Press.

Frye, Marilyn. 1983. *Politics of Reality: Essays in Feminist Theory.* Berkeley, CA: Crossing Press Feminist Series.

Fuest, Veronika. 2008. "'This Is the Time to Get in Front': Changing Roles and Opportunities for Women in Liberia." *African Affairs* 107 (427): 201–224.

Gilligan, Carol and Snider, Naomi. 2018. *Why Does Patriarchy Persist?* Cambridge, UK: Polity Press.

Gines, Kathryn. 2014. "Race Women, Race Men and Early Expressions of Proto-Intersectionality, 1830s–1930s." In *Why Race and Gender Still Matter: An Intersectional Approach*, edited by Maeve M. O'Donovan, Namita Goswami, and Lisa Yount. New York: Routledge, 1: 13–25.

Hartsock, Nancy. 1983. *Money, Sex, and Power: Toward a Feminist Historical Materialism.* Boston: Northeastern University Press.

Haslanger, Sally. 2012. *Resisting Reality: Social Construction and Social Critique.* New York: Oxford University Press.

Held, Virginia. 1993. *Feminist Morality: Transforming Culture, Society, and Politics.* Chicago: University of Chicago Press.

Hughes, Melanie M. 2009. "Armed Conflict, International Linkages, and Women's Parliamentary Representation in Developing Nations." *Social Problems* 56 (1): 174–204.

Irigaray, Luce. 1985. *This Sex Which Is Not One.* Ithaca, NY: Cornell University Press.

Kandiyoti, Deniz. 1988. "Bargaining with Patriarchy." *Gender and Society* 2 (3): 274–290. Accessed September 27, 2020. http://www.jstor.org/stable/190357.

Khader, Serene J. 2011. *Adaptive Preferences and Women's Empowerment.* New York: Oxford University Press.

Krook, Mona Lena. 2006. "Reforming Representation: The Diffusion of Candidate Gender Quotas Worldwide." *Politics and Gender* 2 (3): 303–327.

Lerner, Gerda. 1986. *The Creation of Patriarchy.* Oxford: Oxford University Press.

Lorde, Audre. 1984. *Sister/Outsider: Essays and Speeches by Audre Lorde.* Freedom, CA: Crossing Press.

Lovenduski, Joni, and Azza Karam. 2002. "Women in Parliament: Making a Difference." In *Women in Parliament: Beyond Numbers*, edited by J. Ballington and A. Karam. Stockholm: International Idea, 1–16.

Lukes, Steven. 1986. "Introduction." In *Power*, edited by Steven Lukes. Oxford: Blackwell, 1–18.

———. 2005. *Power: A Radical View*, 2nd expanded edition. London: Macmillan.

MacKinnon, Catharine. 1987. *Feminism Unmodified: Discourses on Life and Law.* Cambridge, MA: Harvard University Press.

———. 1989. *Toward a Feminist Theory of the State.* Cambridge, MA: Harvard University Press.

Miller, Jean Baker. 1992. "Women and Power." In *Rethinking Power*, edited by Thomas Wartenberg. Albany, NY: SUNY Press, 240–248.

Millet, Kate. 1977. *Sexual Politics.* London: Virago Press.

Moghadam, Valentine M. 2004. "Patriarchy in Transition." *Journal of Comparative Studies*, 35(2):137–162.

Nash, Jennifer. 2008. "Re-thinking Intersectionality." *Feminist Review*, 89: 1–15.

Norris, Pippa, and Ronald Inglehart. 2003. *Rising Tide: Gender Equality and Cultural Change around the World.* Cambridge: Cambridge University Press.

Okin, Susan Moller. 1989. *Justice, Gender and the Family.* New York: Basic Books.

Ortner, Sheri B. 1974. "Is Female to Male as Nature Is to Culture?" In *Women, Culture, & Society*, edited by Michelle Zimbalist Rosaldo and Louise Lamphey. Stafford, CA: Stanford University Press, 68–87.

Pateman, Carole. 1988. *The Sexual Contract.* Stanford: Stanford University Press.

Pateman, Carole, and Charles Mills. 2007. *Contract and Domination.* Cambridge: Polity Press.

Pawson, Ray, and Nicholas Tilley. 1997. *Realistic Evaluation.* London: Sage.

Phillips, Anne. 1991. *Engendering Democracy.* Cambridge: Polity Press.

Rai, Shirin. 2005. "Equal Participation of Women and Men in Decision-making Processes, with Particular Emphasis on Political Participation and Leadership:

Background Paper." https://www.un.org/womenwatch/daw/egm/eql-men/docs/BP
.1%20Background%20Paper.pdf.

Rogers, Melvin. 2018. Democracy Is a Habit: Practice It—John Dewey on the culture democracy requires. *Boston Review*. http://bostonreview.net/politics/melvin-roger s-democracy-habit-practice-it.

Rosaldo, Renato. 1993. "Notes towards a Critique of Patriarchy from a Male Position." *Anthropological Quarterly*, 66(2): 81–86.

Saar, Martin. 2010. "Power and Critique." *Journal of Power* 3 (1): 7–20.

Sen, Amartya K. 1999. "Democracy as a Universal Value." *Journal of Democracy* 10 (3): 3–17.

Tripp, Aili Mari. 2002. "Women's Movements and Challenges to Neopatrimonial Rule: Preliminary Observations from Africa." *Development and Change* 32 (1): 33–54.

Walby, Sylvia. 1990. *Theorising Patriarchy*. London: Blackwell.

Wartenberg, Thomas. 1990. *The Forms of Power: From Domination to Transformation*. Philadelphia: Temple University Press.

Waylen, Georgina. 2008. "Enhancing the Substantive Representation of Women: Lessons from Transitions to Democracy." *Parliamentary Affairs* 61 (3): 518–534.

Wollstonecraft, Mary. 1975. *A Vindication of the Rights of Women*. Baltimore: Penguin.

Yeatmann, Anna. 1997. "Feminism and Power." In *Reconstructing Political Theory: Feminist Perspectives*, edited by Mary Lyndon Shanley and Uma Narayan. University Park, Pennsylvania: The Pennsylvania State University Press.

Young, Iris Marion. 1990. *Justice and the Politics of Difference*. Princeton, NJ: Princeton University Press.

———. 1992. "Five Faces of Oppression." In *Rethinking Power*, edited by Thomas Wartenberg, Albany, NY: SUNY Press, 1–20.

Yuval-Davis, Nira. 1997. *Gender and Nation*. London: Sage.

Chapter 2

Intersectionality, Women's Rights in Africa, and the Maputo Protocol

Johanna E. Bond

Common understandings of women's human rights have grown more complex in recent years. The struggle for women's human rights is increasingly understood to encompass systemic discrimination based not only on gender but also on other aspects of identity such as race, ethnicity, class, religion, sexual orientation and gender identity, and disability. "Intersectionality" refers to the insight that systems of oppression intersect and mutually reinforce one another in people's lives. Intersectionality theory has changed the way that scholars and activists alike approach women's human rights violations. The theory offers a lens through which to explore the nuances of privilege, or lack thereof, as it operates in the lives of women around the world.

Although Kimberlé Crenshaw, a critical race feminist from the United States, coined the term *intersectionality* in the late 1980s, the broad parameters of the concept originated much earlier. Sojourner Truth, a former slave and an abolitionist in the United States, for example, famously challenged the combination of race and gender-based oppression in 1851, asking, "Ain't I a woman?" Early critical race feminists in the United States again popularized this notion in the Combahee River Collective's statement in 1977, which recognized that multiple systems of oppression operate simultaneously in people's lives, that these multiple sites of oppression and discrimination intersect, and that one cannot easily tease them apart. At the same time, feminists from the global South were raising parallel critiques of the universalizing tendencies of some feminists in the global North.

In the late 1980s and early 1990s, Crenshaw recognized the mutually reinforcing and intersecting nature of multiple oppressions and popularized the notion of intersectionality. Describing the core insight of intersectionality theory as applied to women of color, Crenshaw explains, "[T]he intersection of racism and sexism cannot be captured wholly by looking at the race or

47

gender dimensions of those experiences separately" (Crenshaw 1993, 1244). Crenshaw articulated the notion that systems of subordination such as racism and sexism intersect in the lives of women of color and result in forms of discrimination that are qualitatively different from the discrimination faced by Black men or White women.

Several scholars have applied the insights of intersectionality theory to the realm of global women's rights (Bond 2003; Goldblatt 2015; Truscan and Bourke-Martignoni 2016). This chapter applies intersectionality theory to the discourse of women's rights in Africa. Specifically, I argue that intersectionality theory is necessary to understand fully the multifaceted discrimination faced by African women. Intersectionality also encourages an appreciation of the agency with which women fight for equality within their families, communities, and countries. I argue that some nongovernmental organizations in sub-Saharan Africa, such as the Coalition for African Lesbians (CAL) (cal .org.za), have already embraced the concept of intersectionality. The theory informs the grassroots human rights work undertaken by these organizations. The chapter also explores the extent to which the human rights instruments of the African Union (AU) facilitate intersectional human rights analysis. In conclusion, I argue that the African Protocol on the Rights of Women in Africa, the "Maputo Protocol," incorporates insights from intersectionality theory and, as a result, offers women in the region a critical tool for pursuing comprehensive remedies for human rights violations.

THE EVOLUTION OF INTERSECTIONALITY
IN HUMAN RIGHTS DISCOURSE

Until the early 2000s, the global women's human rights movement focused primarily on discrimination based on sex. The prevailing understanding of sex-based discrimination gradually morphed into the broader concept of gender-based discrimination (Bond 2003, 124). The move from sex to gender as the focus for women's human rights advocacy reflected broader trends in feminist theory. In particular, "sex" was a limiting term linked to physiological differences between biological males and biological females. Gender is understood as a broader, more fluid term reflecting the relational, socially constructed understandings of feminine and masculine identities. The concept of gender has also opened the door for a richer understanding of sexuality and gender identity that extends beyond the male/female binary.

Despite this evolving understanding of gender, many of the core women's human rights treaties refer to *sex*, because they were drafted before the 1990s. The Convention on the Elimination of All Forms of Discrimination Against Women (CEDAW), for example, refers to sex discrimination and, specifically, discrimination against women as compared to men. The United Nations General Assembly adopted CEDAW in 1979, years before *gender* entered the popular lexicon. In contemporary discussions of CEDAW, however, representatives of the United Nations, scholars, and activists widely refer to gender-based discrimination rather than sex-based discrimination.

Similarly, CEDAW contains no references in its text to intersectionality. The textual focus of the treaty is on discrimination against women *qua* women, with little attention paid to other aspects of identity that could lead to intersecting, mutually constitutive forms of subordination. In the 1970s, when CEDAW was drafted, many women's rights advocates around the world were in the process of raising awareness about the existence of discrimination against women. As a strategic matter, advocacy efforts focused on the concept of women's shared experiences of discrimination as a way of uniting women behind the cause of women's equality. Some scholars in the global North, such as Robin Morgan, promoted the notion of the "global sisterhood" to galvanize support for women's rights advocacy around the world. This appeal to "common" experience, however, failed to capture the many ways in which gender discrimination and subordination is differently experienced across such identity categories as race, ethnicity, religion, class, disability, sexual orientation, and gender identity. Because intersectionality had not yet permeated the consciousness of international legal scholars or human rights activists at the time of CEDAW's drafting, there is very little evidence of intersectional analysis in the text of the treaty.

CEDAW's text, for example, does not explicitly refer to other identity categories that are central to intersectional analysis, such as race, ethnicity, religion, class, sexual orientation, and gender identity. CEDAW does expressly mention the plight of rural women in Article 14 of the treaty. Article 14 recognizes the unique challenges posed by the combination of rurality and gender. The treaty also mentions discrimination against women based on nationality, discrimination against girls, and discrimination based on marital status. These subgroups of women represent a nod toward differentiated experiences of discrimination among women based on other identity categories. The text of CEDAW, however, goes no further in recognizing the insights of intersectionality. In the years since the treaty's drafting, however, the UN treaty bodies have sporadically begun to adopt an intersectional framework in their human rights work.

Within the United Nations human rights system, there are nine primary multilateral human rights treaties. Each treaty has a committee of independent experts that oversees the implementation of the treaty. In some cases, the committees also hear individual complaints from victims of human rights violations that fall within the purview of the relevant treaty. Since the early 2000s, the committee that oversees the implementation of CEDAW (the "CEDAW Committee") has slowly begun to embrace an intersectional understanding of human rights. The other committees with oversight over the major human rights treaties have also begun to use an intersectional framework for examining potential violations of the human rights treaties.

One of the earliest indications that the United Nations human rights treaty bodies might be moving to embrace intersectional analysis came in 2000. In 2000, the Committee on the Elimination of Racial Discrimination (CERD) adopted a general recommendation on the gender-related dimensions of racial discrimination. When the treaty bodies adopt general recommendations, those recommendations are often the most authoritative guide to states' obligations under the terms of the treaty. As such, they represent an important articulation by the Committee of its interpretation of treaty provisions. The fact that the CERD Committee adopted an intersectional interpretation of the Convention on the Elimination of Racial Discrimination is highly significant in the evolving understanding of intersectionality as an analytical lens within the United Nations treaty bodies.

In 2010, the CEDAW Committee adopted a general recommendation that identifies intersectionality as a "basic concept for understanding the scope of State parties' obligations" (CEDAW General Recommendation 28 2010, para. 18). CEDAW's General Recommendation 28 recognizes that "[c]ertain groups of women, including women deprived of their liberty, refugees, asylum-seeking and migrant women, stateless women, lesbian women, disabled women, women victims of trafficking, widows and elderly women, are particularly vulnerable to discrimination through civil and penal laws, regulations, and customary law and practices" (CEDAW General Recommendation 28 2010, para. 31).

In 2014, the CEDAW Committee and the Committee on the Rights of the Child issued a joint general recommendation on harmful practices that explicitly recognized the intersectional nature of certain human rights violations. General Recommendation/Comment 31 states, "Harmful practices are persistent practices and behaviours that are grounded on discrimination on the basis of sex, gender, age, and other grounds as well as multiple and/or intersecting forms of discrimination that often involve violence and cause physical and/or psychological harm or suffering" (CEDAW/CRC Gen. Rec./ Comment No. 31 2014, para. 14).

At times, the CEDAW Committee has raised the issue of "multiple discrimination" that some women may face based on identity categories such as race, ethnicity, religion, and sexual orientation (CEDAW Concluding Observations on the Ninth Periodic Report of Guyana 2019, para. 45). These references typically appear in concluding observations to State parties, in which the Committee offers its views regarding the state's efforts to implement the convention. The Committee is inconsistent, however, in its invocation of intersectional analysis when it responds to State parties' reports through the issuance of concluding observations.

In the years between 2000 and 2018, other United Nations treaty bodies have slowly taken similar steps to explore intersectionality as a framework for addressing complex human rights violations. Although progress has been slow in the last fifteen years, there are encouraging signs that the United Nations treaty system is open to a more robust embrace of intersectionality theory as an analytical lens for its human rights work. There are similar indications that representatives of the African regional human rights system have begun to explore an intersectional framework for human rights work.

INTERSECTIONALITY WITHIN THE DISCOURSE OF GENDER AND HUMAN RIGHTS IN AFRICA: THE EXAMPLE OF SEXUAL VIOLENCE IN ARMED CONFLICT

An intersectional lens deepens our understanding of human rights violations. It opens up space for inquiry about complex, intersecting, and mutually constitutive sources of discrimination and subordination. Rather than evoking a unidimensional analysis of gender discrimination, for example, intersectionality fosters a richer understanding of the many mutually reinforcing ways gender subordination intersects with discrimination based on race, ethnicity, religion, socioeconomic status, disability, sexual orientation, and gender identity. From a human rights perspective, this deeper, more nuanced approach allows for broader human rights remedies that more fully redress the human rights violations in question.

In the context of human rights in Africa, intersectional human rights abuses arise in a variety of contexts. In the context of sexual violence in armed conflict, human rights violations sometimes reflect the combination of subordination based on both gender and ethnicity or race. The 1994 genocide in Rwanda offers an example. The conflict involved two large ethnic groups, the Hutus and the Tutsis. The violent conflict led to the massacre of between 500,000 and 800,000 people in a country of only eight million people, with most of the victims coming from the minority Tutsi group (Drumbl 2007, 71).

In addition to murder, sexual violence was widespread throughout the genocide in Rwanda. Although both men and women were victims of sexual violence in the conflict, the majority of sexual violence victims were female. In those cases, perpetrators targeted women for sexual violence based on both their gender and their ethnicity. Perpetrators subjected women to "rape, gang-rape, the introduction of objects into women's vaginas and pelvic area, sexual slavery, forced incest, deliberate HIV transmission, forced impregnation and genital mutilation" (Davis 2015, 225). Like the genocide in Rwanda, armed conflicts in Darfur, Sudan, and the Democratic Republic of Congo have resulted in widespread sexual violence committed against women that is based on both gender and ethnicity.

To appreciate fully the devastating consequences to victims, human rights bodies must begin to analyze sexual/ethnic violence as intersectional. In any ethnic conflict or in its aftermath, human rights bodies must consider the consequences of that violence within specific communities of women. Aisha Davis notes, "[V]ictims of rape during ethnic conflicts would benefit from having their experiences viewed intersectionally through recognition during indictment, acknowledgement during trial and sentencing, and individualisation when awarding reparations" (Davis 2015, 241). A one-size-fits-all approach to rape in armed conflict may address neither the systematic gender subordination underlying the sexual violence nor the impact on women in particular ethnic communities.

INTERSECTIONALITY WITHIN THE AFRICAN REGIONAL SYSTEM

The 1963 Charter establishing the Organization of African Unity (OAU), which was later replaced by the AU Constitutive Act, obligated states to have regard for the rights embodied in the Universal Declaration of Human Rights. Although the Charter contained no express human rights obligations for states, the OAU, nevertheless, took steps to address human rights issues, particularly in the areas of decolonization, race discrimination, the environment, and migration and refugee populations. The OAU faced the criticism, however, that its early interventions did not include the large-scale human rights violations perpetrated by some authoritarian leaders (Center for Human Rights 2016, 1).

The OAU adopted the African Charter on Human and Peoples' Rights (known as the African Charter or the Banjul Charter) in 1981. All member states of the OAU had ratified the Charter by 1999. As a multilateral, regional human rights treaty, the African Charter provides a legal framework for analyzing human rights in Africa. The African Charter offers protection of both civil and political rights and of economic, social, and cultural rights (Center for Human Rights 2011, 56). It also offers human rights protection to group or collective rights (Center for Human Rights 2011, 56–57). In addition to providing a basic framework for human rights in the region, the Charter created the African Commission on Human and Peoples' Rights (African Commission). The African Commission is charged with promoting, protecting, and interpreting the human rights included in the Charter. The Commission's decisions have influenced domestic law and policy in countries within the region. The Protocol to the African Charter on the Establishment of an African Court on Human and Peoples' Rights (now the African Court of Justice and Human Rights) was adopted in 1998 and entered into force in 2004. The African Court, with the ability to issue legally binding decisions, established itself as a critical source of human rights jurisprudence in the region (Center for Human Rights 2011, 53).

In addition to the African Charter, the African Charter on the Rights and Welfare of the Child was adopted by the OAU, in 1990. The Charter on the Rights and Welfare of the Child entered into force in 1999. The Charter prohibits discrimination and promotes children's healthy development. It addresses children's rights in the context of *inter alia* child marriage, child labor, child abuse, juvenile justice, armed conflict, and sexual exploitation and human trafficking (Center for Human Rights 2011, 12). Without explicitly stating it, the Charter embraces intersectionality theory by recognizing that gender and age bias may combine to subject young girls to mutually reinforcing forms of subordination (African Charter on the Rights and Welfare of the Child 1990, art. 21). Similarly, the Charter includes special protection for disabled or, in the words of the Charter, "handicapped" children, along with protection against harmful social and cultural practices that might be discriminatory toward girl children (African Charter on the Rights and Welfare of the Child 1990, art. 13).

In 2003, the African Union (AU, formerly the OAU) adopted a supplemental protocol to the Charter dealing with women's human rights. The Protocol to the African Charter on Human and Peoples' Rights on the Rights of Women in Africa (the "Maputo Protocol") came into force in November 2005. Although the African Charter includes basic guarantees of gender equality, activists and member states felt the need for a supplemental protocol that would specifically and broadly protect women from discrimination and inequality (Center for Human Rights 2011, 13).

The Maputo Protocol offers broad protection against gender-based discrimination. It includes provisions related to the rights to "life, integrity and security of person"; right to be free from "harmful practices"; and to "equal rights in marriage" (Protocol to the African Charter on Human and Peoples' Rights on the Rights of Women in Africa 2003, arts. 3–7). The Maputo Protocol guarantees several other human rights designed to comprehensively protect aspects of women's public and private lives. This comprehensive articulation of women's rights to non-discrimination and gender equality has become a critical human rights instrument for women in the region.

INTERSECTIONAL INSIGHTS REFLECTED
IN THE MAPUTO PROTOCOL

Compared with the text of CEDAW and the African Charter, the text of the Maputo Protocol reflects a slightly deeper commitment to intersectionality theory. The Maputo Protocol, however, does not specifically use the term *intersectionality*. Because the AU adopted the Protocol in 2003, much later than many of the core United Nations human rights treaties, the Protocol's text reflects a more nuanced, more contemporary understanding of women's rights. For example, Article 22 of the Protocol provides special protection for elderly women. The insight that gender discrimination may intersect with age discrimination and affect older women differently than it does younger women is, at its core, an intersectional insight.

Article 22 requires ratifying states to "provide protection to elderly women and take specific measures commensurate with their physical, economic, and social needs as well as their access to employment and professional training." The provision also offers older women protection from violence, including sexual violence. In so doing, the Maputo Protocol implicitly recognizes intersectionality by acknowledging that older women face a combination of discrimination based on age and gender.

HelpAge International, an organization dedicated to combating age discrimination, describes the kind of intersectional discrimination that older African women sometimes experience. HelpAge notes:

> Their age can make them a scapegoat when something goes wrong in the community; when a relative dies, a child goes missing, someone becomes ill or even if they just have red eyes due to years of poor cooking conditions. The need to blame someone has led to many older women becoming victims of verbal and physical abuse and often leads to them being excluded from their families and communities. (Cummingsjohn 2011, para. 3)

In addition to facing unfounded blame and accusations of witchcraft, older African women are often unable to get bank loans or credit and are more likely than men to live in poverty (Ogonda 2006, 6). Widows are sometimes unable to inherit marital property because of discriminatory laws or discriminatory enforcement of laws. Job Ogonda describes the fate of many older widows in Africa:

> [Older widows] are more susceptible to all forms of abuse, including murder, in the quest by relatives, including sons, to disinherit them of property entitled to them after their husbands pass away. In many cases, family resources (land, the

house and money) are allocated to a male relative, often along with the widow herself, especially if she is young. The older ones are usually abandoned by a society that sees no need for them. (Ogonda 2006, 6)

The discrimination and abuse faced by older women bears some resemblance to the discrimination faced by other women. It shares the same patriarchal roots. Discrimination faced by older women, however, is qualitatively different in important ways. If human rights mechanisms are to address properly discrimination against older women, there must be a recognition of the ways in which gender and age subordination intersect to produce a qualitatively different form of discrimination. By specifically protecting older women, the Maputo Protocol opens the door for consideration of intersectionality. The recognition of this different experience of discrimination reflects the foundational contribution of intersectionality theory.

Similarly, the Maputo Protocol specifically protects women with disabilities. By so doing, the Protocol embraces an intersectional analysis grounded in the recognition that women with disabilities experience qualitatively different and mutually reinforcing forms of discrimination that are greater than those faced by men with disabilities and by women without disabilities (Protocol to the African Charter on Human and Peoples' Rights on the Rights of Women in Africa 2003, art. 23). The barriers faced by disabled people increase when combined with gender, poverty, and certain other aspects of identity. Disability rights scholar Mark Priestly writes, "In a global context, most disabled people encounter both disabling barriers *and* barriers to scarce resources. Access to resources is highly gendered, and the life experiences of disabled women require specific attention" (Priestly 2001, 4).

Over one billion people around the world live with a disability. Eighty percent of that one billion live in developing countries, with 20 percent of those among the poorest in the world (Disability Rights Fund 2013, at 10). Disability, female gender, and poverty have a mutually reinforcing relationship, with the combination producing a qualitatively different experience of discrimination than that experienced by those who are privileged along any or all of those axes. The links between the female gender and poverty are well established (Goldblatt 2015). Disability in women may affect their ability to work or marry, both of which may affect their socioeconomic status. In countries with a dowry or brideprice, a daughter with a disability is often seen as adversely affecting the family's finances (Humphrey 2016, 15). Discrimination and maltreatment sometimes begin in the family and continue throughout the life of a disabled woman. The intersection of disability, race, class, and gender in a woman's life also affect the ways in which women with disabilities seek help and the extent to which they are able to access service providers (Cramer and Plummer 2009, 162).

Women and girls with disabilities are at high risk for violence. Girls with disabilities are at a higher risk of, for example, mercy killings and infanticide than are boys with disabilities (Humphrey 2016, 24). In the context of gender-based violence, women with disabilities who are survivors of violence will have different service needs than nondisabled women. "Intersectionality provides a conceptual framework for understanding the complicated reasons why, how, and from whom abused women seek assistance and their experiences with service providers," note Cramer and Plummer (2009, 176). Some programs that incorporate an intersectional approach to advocacy and services have enjoyed success, including programs that incorporate indigenous values and disability awareness into strategies for combating violence.

By specifically including protection for women with disabilities, the Maputo Protocol reflects an evolving commitment to intersectionality. This more nuanced, intersectional understanding of human rights violations invites the African Commission and related regional human rights institutions to implement a sophisticated and more holistic human rights remedy. For example, a poor, disabled woman in rural Kenya may need different human rights remedies than a wealthy disabled woman from Nairobi, given the generally high cost of additional medical services and specialized assistive devices (Humphrey 2016, 8). The intersectional framework embodied in the Protocol invites a deep, rich inquiry about how best to provide access to services across identity categories, including, for example, in rural and impoverished areas of the region, within specific religious or ethnic communities, or within LGBTQI communities.

The Protocol also provides "special protection for women in distress" in Article 24. This article requires states to "ensure the protection of poor women and women heads of families including women from marginalised population groups and provide an environment suitable to their condition and their special physical, economic and social needs." Here, too, the Maputo Protocol fosters an intersectional approach that recognizes that poor women are differently positioned than both men living in poverty and women who enjoy higher socioeconomic status. It goes further to address women living in poverty who may also be from marginalized population groups.

WHERE THE AU FALLS SHORT OF A COMMITMENT TO INTERSECTIONALITY: LGBTQI RIGHTS

In May 2008, the Coalition for African Lesbians (CAL) applied for observer status at the African Commission. Prior to submission, CAL had satisfied all the requirements for observer status, having submitted the required documentation and otherwise met the legal and administrative criteria. The African Commission postponed a decision on CAL's observer status on three separate occasions before rejecting the application in October 2010. The African Commission noted, "[T]he activities of the said Organisation [CAL] do not promote and protect any of the rights enshrined in the African Charter" (Centre for Human Rights and African Commission 2011, 40). This approach fails to recognize that many people who identify as LGBTQI are frequently targeted for violence and denied the very rights enshrined in the Charter on the basis of their real or perceived sexual orientation or gender identity, making them victims of gender discrimination as it is commonly defined in contemporary human rights analysis.

In 2014, CAL submitted another application for observer status. Also, in 2014, the African Commission adopted a resolution titled "Protection against Violence and other Human Rights Violations against Persons on the basis of their real or imputed Sexual Orientation or Gender Identity." In Resolution 275, the African Commission expressed alarm at the increasing rate of violence against LGBTQI communities in the region and at the violence directed at the human rights defenders and civil society organizations who are working to protect those communities. Resolution 275 condemns such violence and urges states to take action to combat violence against people "on the basis of their imputed or real sexual orientation or gender identities" (Resolution 275 2014). In the wake of this landmark resolution, the African Commission granted CAL observer status at the Commission's 56th Ordinary Session in 2015.

After taking the important step of granting CAL observer status and after passing a resolution on LGBTQI rights, the African Union, as a whole, has wavered significantly in its commitment to LGBTQI rights. The Executive Council of the AU (the Executive Council), for example, has been reluctant to recognize LGBTQI rights. The Executive Council supports the AU Assembly, reports to the AU Assembly of Heads of State and Government, and supports work on issues of common concern to member states. The Executive Council has injected itself into the Commission's work on LGBTQI rights, asserting pressure on the Commission to review its 2015 decision to grant observer status to CAL. In requesting a review of CAL's observer status, the Executive Council called on the African Commission to consider "African values" when reviewing applications for observer status (Article19 2018). After initially resisting pressure from the Executive Council, the African Commission implemented a June 2018 decision to revoke CAL's observer status. Human rights organizations have expressed concern that the African Commission is not operating as an independent human rights body. The decision calls into question the African Commission's commitment to LGBTQI rights.

The campaign for LGBTQI rights must be an intersectional one if it is to address the needs and priorities of diverse members of LGBTQI communities within the region. Although few of the core human rights treaties explicitly mention LGBTQI rights, human rights bodies have developed an approach for addressing rights violations based on sexual orientation or gender identity. That approach considers gender to be a social construct and recognizes that perpetrators often target those who do not conform to societal expectations around gender, masculinity, femininity, and sexuality. Some human rights treaties, such as the 1966 International Covenant on Civil and Political Rights (ICCPR) and the 1966 International Covenant on Economic, Social, and Cultural Rights (ICESCR), prohibit discrimination based on a number of enumerated categories and include a catch-all category for "any other status." Going further, the Human Rights Committee, which oversees the implementation of the ICCPR, has held that the prohibition on sex discrimination in the treaty encompasses discrimination based on sexual orientation and gender identity (Bond 2016, 75). Other human rights bodies have followed suit and recognized human rights violations based on sexual orientation and gender identity.

The intersection of gender discrimination and discrimination based on sexual orientation or gender identity is evident in the sexual violence sometimes perpetrated against lesbians as a method of brutally enforcing gender norms. Perpetrators of gender-based violence may police social norms around sexuality in attempts to enforce compliance with sociocultural expectations of masculinity and femininity. In this way, perpetrators use violence to regulate sexuality. African human rights activists have also noted, "It is . . . imperative that an understanding of the violence and violations faced by LGBTI individuals be placed within the context of gender-based violence broadly conceived" (African Men for Sexual Health & Coalition of African Lesbians 2013, 6).

In South Africa and other sub-Saharan African countries, perpetrators of sexual violence have targeted lesbians and women and girls whom they perceive to be lesbians. Sometimes called "curative" rape, targeted homophobic sexual assault is motivated by a desire to "correct" or "cure" lesbians of their sexual orientation. One study reported that at least 500 women in South Africa alone are victims of targeted homophobic sexual assault each year (Di Silvio 2011).

An intersectional framework would allow the African Commission to explore human rights violations perpetrated against LGBTQI people as gender-based human rights violations. There is precedent among human rights institutions for treating violations based on sexual orientation and gender identity as derivative of gender-based rights. Some civil society organizations, such as CAL, have explicitly embraced intersectionality as a way of securing basic human rights for LGBTI communities. CAL's website notes, "We believe that our multiple identities intersect and are linked. Our race, class, gender, sexual orientation, [dis]ability, geographic location, and other identities are connected in a web of oppression" (2011, "What We Believe," para. 4). The explicit commitment to intersectionality in CAL's mission statement may pave the way for regional human rights bodies to similarly adopt an intersectional framework for human rights violations. A more robust embrace of intersectionality would represent progress in the evolution of our understanding of human rights violations and how best to combat them.

CONCLUSION

Intersectionality theory offers a new way to analyze international human rights law. Intersectional approaches examine how systems of oppression and discrimination interact and mutually reinforce one another to produce complex, multifaceted human rights violations. The post–World War II human rights regime, however, was not designed to take into account the intersectional nature of human rights violations. The primary human rights mechanisms tend to silo human rights violations as separate violations based on *one* aspect of identity, such as gender, race, class, ethnicity, age, disability, or sexual orientation and gender identity, rather than as a potential intersection of multiple forms of subordination. The text of the treaties largely reinforces this unidimensional approach to human rights violations. Nevertheless, the UN treaty bodies are cautiously moving to embrace an intersectional framework for human rights.

The Maputo Protocol also offers the potential to address human rights violations in Africa using an intersectional framework. The embrace of intersectionality, even within the text of the Maputo Protocol, has been gradual and modest. There is much work to be done in the African region, particularly with respect to LGBTQI rights. The Protocol, however, represents progress in the pursuit of an intersectional framework for human rights analysis, one that will capture the true complexity of people's experiences of discrimination and subordination.

REFERENCES

African Men for Sexual Health and Coalition of African Lesbians. 2013. *Realities and Rights of Gender Non-Conforming People and People Who Engage in Same-Sex Sexual Relations in Africa: A Civil Society Report.* https://www.oursplatform.org/resource/realities-and-rights-of-gender-non-conforming-people/.

African Union. 2003. *Protocol to the African Charter on Human and Peoples' Rights on the Rights of Women in Africa.* https://www.un.org/en/africa/osaa/pdf/au/prot ocol_rights_women_africa_2003.pdf.

Article 19. 2018. *ACHPR: Withdrawing Coalition of African Lesbians' Observer Status Threatens Civil Society Participation.* https://www.article19.org/resources /achpr-concern-with-decision-to-withdraw-coalition-of-african-lesbians-observer-status/.

Bond, J. 2003. "International Intersectionality: A Theoretical and Pragmatic Exploration of Women's International Human Rights Violations." *Emory Law Journal* 52: 71–186. https://papers.ssrn.com/sol3/papersc.cfm?abstract_id=21 09878.

Center for Human Rights, University of Pretoria, and the African Commission for Human and Peoples' Rights. 2011. *Celebrating the African Charter at 30: A Guide to the African Human Rights System.* http://www.pulp.up.ac.za/pulp-guides /celebrating-the-african-charter-at-30-a-guide-to-the-african-human-rights-system.

Center for Human Rights, University of Pretoria, and the African Commission for Human and Peoples' Rights. 2016. *A Guide to the African Human Rights System.* http://www.pulp.up.ac.za/pulp-guides/a-guide-to-the-african-human-righ ts-system-celebrating-30-years-since-the-entry-into-force-of-the-african-charter-o n-human-and-peoples-rights-1986-2016.

Coalition of African Lesbians [CAL]. 2011, October 14. *Blog Post.* http://coalitionafri canlesbians.blogspot.com/2011/10/cal-at-ngo-forum-and-50-th-session-of.html.

Crenshaw, Kimberlé. 1993. "Mapping the Margins: Intersectionality, Identity Politics, and Violence Against Women of Color." *Stanford Law Review* 43: 1241–99. https://www.jstor.org/stable/i252725.

Cramer, Elizabeth P., and Sara-Beth Plummer. 2009. "People of Color with Disabilities: Intersectionality as a Framework for Analyzing Intimate Partner Violence in Social, Historical, and Political Contexts." *Journal of Aggression, Maltreatment & Trauma* 18: 162–81. https://doi.org/10.1080/109267708026 75635.

Cummingjohn, Glynnis. 2011. "Rights of Older Women in Africa Raised at the UN." *HelpAge International.* https://www.helpage.org/blogs/glynnis-cumming sjohn-2536/rights-of-older-women-in-africa-raised-at-the-un-323/.

Di Silvio, Lorenzo. 2011. "Correcting Corrective Rape: Charmichele and Developing South Africa's Affirmative Obligations to Prevent Violence Against Women." *Georgetown Law Journal* 99 (5): 1469–1516. https://ssrn.com/abstract=1709629.

Disability Rights Fund. 2013. *One in Seven: How One Billion People Are Redefining the Global Movement for Human Rights.* Boston: DRF. http://disabilityrightsfund .org/wp-content/uploads/2015/12/DRF_report_OneinSeven-1.pdf.

Drumbl, Mark. 2007. *Atrocity, Punishment, and Criminal Law.* Cambridge: Cambridge Univ. Press.

Goldblatt, Beth. 2015. "Intersectionality in International Anti-Discrimination Law: Addressing Poverty in Its Complexity." *Australian Journal of Human Rights* 21 (1): 47–70. https://doi.org/10.1080/1323238X.2015.11910931.

Humphrey, Megan. 2016. "The Intersectionality of Poverty, Disability, and Gender as a Framework to Understand Violence Against Women with Disabilities: A Case Study of South Africa." *International Development, Community and Environment (IDCE)*, Paper 36.

International Justice Resource Center. 2018. *African Commission Bows to Political Pressure, Withdraws NGO's Observer Status.* https://ijrcenter.org/2018/08/28/ac hpr-strips-the-coalition-of-african-lesbians-of-its-observer-status/.

Morgan, Robin. 1984. *Sisterhood Is Global.* New York: Anchor Press/Doubleday.

Priestly, Mark. 2001. *Disability and the Life Course: Global Perspectives.* Cambridge: Cambridge University Press.

Ogonda, Job. 2006. *Age Discrimination in Africa.* https://www.ifa-fiv.org/wp-con tent/uploads/2012/11/061_Age-Discrimination-in-Africa-Age-Concern-England -DaneAge-Association-IFA-2006.pdf.

Organization of African Unity (OAU). 1990. *African Charter on the Rights and Welfare of the Child*, CAB/LEG/24.9/49. https://www.refworld.org/docid/3ae6 b38c18.html.

UN Committee on the Elimination of Discrimination against Women (CEDAW). 2010. *General Recommendation No. 28 on the Core Obligations of States Parties under Article 2 of the Convention on the Elimination of All Forms of Discrimination against Women*, CEDAW/C/GC/28. https://www.refworld.org/ docid/4d467ea72.html.

United Nations Committee on the Elimination of Discrimination against Women. 2019. *Concluding Observations on the Ninth Periodic Report of the Guyana.* https ://digitallibrary.un.org/record/3827972?ln=en#record-files-collapse-header.

Chapter 3

Building the Patriarchy Index for Sub-Saharan Africa

Perceptions and Acceptance of Violence Matter Most

Verena Tandrayen-Ragoobur

Patriarchy represents an important hurdle to women's progress and development. Although the level and nature of domination differ across countries, communities, and households, the patriarchal principles are the same, with male domination prevailing in both the public and private domains. Patriarchal ideology further strengthens biological differences between men and women, so much that men have the dominant or masculine roles and women have the subordinate or feminine ones (Sultana 2011). Patriarchal institutions and social relations further contribute to the inferior or secondary status of women (Sultana 2011).

Across many sub-Saharan African (SSA) societies, patriarchy as a way of doing things prevails in norms, values, and customs. It is deeply entrenched in most African settings, so much so that it cannot be disentangled from the African culture. The systems and structures of patriarchy have worked for centuries for men who have benefited strongly from having privileged positions. Men in most African cultures have an inherently higher status because society values men and boy children. The practices of polygamy, paternal control of the choice of marriage partners, emphasis on women's role in fertility, and decision-making in the household create various obstacles for women's advancement. Patriarchy uses women, especially older women, to be its guardian and to keep its systems functioning and sustainable. In fact, patriarchy uses women to suppress and oppress other women (Bvukutwa 2014). Many women support patriarchy because it is still one of society's dominant forces—one that is actively denying their rights, minimizing their accomplishments, erasing their concerns, and keeping them poor and deprived. In a nutshell, patriarchy is limiting women's possibilities. Thus, "patriarchy has been particularly difficult to dismantle in African societies" (Bvukutwa 2014, para. 5).

Over the years, there has been an increasing need to overcome the belief and practice of patriarchy; and gradually, many of the overt emblems of patriarchy are changing. For example, although African women are still expected to marry and have children, they now exercise somewhat more control over birth spacing and birth control options than they traditionally did. One example is from Northern Ethiopia, where women are more willing to use contraceptives because of the "perceived severity of unwanted pregnancy and higher self-efficacy surrounding contraceptive use" (Kahsay et al. 2018, Abstract para. 4).

Patriarchal control, exploitation, and oppression have important implications for women. Existing empirical studies on developing countries have incorporated only dummy variables to measure the country or regional aspect of culture (Psacharopoulos and Tzannatos 1989). More detailed works that have factored in the role of patriarchal culture are mostly country based (World Bank 2015 for Morocco) or have focused on Muslim or Arab countries (Cinar 2001; Dildar 2015; Gaddis and Klasen 2013; Hayo and Caris 2013).

In the patriarchy literature, it is well accepted that patriarchal values dominate and hinder women's potential, but as of this writing, this has not been analyzed in the African literature. To the best of my knowledge, no study has attempted to measure patriarchy and build in a composite index by combining different variables that affect women in SSA. The absence of a direct measurement of patriarchal culture that explains country differences makes it difficult to study the influence of country norms and individual values on women's development (Diwan and Vartanova 2017). To this end, this chapter fills in the gap in the literature by building a patriarchy index for SSA. The methodology is based on data from the Demographic Health Surveys (DHS) of twenty SSA countries over the period 2010 to 2015. The patriarchy index is computed by combining a range of variables such as intimate partner violence, decision-making in the family structure on health issues and household expenditure, polygamy, and fertility preference of the husband/partner.

The chapter is structured as follows: the section "Literature Survey" reviews the existing literature and empirical studies on patriarchy and women in different countries. Section "Conceptualizing Patriarchy in SSA" adopts a conceptual framework of patriarchal beliefs, ideology, and a system relevant to SSA. Section "Data Source and Analysis" builds the patriarchy index for the region, and section "The Patriarchy Index for SSA" discusses the results. Section "Conclusion and Policy Options" concludes the chapter with relevant policy options.

LITERATURE SURVEY

Patriarchy is "a form of mental, social, spiritual, economic and political structuring of society produced by the gradual institutionalization of sex-based political relations, created, maintained and reinforced by different institutions linked closely together to achieve consensus on the lesser value of women and their roles" (Facio 2013, 1). Patriarchy is not a static phenomenon, as it changes over time through different mediums. It permeates various institutional structures, societal norms, cultural practices, religious teachings, and negative portrayals of gender roles in the media. It is present at all levels of a society—that is, at the household/family, community, workplace, and state levels (Isran and Isran 2012; Rawat 2014; Sultana 2011; Walby 1990). It has a multifaceted nature which, as Halpern et al. (1996) noted in a discussion of Balkan patriarchy, "has been historically anchored in the interlocking combination of the rule of the father, the eldest or the husband (Halpern et al. 1996)" (as cited in Szoltysek et al. 2016, 1).

Feminist studies focus on the patriarchal structure to explain the perpetuation of gender inequality (Walby 1994). Two dimensions of patriarchy are often probed: private and public patriarchal systems. Private patriarchy is based upon household production as the main site of women's oppression. Public patriarchy is built primarily in public sites like employment and the state (Sultana 2011; Walby 1990). Both housework and wage labor are important sites of women's exploitation and subordination (Hartmann 1981). Within paid work, occupational segregation is applied, whereby access to the best-paid jobs is kept for men, to the detriment of women. Within the household, women spend more time on unpaid work than men, even though they also work for money outside the home (ILO 2018; OECD/CAWTAR 2014). Private and public patriarchal systems reinforce each other. For example, women are disadvantaged compared to their male counterparts in paid work. They are mostly unemployed and faced major difficulties in getting a job or operate predominantly in the informal sector or in low-paid jobs. This weakens their financial position and independence and makes them more vulnerable.

Women's labor power is not the only aspect of their lives affected by the patriarchal system. Patriarchy also influences a woman's reproduction, sexuality, mobility, and property ownership (Walby 1990). This control over and exploitation of areas of women's lives means that men benefit materially from patriarchy, deriving concrete economic gains from the subordination of women (Sultana 2011).

Few existing studies have attempted to combine a range of factors to compute a patriarchy index for a particular country or region. The only empirical works are those of Gruber and Szoltysek (2015) and Szoltysek et al. (2017), who build a new measure of patriarchy by combining a range of variables across European economies. These variables relate to familial behavior, such as patterns of marriage and post-marital residence, living arrangements, the position of the aged and seniority patterns within domestic groups, and the sex of the offspring. Their results reveal a strong correlation between historical and contemporary inequality patterns, in addition to important associations between demographic, institutional, socioeconomic, and environmental characteristics of the regional populations and the spatial variation in the patriarchy levels. There is no study that has attempted to compute a patriarchy index for sub-Saharan Africa or for the African continent.

CONCEPTUALIZING PATRIARCHY IN SSA

The patriarchal system in SSA economies covers various specific characteristics at different levels. A few examples are son preference, burden of

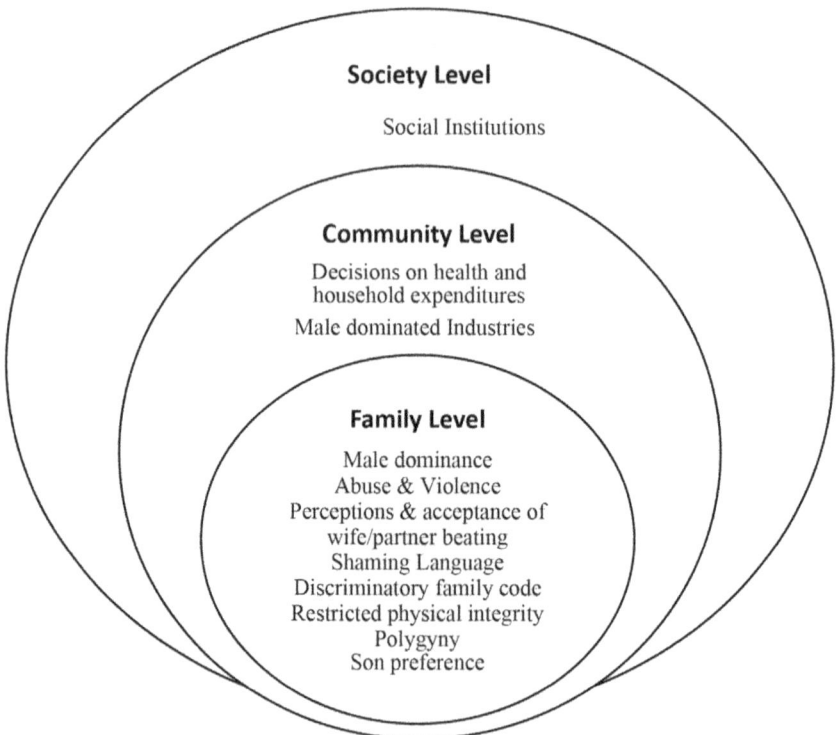

Society Level
Social Institutions

Community Level
Decisions on health and
household expenditures
Male dominated Industries

Family Level
Male dominance
Abuse & Violence
Perceptions & acceptance of
wife/partner beating
Shaming Language
Discriminatory family code
Restricted physical integrity
Polygyny
Son preference

Figure 3.1   The Patriarchal Framework. *Source:* Author's compilation.

household work on women, lack of educational opportunities for girls, and lack of freedom and mobility for girls, along with domestic violence. Other common examples of male control over women are sexual harassment at the workplace, lack of inheritance or property rights for women, male control over women's bodies and sexuality, and women having no control over their fertility or reproductive rights.

A theoretical conceptual framework is used to explain the different characteristics pertinent to patriarchal norms, values, and customs that are deeply entrenched in most SSA countries. A patriarchy index was calculated based on the different characteristics outlined on the family, community, and society levels in figure 3.1.

Family Level

The family or close relationship level of patriarchy consists of several factors that lead to women being subordinated within the household. First, across SSA, male domination is an important element of the patriarchal system and is captured by the head of the household, who is most often a man (Szoltysek et al. 2017). Furthermore, shaming language within the household that constitutes humiliation or emotional violence faced by women also forms part of the patriarchal system. Likewise, the perceptions and acceptance of wife beating is an effective tool for assessing the status of women in a specific social, religious, and cultural environment. It also reveals the degree of gender equity in a particular society (Rani and Bonu 2009). Two additional characteristics are included in the framework to compute the patriarchy index. These are the discriminatory family codes and restricted physical integrity index obtained from the Social Institutions and Gender Index (SIGI) (OECD 2019). Discriminatory family codes account for laws on child marriage, household responsibilities, inheritance, and divorce. The restricted physical integrity index measures the restrictions women and girls face over their bodies. These two aspects limit women's decision-making power and undervalue their status in the household.

Still referring to the family level, polygamy is included because it is common in many religious and cultural communities in Africa and is strongly correlated with various types of violence against women and children (McDermott and Cowden 2014; Tandrayen-Ragoobur 2018). The more wives a man has, the less power the women have. Polygamy is almost impossible without extreme patriarchy—so much so that the two are highly correlated. Finally, as was seen in Szoltysek et al. (2017), son preference is accounted for. The sex ratio imbalance at birth is closely related to son preference, which is often attributed to "conservative thoughts and conventional family customs and traditions" (Huiying 2016, Abstract Para 4). Discrimination that starts before birth or at infancy has always been seen as an important indicator of the lower status of women (Cain 1993; Das Gupta et al. 2003; Mason 1993) and as one of the effects of a patriarchal system (Chakraborty and Kim 2010; Guilmoto 2012). Cain (1993) and Mason (1993) argue that women in patriarchal societies prefer sons over daughters because sons are viewed as safeguards who will protect their mothers against a miserable life.

Community Level

The next dimension in the framework is the community level. Decisions about household expenditure, health, and even education are in many cases made by the male head of household. Traditional gender roles and stereotypes are very much relevant at the level of the community in many African economies. Along those lines, gender wage disparity (unequal pay) has been a major concern in many parts of the continent (Tandrayen-Ragoobur and Pydayya 2016). Gender pay differentials across occupations and sectors perpetuate gender inequality and very often prevent women from taking up higher-level occupations. Glass ceiling is a common problem for women around the world and in particular those in developing regions. According to Sultana (2011, 11), "Patriarchal institutions . . . are responsible for the inferior or secondary status of women in the capitalist wage-labour market." Women often find themselves in administrative positions or low-level occupations with low wages, while men have more responsibilities in higher-level occupations. Furthermore, in male-dominated and higher positions, men have more power to enforce discriminatory practices and policies.

Society Level

Within the societal dimension of the conceptual framework, important dimensions are included. These include women's restricted civil liberties and women's restricted access to financial resources and assets. Restricted civil liberties measure the "discriminatory laws and practices that restrict women's access to public space, their political voice and their participation in all aspects of public life" (Ruyssen and Salomone 2018, 159). For instance, women may not be able to vote or run for elections. There is an important gender gap in political ambitions, and women are highly under represented on the political front. A number of reasons can explain this gender disparity and one of them being the negative attitudes and views of voters toward women's capabilities. Similarly, the prevalence of discriminatory laws in many parts of SSA deny women the right to own, control, or use land and non-land assets as well as their rights to decent work and financial services. Women's unequal access to land, assets, and financial services place them in a more vulnerable position and impact negatively on their well-being. In other words, these discriminations are more likely to leave women in difficult financial straits, whereas the absence of these discriminations would improve their financial outlook.

DATA SOURCE AND ANALYSIS

Data Source

Micro-data from the DHS (2019) for twenty SSA countries from 2010 to 2015 was used as a model to compute the patriarchy index for SSA (DHS 2019). Comparable data across countries was collected via standard model questionnaires, and similar survey procedures were followed in each country. The surveys used were conducted on a sample of female respondents and contain information about several variables: household and respondent characteristics, wealth and health indicators, women's empowerment and decision-making power, education, employment and intimate partner violence, among others. Data from the OECD Gender, Institutions, and Development Database 2014 was merged with the sample of SSA economies, and different sub-indices are analyzed. This database allows for data at the society level, namely data on social institutions, restricted civil liberties, and access to resources.

Data Analysis

Two indicators were selected to analyze the extent of patriarchy within countries and the difference in the levels of patriarchy across nations based on the DHS data of twenty SSA countries. The two indicators refer mainly to gender roles/stereotypes and to perceptions and acceptance of wife/partner beating. Gender roles or stereotypes are measured by decisions in the household regarding health care of women, household purchases, and visits to the woman's family. If the husband or partner is the only one who makes these decisions, then he exerts some form of control or power over the household and over the wife or partner. In table 3.1 (columns 1–3), countries such as Burkina Faso, Cameroon, Democratic Republic of Congo, Cote d'Ivoire, Guinea, Mali, and Senegal provided data showing that more than 50 percent of women reported that their husband make all decisions. In Togo and Tanzania, husbands make at least one of these decisions for more than 50 percent of women.

On the DHS surveys, men were also asked about decision-making in the household across all the household matters discussed above. When men

Table 3.1 Gender Roles and Stereotypes across SSA Economies: Decision-Making in the Household

Country	(1) Husband/ Partner decides on health care of women	(2) Husband/ Partner decides on major household purchases	(3) Husband/ Partner decides on visits to her family	(4) Husband/ Partner have final say in all the decisions	(5) Women have final say in all of the decisions
Angola	24.7	18.5	12.0	61.6	65.4
Benin	36.2	42.0	30.8	91.6	48.3
Burkina Faso	74.9	78.5	46.6	91.6	12.0
Burundi	27.7	30.6	18.7	94.5	60.3
Cameroon	58.6	49.1	43.8	–	23.7
Chad	73.9	59.0	51.8	91.1	17.4
Comoros	48.3	39.6	39.2	67.7	34.6
Congo Democratic Republic	52.8	39.4	45.2	82.8	33.5
Cote d'Ivoire	64.1	60.6	51.1	88.7	23.6
Eritrea	9.3	37.4	19.8	–	50.1
Eswatini	28.5	35.4	44.9	–	36.7
Ethiopia	18.2	21.4	16.0	93.9	70.6
Gabon	38.8	23.8	27.2	–	43.7
Gambia	27.2	49.4	27.8	94.0	39.2
Ghana	22.5	25.3	12.7	86.9	61.6
Guinea	65.7	51.6	57.0	79.2	23.2
Kenya	20.9	27.0	26.1	86.1	55.8
Lesotho	9.0	9.0	24.9	80.0	65.4
Liberia	22.1	17.1	20.6	79.6	65.9
Madagascar	10.8	12.6	10.0	–	73.9
Malawi	31.7	44.1	21.4	78.5	46.9
Mali	83.6	80.1	75.4	85.7	8.9
Mozambique	20.5	23.2	19.0	84.1	64.7
Namibia	10.8	16.0	11.3	79.7	74.6
Niger	76.3	77.3	58.1	92.8	12.3
Nigeria	55.7	61.6	44.4	–	32.1
Rwanda	16.0	26.2	14.2	93.1	65.4
Sao Tome and Principe	28.9	42.6	25.0	–	46.9
Senegal	70.8	60.0	57.1	71.9	14.1
Sierra Leone	44.9	43.2	37.2	79.8	45.4
South Africa	5.4	7.4	5.7	83.3	87.2
Tanzania	27.5	52.4	40.8	92.1	35.2
Togo	57.0	51.6	34.3	94.9	29.4
Uganda	26.0	35.8	27.7	81.9	51.1
Zambia	25.4	33.2	24.4	83.2	53.8
Zimbabwe	14.3	12.7	11.4	74.6	72.1

Source: Author's Compilation from the DHS Survey Data, 2019.

reported their participation in the decision-making process, the figure across countries was much higher, ranging from 61.6 to 94.5 percent of men reporting that they made all decisions in the household. A different picture is obtained when women report on their final say in household decisions. The percentage is as low as 8.9 percent in Mali, 12 percent in Burkina Faso, 12.3 in Niger, and 14.1 percent in Senegal (see table 3.1). Autonomy is considered essential for decision-making, whether regarding health decisions, household decisions, or family relations. The data indicates that women in these countries have little independence to make their own choices and decisions.

The next aspect of patriarchy analyzed is perception and acceptance of any form of violence by women in the region. From table 3.2, it can be observed that countries such as Chad, Guinea, Ethiopia, and Niger have more than 30 percent of women justifying wife beating on all five issues relating to burning of food, argument with husband/partner, going out without telling the husband, neglecting children, and refusing to have sex. Countries with at least one of these issues being accepted as grounds for beating by a high percentage of women (exceeding 30%) are Burkina Faso, Burundi, Democratic Republic Congo, Eritrea, Mali, Senegal, Sierra Leone, Tanzania, Uganda, and Zambia. Patriarchy analyzed by gender roles along with the perception and acceptance of wife beating is seen to be more prominent in Western and Central Africa relative to other parts of the continent.

THE PATRIARCHY INDEX FOR SSA

The patriarchal index is estimated using the Principal Component Analysis (PCA) and is a composite measure that combines a range of variables in accordance with the conceptual framework discussed above. The PCA is a dimension-reduction tool that is applied to reduce a large set of variables to a small set that still contains most of the information in the large set. The procedure "transforms a number of (possibly) correlated variables into a (smaller) number of uncorrelated variables called *principal components*. The first principal component accounts for as much of the variability in the data as possible, and each succeeding component accounts for as much of the remaining variability as possible" ("Principal Component Analysis" 2016, para. 2).

In this chapter, a patriarchy index is constructed for SSA using the PCA tool. The index comprises twelve variables for each country and measures the relative position of a country considering a set of observables (see table 3.3). The first principal component is a measure of perceptions and acceptance of wife or partner beating if she either neglects children or argues with her husband or partner. These perceptions also hold if the woman either goes out without informing her husband or refuses sex or burns food. Hence,

Table 3.2   Perception and Acceptance of Wife/Partner Beating across SSA Countries

Country	Wife beating justified if she burns the food	Wife beating justified if she argues with him	Wife beating justified if she goes out without telling him	Wife beating justified if she neglects the children	Wife beating justified if she refuses to have sex with him	Married women disagree with all reasons justifying wife beating
Angola	10.5	15.2	14.5	16.3	11.5	66.0
Benin	6.0	10.6	7.7	8.8	6.5	75.7
Burkina Faso	9.8	30.8	30.3	30.4	19.7	52.8
Burundi	22.0	30.1	39.2	51.8	41.8	32.9
Cameroon	13.6	20.7	26.5	37.4	14.1	47.7
Chad	48.6	49.8	59.0	59.7	40.6	22.4
Comoros	12.7	15.7	28.4	29.7	20.0	53.0
Congo Democratic Republic	24.4	57.7	49.1	51.4	43.5	18.7
Cote d'Ivoire	16.4	34.3	26.6	32.7	21.5	47.7
Eritrea	29.1	44.6	51.7	51.0	47.9	16.9
Eswatini	2.9	17.1	9.2	11.1	3.3	79.3
Ethiopia	39.8	42.2	43.3	47.5	34.7	25.1
Gabon	10.6	26.1	19.0	40.2	8.8	39.1
Gambia	10.6	24.1	42.0	35.3	44.7	29.7
Ghana	7.4	15.6	16.5	20.9	12.2	64.1
Guinea	46.2	77.6	82.7	81.0	69.7	5.1
Kenya	7.0	21.0	21.8	33.3	15.1	47.9
Lesotho	6.3	24.6	10.7	22.0	9.4	45.0
Liberia	7.4	33.1	28.5	32.2	10.7	54.2
Madagascar	7.2	6.0	19.2	28.2	9.2	55.5
Malawi	5.5	6.7	6.9	8.8	8.3	80.9
Mali	26.3	58.4	55.0	48.7	58.9	21.3
Mozambique	2.4	6.5	7.5	4.2	5.4	86.0
Namibia	10.0	11.5	12.9	19.9	7.8	67.0

Niger	34.6	50.4	42.7	42.0	50.1	42.4
Nigeria	14.2	21.3	25.3	24.6	18.8	58.8
Rwanda	8.9	20.4	22.3	29.4	24.4	48.0
Sao Tome and Principe	6.4	7.0	10.2	11.7	5.6	65.4
Senegal	22.1	35.4	33.2	35.4	35.2	41.4
Sierra Leone	18.3	47.6	52.9	52.9	25.8	32.5
South Africa	1.0	2.2	2.1	3.8	1.0	95.6
Tanzania	20.2	42.0	40.9	47.9	30.5	27.8
Togo	11.2	19.5	17.8	18.9	9.6	65.8
Uganda	13.6	26.1	30.0	38.5	18.1	45.0
Zambia	23.5	33.5	29.7	33.1	28.9	38.9
Zimbabwe	8.1	16.7	22.8	21.4	14.5	56.2

Source: Author's Compilation from the DHS Survey Data, 2019.

Table 3.3 Patriarchy Index for SSA Computed from PCA

	Comp* 1	Comp 2	Comp 3	Comp 4	Comp 5	Comp 6	Comp 7
Family/Close Relationship Level							
Gender Roles—Sex Household Head			0.208	−0.320	0.466		0.300
Violence—Less Severe Physical Violence		0.531					
Violence—Severe Physical Violence		0.497					
Violence—Sexual Violence		0.446					
Perceptions and acceptance of wife/partner beating—If she goes out without informing him	0.452						
Perceptions and acceptance of wife/partner beating—If she neglects children	0.471						
Perceptions and acceptance of wife/partner beating—If she argues with husband	0.464						
Perceptions and acceptance of wife/partner beating—If she refuses sex	0.431						
Perceptions and acceptance of wife/partner beating—If she burns food	0.412						
Shaming Language (Emotional Violence)		0.516					
Discriminatory family code				0.639			
Restricted physical integrity				0.450	0.238		
Polygamy (Husband has 2 wives)				0.291		−0.573	0.111
Polygamy (Husband has more than 2 wives)				0.115		0.813	0.113
Son Preference			−0.393	−0.320			
Community Level							
Gender Roles-Decision on health of woman				0.111	0.564		
Gender Roles-Decision on home purchase					0.623	−0.144	
Unequal Pay				−0.194			
Society Level							
Restricted access to productive and financial resources			0.661				
Restricted civil liberties			0.574	0.208			0.911

Rotated component matrix. Extraction Method: Principal Component Analysis. Rotation Method: Varimax with Kaiser Normalization. Threshold for exclusion=low correlations (< 0.1). *Comp means component. *Source:* Author's Computation.

perceptions and acceptance of wife beating represent an important element in the patriarchy index. As Sweeney (2016, 23) notes, "Patriarchy influences the perception of domestic violence in many areas." This conclusion is supported in the literature Yount et al. (2013, para. 6) reported the findings of many scholars, noting that "very often the wife exchanges *obedience* for her husband's *maintenance* (e.g. Alam 2007; Kabeer 1988; Yount and Li 2010) and thus respects his authority to punish disobedience" (Yount and Lee 2010). Compliance with existing gender norms, however, may be a deliberate strategy for some women (Komter 1989, as cited in Yount et al. 2013, para. 8). These women feel powerless to change their current conditions and thus agree with prevailing norms. Moreover, women sometimes are too frightened to report that they have been attacked because it is possible that they will be told that they bear the responsibility for such acts (UN Women 2019, para. 2).

The second principal component of the patriarchy index for SSA is highly related to shaming and humiliation, which are illustrated by emotional violence. This is followed by other types of violence ranging from less severe violence to sexual violence. This result is in line with feminist analysis, which "underlines the various ways in which patriarchal gender norms and 'hegemonic masculinities' (Connell and Messerschmidt 2005)—normative ideals that define and reinforce men's dominance, privilege and power—serve to produce gender hierarchies and validate men's use of violence against women" (Namy et al. 2017, para. 4). Existing literature has shown that men who have strong patriarchal beliefs about gender roles are more likely to engage in violence against women. Violence against women is very often viewed as a private matter, although it is a severe violation of human rights. These different forms of violence have major health consequences and may even end with fatalities.

Furthermore, restricted access to productive and financial resources and restricted civil liberties also seem to correlate well with the third component, depicting that it is an important element in the patriarchy index. Women face gender-specific barriers to gaining access to and control over land and other assets. These barriers can be viewed in terms of the fact that women have less access to information and they may be affected by cultural, religious, community, or family dynamics that discriminate against them. Restricted civil liberties encompass several elements, such as restricted freedom of speech, opinion, and movement, along with the right to information. Hallman and Roca (2007) point out that restrictions on mobility are closely related to girls' exclusion from social, political, and economic life (and thus from participation), and as such are part of the processes that perpetuate disparities in education, health, and economic development, and exacerbate poverty. These disparities are further accentuated by discriminatory family codes and

restricted physical integrity, which are important components of the patriarchy index for SSA.

CONCLUSION AND POLICY OPTIONS

This chapter develops a conceptual framework to analyze the patriarchal system in SSA. From the conceptual model, a patriarchy index was built using
Demographic Health Surveys for twenty SSA countries from 2010 to 2015.
The results reveal that patriarchy still has deep roots in Africa and it is not
easily pulled out from society. The patriarchal system in SSA is supported
by powerful traditional cultural and social norms and values. The patriarchy
index generated in this study shows that perceptions and acceptance of wife
or partner beating, followed by physical, sexual, and emotional violence are
important components of SSA's patriarchal culture. Intimate partner violence
and abuse against women are well anchored in social and cultural conditions.
    Patriarchal culture thus remains one of the biggest barriers to ending vio-
lence against women on the African continent. Challenging patriarchy is not
new and has been ongoing for countless generations, and it will take many
more before it can finally be eliminated. Attempts to dismantle a patriarchal
system necessitate initiatives by both men and women. There should be
a holistic approach for breaking down the traditional patriarchal structure
and practices of women's subjugation, with different stakeholders working
together, namely the government, civil society, religious groups, community
groups, and nongovernmental organizations, among others.
    Mainstreaming of gender equality in national politics can help change the
internal dynamics of political parties in a way that will enable women to
participate in decision-making bodies. Women can also reinvent themselves
creatively and radically to be able to tackle the systems of oppression. By
connecting, organizing, and forming alliances, women can together better
face and change the traditional cultural and social norms that govern their
society or community. A patriarchal system can gradually change by shifting
political, economic, and social systems from being based on men's domination and women's subjugation to being based on equality and justice.
    Furthermore, more opportunities must be made available to women to
attain higher education so that they can gain self-realization about their
agency and their role in society. Laws concerning access to resources, namely
land and property, must be more gender friendly so that women can also own
assets and other resources, as men do. Supporting women by providing financial, legal, and therapeutic help is crucial for them to build their confidence
and stand up for their rights. Lastly, there is a need for both men and women
to fight against patriarchal ideology; it should not only be a woman's battle.

Toxic masculinity, male privilege, and gender inequality should be eliminated as gender violence, intimidation, and sexual assaults are all well related and entrenched in society's gender stereotypes and norms. Patriarchal culture remains one of the major obstacles in SSA to protect women against violence and empower them and help their children have a decent living. To combat patriarchy, greater gender equality needs to be promoted and mainstreamed into policies by African leaders, social groups, civil society, and policymakers.

REFERENCES

Alam, Mohd. Sanjeer. 2007. "Interrogating Gendered Inequality in Educational Attainment in India." *Social Change* 37 (4): 153–79. doi:10.1177/0049085 70703700408.

Bvukutwa, Goddess. 2014. "Gender Equality Is Not a Western Notion." *Imagining Equality*. http://imaginingequality.globalfundforwomen.org/content/gender-equalit y-not-western-notion.

Cain, Mead T. 1993. "Patriarchal Structure and Demographic Change." Pp. 43–60 in *Women's Position and Demographic Change*, edited by N. Federici, K. O. Mason, and S. Sogner. Oxford: Clarendon Press.

Chakraborty, Tanika, and Sukkoo Kim. 2010. "Kinship Institutions and Sex Ratios in India." *Demography* 47 (4): 989–1012. doi:10.1007/BF03213736.

Cinar, E., ed. 2001. *The Economics of Women and Work in the Middle East and North Africa*. Research and Middle East Economics, vol. 4. Amsterdam: JAI Press.

Connell, R. W., and James W. Messerschmidt. 2005. "Hegemonic Masculinity: Rethinking the Concept." *Gender & Society* 19 (6): 829–59. doi:10.1177/089124 3205278639.

Das Gupta, Monica, Jiang Zhenghua, Li Bohua, XieZhenming, Woojin Chung, and Bae Hwa-Ok. 2003. "Why Is Son Preference So Persistent in East and South Asia? A Cross-country Study of China, India and the Republic of Korea." *Journal of Development Studies* 40 (2): 153–87. doi:10.1080/00220380412331293807.

DHS [Democratic Health Surveys]. 2019. https://www.dhsprogram.com/. Accessed on January 5, 2019.

Dildar, Yasemin. 2015. "Patriarchal Norms, Religion, and Female Labour Supply: Evidence from Turkey." *World Development* 76: 40–61. doi:10.1016/j. worlddev.2015.06.010.

Diwan, Ishac, and Irina Vartanova. 2017. "The Effect of Patriarchal Culture on Women's Labour Force Participation." Working Papers 1101, Economic Research Forum.

Facio, Aldo. 2013. *What Is Patriarchy?* Translated by Michael Solis. http://www.lear nwhr.org/wp–content/uploads/D–Facio–What–is–Patriarchy.pdf.

Friends of the Earth International. n.d. "Gender Justice and Dismantling Patriarchy." https://www.foei.org/what-we-do/gender-justice-dismantling-patriarchy.

Gaddis, Isis, and Stephen Klasen. 2013. "Economic Development, Structural Change, and Women's Labour Force Participation." *Journal of Population Economics* 27 (3): 639–81. doi:10.1007/s00148-013-0488-2.

Gruber, Siegfried, and Mikołaj Szołtysek. 2015. "The Patriarchy Index: A Comparative Study of Power Relations across Historical Europe." *History of the Family* 21 (2): 133–74. doi:10.1080/1081602X.2014.1001769.

Guilmoto, Christophe Z. 2012. "Son Preference, Sex Selection, and Kinship in Vietnam." *Population and Development Review* 38 (1): 31–54. doi:10.2307/41857356.

Halpern, Joel M., Karl Kaser, and Richard A. Wagner. 1996. "Patriarchy in the Balkans: Temporal and Cross-Cultural Approaches." *History of the Family* 1 (4): 425–42. doi:10.1016/S1081-602X(96)90011-1.

Hallman, Kelly, and Eva Roca. 2007. "Reducing the Social Exclusion of Girls." Promoting Healthy, Safe and Productive Transitions to Adulthood. Brief no. 27. New York: Population Council. doi:10.31899/pgy12.1038.

Hayo, Bernd, and Tobias Caris. 2013. "Female Labour Force Participation in the MENA Region: The Role of Identity." *Review of Middle East Economics and Finance* 9 (3): 271–92. doi:10.1515/rmeef-2013-0021.

Huiying, Li. 2016. "Son Preference and the Tradition of Patriarchy in Rural China." Pp. 137–56 in *Revisiting Gender Inequality*, edited by Qi Wang, Min Dongchao, and Bo Ærenlund Sørensen. New York: Palgrave Macmillan.

ILO [International Labour Office]. 2018. "World Employment and Social Outlook: Trends for Women 2018." https://www.ilo.org/global/research/global–reports/weso/trends–for–women2018/WCMS_619577/lang—en/index.htm. Accessed on August 5, 2019.

Isran, Samina, and Manzoor Ali Isran. 2012. "Patriarchy and Women in Pakistan: A Critical Analysis." *Interdisciplinary Journal of Contemporary Research in Business* 4 (6): 835–59.

Kabeer, Naila. 1988. "Subordination and Struggle: Women in Bangladesh." *New Left Review* 168 (1): 114–15.

Kahsay, Znabu Hadush, Mussie Alemayehu, Araya Abrha Medhanyie, and Afework Mulugeta. 2018. "Drivers to Have More Children in the Pastoralist Communities of Afar, Ethiopia: An Explorative Qualitative Study." *Ethiopian Journal of Health Development* 32: 21–27.

Komter, Aafke Elisabeth. 1989. "Hidden Power in Marriage." *Gender & Society* 3 (2): 187–216. doi:10.1177/089124389003002003.

Lefkowitz, Eva S., Cindy L. Shearer, Meghan M. Gillen, and Graciela Espinoza-Hernandez. 2014. "How Gendered Attitudes Relate to Women's and Men's Sexual Behaviors and Beliefs." *Sexuality and Culture* 18 (4): 833–46. doi:10.1007/s12119-014-9225-6.

Martin, Phinoa, and Antoni Barnard. 2013. "The Experience of Women in Male-dominated Occupations: A Constructivist Grounded Theory Inquiry." *South African Journal of Industrial Psychology* 39 (2): 1–12. doi:10.4102/sajip.v39i2.1099.

Mason, K. O. 1993. "The Impact of Women's Position on Demographic Change during the Course of Development." Pp. 19–42 in *Women's Position on Demographic Change*, edited by N. Federici, K. Mason, and S. Sogner. Oxford: Clarendon Press.

Mathur-Helm, Babita. 2006. "Women and the Glass Ceiling in South African Banks: An Illusion or Reality?" *Women in Management Review* 21 (4): 311–26. doi:10.1108/09649420610667028.

McDermott, Rose, and Jonathan A. Cowden. 2014. "Polygyny and Violence against Women." *Emory Law Journal* 64: 1767–1814.

Namy, Sophie, Catherine Carlson, Kathleen O'Hara, Janet Nakuti, Paul Bukuluki, Julius Lwanyaaga, Sylvia Namakula, Barbrah Nanyunja, Milton L. Wainberg, Dipak Naker, and Lori Michau. 2017. "Towards a Feminist Understanding of Intersecting Violence against Women and Children in the Family." *Social Science & Medicine* 184: 40–48. doi:10.1016/j.socscimed.2017.04.042.

OECD/CAWTAR. 2014. *Women in Public Life: Gender, Law and Policy in the Middle East and North Africa.* Paris: OECD Publishing. doi:10.1787/9789264224636-en. Accessed on August 5, 2019.

OECD. 2019. *SIGI 2019 Global Report.* Social Institutions and Gender Index (SIGI). https://www.genderindex.org/. Accessed on January 25, 2019.

"Principal Component Analysis." 2016. https://www.fon.hum.uva.nl/praat/manual/Principal_component_analysis.html.

Psacharopoulos, George, and Zafiris Tzannatos. 1989. "Female Labor Force Participation: An International Perspective." *World Bank Research Observer* 4 (2): 187–201. https://documents.worldbank.org/en/publication/documents-reports/documentdetail/655261468767058052/female-labor-force-participation-an-international-perspective.

Rani, Manju, and Sekhar Bonu. 2009. "Attitudes toward Wife Beating: A Cross-country Study in Asia." *Journal of Interpersonal Violence* 24 (8): 1371–97. doi:10.1177/0886260508322182.

Rawat, Preeti S. 2014. "Patriarchal Beliefs, Women's Empowerment, and General Well-being." *Vikalpa* 39 (2): 43–56. doi:10.1177/0256090920140205.

Ruyssen, Ilse, and Sara Salomone. 2018. "Gender Discrimination as a Driver of Female Migration." Pp. 149–72 in *Gender and Migration: A Gender-sensitive Approach to Migration Dynamics*, edited by Christiane Timmerman, Maria Lucinda Fonseca, Lore Van Praag, and Sónia Pereira. Belgium: Leuven University Press.

Serres, Drew. 2014, January 9. "Why Patriarchy Persists (and How We Can Change It)." Organizing Change. https://organizingchange.org/patriarchy-persists-can-change/.

Schuler, Sidney Ruth, Syed M. Hashemi, Ann P. Riley, and Shireen Akhter. 1996. "Credit Programs, Patriarchy and Men's Violence against Women in Rural Bangladesh." *Social Science & Medicine* 43 (12): 1729–42. doi:10.1016/S0277-9536(96)00068-8.

Sultana, Abeda. 2011. "Patriarchy and Women's Subordination: A Theoretical Analysis." *Arts Faculty Journal* 4: 1–18. doi:10.3329/afj.v4i0.12929.

Sweeney, Kelly. 2016. "Factors Contributing to the Social Acceptance of Domestic Violence: A Systematic Review." Master of social work clinical research paper, St. Catherine University. https://sophia.stkate.edu/cgi/viewcontent.cgi?article=1681&context=msw_papers.

Szoltysek, Mikolaj, Radosław Poniat, Siegfired Gruber, and Sebastian Klüsener. 2016, December. *The Patriarchy Index: A New Measure of Gender and Generational*

Inequalities in the Past. MPIDR Working Paper WP 2016-014. Max Planck Institute for Demographic Research. https://www.demogr.mpg.de/papers/working /wp-2016-014.pdf.

Tandrayen-Ragoobur, Verena. 2018. "Intimate Partner Violence and Women's Labour Force Participation in Sub Saharan Africa." *Community, Work & Family* 23 (1): 1–25. doi:10.1080/13668803.2018.1540400.

Tandrayen-Ragoobur, Verena, and Rajeev Pydayya. 2016. "Gender Wage Differential in Private and Public Sector Employment: A Distributional Analysis for Mauritius." *Gender in Management: An International Journal* 31 (3): 222–48. doi:10.1108/ GM-08-2014-0071.

UN Women. 2019. "Take Five: 'Patriarchal Culture Is One of the Biggest Barriers in Ending Violence against Women.'" https://eca.unwomen.org/pt/news/stories/2019/ 02/take-five-patriarchal-culture-is-one-of-the-biggest-barriers-in-ending-violence -against-women.

Walby, S. 1990. *Theorizing Patriarchy*. Oxford: Blackwell.

Walby, S. 1994. "Methodological and Theoretical Issues in the Comparative Analysis of Gender Relations in Western Europe." *Environment and Planning A* 26 (9): 1339–54. doi:10.1068/a261339.

Wilcox, Annika M. 2015. "A Study of Domestic Violence and Patriarchal Ideologies in Popular Men's Magazines." Senior Honors Project, James Madison University. https://commons.lib.jmu.edu/cgi/viewcontent.cgi?article=1013&context=honors 201019.

World Bank. 2015. "Morocco Mind the Gap Empowering Women for a More Open, Inclusive, and Prosperous Society Middle East and North Africa." http://document s1.worldbank.org/curated/en/798491468000266024/pdf/103907-WP-P144621-P UBLIC-Non-BOARD-VERSION-Morocco-Gender-ENG-3-8-16-web.pdf

Yount, Katheryn M., and Li Li. 2010. "Domestic Violence against Married Women in Egypt." *Sex Roles* 63 (5–6): 332–47. doi:10.1007/s11199-010-9793-3.

Yount, Katheryn M., Nafisa Halim, Sidney Ruth Schuler, and Sara Head. 2013. "A Survey Experiment of Women's Attitudes about Intimate Partner Violence against Women in Rural Bangladesh." *Demography* 50 (1): 333–57. doi:10.1007/ s13524-012-0143-7.

Chapter 4

Patriarchy and Gender Challenges in Africa

Burdens of Wedlock Children in Cameroon

Chick Loveline Ayoh Epse Ndi

In precolonial times, African communities had a hierarchical structure that put men at the top and front positions of the social, political, economic, and cultural issues of their communities (Hess, Markson, and Stein 1988). In the same way, patriarchy describes a system of governance that depends on the philosophy by which men control and rule the most important resources of a community. This definition is gender-challenged and demonstrates the idea behind the construction of Africa, where the idea of considering men and women on the same scale was left out. One consequence of colonialism is the clash between African traditional values and modern social values. Colonialism has destabilized many communities, creating challenges to pertinent African values of oneness, unity, and love. This is true in the case of children, who were once believed to belong to the community and not to an individual. Children are defined in relation to the type of union from which they are born: A distinction is made between children born in a recognized union of marriage and those born out of free unions. Children born in free unions are called *wedlock children* and are clearly differentiated from other children by their labeling in the Mbu community of the north-west region of Cameroon, where this study was carried out. A child born out of wedlock is called *Wan-mbom*, meaning "a natural child." "Natural child" is a term used in the place of "illegitimate child" to reduce the stigma that is associated with the wedlock child.

A simple or pure natural child is a product of two single parents. A child born from a relationship between a single parent and a married parent is called an "adulterous natural child." Such a child originates from either a married man having a child with a woman who is not his wife or a married woman having a child with a man who is not her husband. The concept of wedlock opposes the concept of a legitimate child, which describes the product of an approved or official union between the two parents of a child. According to Hess, Markson, and Stein (1988, 297), every community has rules to govern courtship and marriages and family relationships and designs to control sexuality, to pair off potential parents, to maintain order within the household, and to meet human needs for intimacy.

The aim of such rules is to limit any negative consequences, such as unwanted pregnancies, that could arise from sexual misconduct. Sexual misconduct is more strongly reprimanded in single girls than in single boys in this community. Ownership or guardianship of a child resulting from misconduct has been problematic in this patriarchal system, where most power and authority over decisions is given to the men. The single girl/mother is more negatively sanctioned by the powerful men than is the boy/father who is the cause of the pregnancy. The degree of sanction is not only social but psychological, as the boy may deny his responsibilities. Men simultaneously cause and sanction this situation. Preferential treatment is given to the boy/father of the unwedded pregnancy and not to the single girl/mother, as she is blamed for not having mastered her fertility period.

THE PROBLEM SITUATION

The wedlock child has been a source of conflict and differential treatment in the Mbu community, where the boys/men who are the cause of the unwanted pregnancy have often not only narrowly escaped from their responsibilities as fathers but most often refused to participate in their duties as a parent to care for such a child. Conflicts have arisen between individuals, families, and the community at large, resulting from the anger of those whose single daughters are abandoned to companionless parenthood. This community had therefore developed strategies to manage such situations that bring shame to the family of the girl, as her chances of getting married are reduced. If she is to get married, her bride price will be lower than that of a girl who has not yet had a child. The issue of a wedlock child illustrates gender challenges in this patriarchal system, where the burden of care is relegated to the single girl/mother. The single girl/mother who is in the process of raising her child born out of wedlock in a male-dominated system faces challenges as gender roles are defined in this community. Despite the dynamic nature of cultures, modernism has not succeeded in imposing a significant change on this community in respect to gender roles; it continues to function in a total patriarchy in most aspects of life, maintaining feminine subordination.

As a social welfare worker, I registered a lot of family conflicts involving children who were vulnerable as a consequence of wedlock pregnancy. The complicated nature of these cases led to the breakdown of most marriages and homes in this community and in its environs. Statistics from the social affair register in many social centers in Cameroon show that seven out of ten vulnerable children are born to single parents (single mothers) and that six out of ten marriages that have been dissolved broke down because of conflicts arising from wedlock children. Husbands feel cheated by their wives who have contact with the biological father of a child they had before marrying. But the reverse is not true; men openly bring children born out of wedlock into their marital homes. An analysis of the conflict's origin revealed a conflict between Western and African values. A wedlock child is born from a broken home and is believed not to have enough affection from both parents to ensure that the child will be psychologically, morally, and emotionally balanced in life. No matter where the child grows up, be it with an adoptive parent or the maternal grandparents, the child's needs are not fully attended to, as are the needs of legitimate children. In some cases, the wedlock child is blamed and punished heavily for the bitterness that arises in the marriage.

METHODOLOGY

The methodological approach is qualitative and centers on action research based on my work as a social welfare officer over the past decade in the field in social action services in Cameroon. Research techniques included collecting participant observations, social inquiries, and in-depth interviews in an attempt to bring together action and reflection, theory and practice, in participation with others and in the pursuit of practical solutions to the pressing issue of wedlock children in these communities. Data was collected using the narration of life experiences of a sample population consisting of cases registered in my duty post in this community and of those received during the exercise of my duties as a social welfare officer. The sample units were selected using a criterion technique and consisted of children born out wedlock, victims of wedlock pregnancy, and their families.

GENDER EXPRESSION IN THE MBU COMMUNITY

Patriarchal philosophy creates and maintains norms that permit men to possess authority and to heavily influence all aspects of the social, cultural, and political structures, to the detriment of women. One of the consequences of this system is the challenge faced by the women in raising children born out of wedlock within this community, where sex education and sex initiation rites are passed on to teenagers to create awareness and to unveil the mystery behind sexuality in efforts to avoid unwanted pregnancies. Early marriage, especially for young girls, is highly encouraged as a measure for avoiding sexual misbehavior. The marriage of a young girl is considered an achievement for her parents, and the most appreciated parent is the mother, who has the role of bringing up her daughter in a way that will make her fit as a future wife and mother. Any delay in this process of marriage invokes fear and panic in parents, who see their child growing old at home without someone coming to ask for her hand in marriage. Singleness or celibacy is highly reprimanded in these communities and is usually labeled with stereotypic and stigmatizing names. In this community, singleness, whether of a man or a woman, is stigmatized with names such as *Rekwek* and *Kware*, respectively. For the man, it is less stigmatizing, because the name *Rekweh* simply means "unmarried," but *Kware* is more stigmatizing and means "prostitute." These labels endlessly stigmatize single women in their social and cultural lives. Single mothers are exposed to social sanction more than single fathers.

The customs and traditions of these people favor the single man over the single woman in the sense that a single mother has a smaller chance of getting married than does a single man who is a father. Men can change their social status by marrying at any age, whereas women must marry before they are considered too old. Age is a determining factor in this community because marriage is directly linked with matrimonial duties, one of which is childbearing. Given that a woman's chances of bearing children when she is in her late forties are slimmer, many single women are less likely to escape the stigma of being unmarried in such a community, since men refuse to ask for their hands in marriage. To avoid the shame and humiliation that may result from singleness or celibacy, the single girl/woman makes every effort to cultivate behavior that will attract a man to marry her. For example, girls/women tend to be sober toward potential male suitors. They might even be willing to enter into an arranged marriage to someone of whom they are not enamored. If she is pregnant, she might be forced to accept a man who is not responsible for her pregnancy; otherwise, she will deliver in her parents' house and bring shame to both herself and her parents. In efforts to avoid or minimize the shame associated with an unwanted pregnancy, certain conditions are created to ensure that children will be cared for and protected. One example is doing everything possible to keep the child from knowing who their biological father is. The information is kept as a family secret, and any attempts to unveil this secret are seen as taboo (Dorothy 1995).

Assessing the Influence of Patriarchy on Gender Identities in this Community

Patriarchy is a philosophy practiced inappropriately and almost universally in the world, with the exception of some few communities that are matriarchal in Africa—more precisely, in Cameroon. An illustration of such a system, where the matrilineal linage has power, is found in the Bikum community of the north-west region of Cameroon. The Bikum community is a matriarchal community with matrilineal linage, where women have much power but do not have the authority to make decisions about certain pertinent community issues. This can be seen in the case of inheritance, where the right to inherit property is matrilineal—that is, the maternal bloodline has greater influence in this process. For example, the children of the daughters are more valued and respected in terms of inheritance than the children of the sons. But the authority is not given solely to the women, because certain rights, such as child naming and bride price, are still under the auspices of the men. The women in this community do not inherit, nor do they receive other social and cultural benefits, such as the power to decide whether to accept or give a daughter's hand in marriage. Other important rights, such as land ownership and control over other important resources, are reserved for the men. Thus, even here, where matriarchy is embraced, it has limitations in a larger context of patriarchal domination where the men own and control all important aspects of the community.

Gender challenges in this community consist of all the socially constructed rights and duties—those kept from the women by virtue of their sex and those that act as obstacles and barriers to the equal acquisition and distribution of duties and responsibilities toward the care for a child born out of wedlock. The task of caring for such children becomes a burden, because the responsibility usually weighs on the mother of the child more than on the father. The case of wedlock children represents the influence of patriarchy on gender identities.

The Philosophy of African Patriarchy

The philosophy of patriarchy viewed from an African perspective is different from patriarchy in other contexts, because of its roots in the unique phenomenon of the extended family. In some parts of Africa, and Cameroon in particular, lineage is regarded as the family built around blood brothers, sisters, and relations. Drawing from my own research in this community, a presentation of a family organization based on an African patriarchy is patriarchal-based, where the male sex is dominant in most social, political, cultural, and economic issues. Kinship roles and categories are gender-differentiated, and power within the family is centralized and gender-specific. The fundamental organizing principle within the family is based on gender, in that it considers the sex of persons first rather than seniority or any other social category. Hence, families are honored and referred to in this community in relation to the family head, who is always a man. Families are named after the male family head. For example, *Nehy* refers to the most honored male head of a family. If the family head is named "NDI," then this family is called *Nehy* NDI. It is a reference principle that is gendered, static, and rigid (Oyeronke 1997). That is, the children of the same families are referred to using their father's name from generation to generation. For example, NDI Blessing and NDI Harmony are the children of Mr. NDI.

Within the Mbu community, the social organization is also gendered. Marriage, for example, is an important social and cultural event that is highly valued. It is an occasion for creating new social bonds between two families or communities. The families concerned have to organize a ceremony to celebrate the new bond that is about to be formed. The negotiation starts with the formal introduction of the groom's family to the bride's family. At the end of the process, a send-off party is held that is meant to officially hand over the bride to her in-laws. Throughout the marriage process, gender principles are respected and played out. The men from both families are at the forefront of the formal negotiations. Meanwhile, the women sit back and await the outcome of the activities. It is understood that this process is a formal way of turning the bride over to the groom: she becomes his possession.

In some communities, women or wives are counted as the wealth of their husbands. Their names change as they bear the names of their husbands in all circumstances and on official documents. Women are referred to by their husband's names. Marriage is hierarchized in the sense that parents give privilege to certain families with respect to others as it concerns the choice of their children for marriage. That is, family backgrounds and social statuses are considered when choosing a wife or a husband. Same-sex marriage is not even considered as a possibility. As mentioned above, celibacy is socially stigmatized in this community, with the women more highly stigmatized and socially reprimanded than the men. Thus, relationships and gender roles are situational and continuously place individuals in gender-dependent hierarchies.

From a functional perspective, the political organization in a community is set up to respond to some basic needs of survival, such as the need for internal order and defend against external enemies. In its structural–functional organization, the head of the community, called the *Fon*, must be a man. Being the highest authority and occupying the top position in the hierarchy ranking, he is assisted by his kinsmen, who are directly beneath him. The power scale is purely masculine-gendered, and kinship and hereditary issues move from one generation to another, with powers designated by a father to his son. Power possession is masculine and is demonstrated during official ceremonies in the way the men dress during official ceremonies. Their seating positions in social gatherings and public places portray the power and authority bestowed on the men. There are special designs in the traditional wear called *Togho*, illustrated by the style and symbols that portray power and masculinity.

Gender Challenges in African Patriarchy

With respect to the African patriarchal philosophy discussed above, there is a clash between African and Western values that hinder gender equality. Division of labor in this community is based on biological differences rather than social differences, with the men being perceived as strong and powerful and having more freedom than the women. In the same case, the responsibilities for the care and upbringing of children, in general, and for children born out of wedlock, in particular, weigh more heavily on the mother than on the father. As in the present case of children born out of wedlock, the maternal family spends almost all their time caring for the child, to the detriment of other outside activities that could develop and empower their daughter for the future. Meanwhile, the paternal family keeps on with life activities with little or no disturbance. The fathers of such children often run away, show no interest in the child, or completely avoid the single mother, leaving her to carry out the childrearing duties single-handed.

Gender challenges are further demonstrated in the negotiation of the gifts offered during marriage negotiations. If the woman has a wedlock child, her family will receive a smaller share of the gifts than the man's family. Men make the decisions in the negotiations about the gifts. When they are satisfied, they can then order the groom to see the women to receive a symbolic gift. The extra duties performed single-handedly by the woman raising a wedlock child are not considered. Such cultural practices demonstrate the marginalization of women. They are an illustration of how African patriarchy created a powerful set of norms that limit the rights of girls and women yet allocate substantive rights to men. Such practices help us to understand how the struggle of women regarding wedlock children has been influenced by the area's customs and traditions.

THE ISSUE OF WEDLOCK CHILDREN IN CAMEROON

Before introducing the concept of the biological father in the context of Cameroon in particular, I want to emphasize that African communities consider a child as community wealth and not as belonging to an individual or a family. Measures were put in place to ensure that care and protection were provided to all children, without making a distinction between children born out of wedlock and those born in marital unions. Marriage was encouraged, and behavior in young and adolescent girls and boys was controlled to avoid unwanted pregnancies that served as a source of conflict between families and communities. To avoid such conflicts arising from unauthorized sexual activities, measures were created to control sexuality in teenage girls. Sexuality is controlled in girls because the teenage mother's bride price package is lowered due to the new status attributed by her community for losing her virginity. Single mothers are also more likely to have conflicts in their future marital homes that result from the pressure put on them by the wedlock children, who are often left behind with their maternal grandparents.

To avoid shame and future conflicts between families, many families force girls with wedlock pregnancies into marriage with a man—even if he is not the one responsible for the pregnancy. This type of marriage is not celebrated until the child is delivered. After the birth, marital negotiations could begin between the family of the forcibly wedded girl/mother and that of the man. In the Muslim communities of northern Cameroon, for example, unwedded teenage pregnancy is taboo. These pregnant girls are forced into marriage with the person who is responsible for the pregnancy, or the pregnancy is terminated in a ritual cleansing (field data, 2015).

One category of wedlock child, mentioned earlier, includes those who are born of a married man and a single woman who is not his wife or of a married woman and a man who is not her husband. Because they are frightened and not ready to marry, most young boys who are responsible for teenage pregnancies deny ownership. My field data from 2017 indicates that when the girl gives birth, the child is considered as "a family child," "a natural child," or "a child born out of wedlock" and is considered a source of shame to the family. The fact that these children's biological fathers are not married to their mothers creates bitterness between the parents of the single mother and those of the biological father, which often turns to hatred. This hatred and pain in the girl's family is managed by keeping the situation as a family secret and creating barriers to prohibit the child from finding out who their biological father is. Modernization has brought a new perspective and opportunities to the concept of the biological father, and some individuals have started to violate the custom by secretly searching for their biological fathers. Despite all the efforts expended by families to keep the secret, the truth can come out. Some parents and family members of the wedlock child see the biological father as having bad fate, and the teenage mother who exposes this secret is accused of violating the customs and traditions. Her doing so is a cause of conflict that fuels ongoing acrimony between the biological father and the teenage mother, even when the wedlock child secretly or openly reclaims the biological father, either under or without social pressure.

To avoid the recurrence of this phenomenon, certain norms are created to manage issues that usually cause problems between individuals and families, and within communities. The wedlock child is claimed with the belief that the claimer will be compensated in the future, either through the bride price if the child is a female or as a source of addition to the family wealth if the child is a boy. If the man said to be the father of the wedlock child comes to ask for the teenage mother's hand in marriage, he will be given two alternatives: (1) to pay a bride price for their daughter and another package of bride price for the wedlock child or (2) to agree to disclaim the wedlock child, who will then remain as a natural child belonging to the maternal grandparents of the girl. The second option is the one selected most frequently, since many boys do not end up marrying the mothers of their children. But modern social values hold that each child should be officially recognized by their biological father to enhance the psychological equilibrium of the child. Most wedlock children who have attempted to transgress this customary practice are victims of evil attacks as their community rejects them.

Contribution to Gender Challenges

From a general perspective, wedlock children are gender-differentiated in all aspects of their social and cultural lives in this community. Throughout their life processes, there are gender challenges experienced through discriminatory practices that start from the conception of pregnancy, where the girl is blamed for being careless. This blame takes different forms of sanctions and punishment leveled at the girl as she becomes a victim of unwanted and unwedded pregnancy. Most often, when it happens in her youth, she loses the chance of continuing her education, either because she is dismissed from school or because she must withdraw because of the shaming she experiences from her schoolmates. Meanwhile, the boy continues going to school or learning a trade without any shame, hindrances, or deterrence. Out-of-wedlock pregnancy has caused setbacks for many girls/women in this community. The period lost while taking care of the baby creates an important gap in the girl's life at a time that would have been used to move forward or to achieve something for her future. Most families deny these girls a second chance because they are so angry. In some situations, the girls' parents chase the girl out of the house for bringing them shame, causing frustration and a mess in their lives.

In the same way, the wedlock children who are adopted as natural children by their maternal grandparents are treated differently depending on their sexes. Depending on whether the child is a girl or a boy, these gender differences become more pronounced in their lives through events such as naming, marriage, inheritance, and sometimes funeral arrangements.

Naming of Wedlock Children

Children are not named at random; their names are symbolic and have meanings. Children are given names according to the period and circumstances that surround their birth. With regard to the negative social regard of wedlock children in this community, and the conflict that may occur during the conception period of these children, their names at times do not reflect the period or true circumstances that surround their birth. The absence of the biological father during the birth of the wedlock child most often leaves the maternal grandparents with the full right to name the child. That being the case, most of the names given express either the circumstance surrounding the birth, the time, or grievances (for example, the name Yimfeng given to a wedlock child means "Endurance" and refers to the situation that the unwedded girl and her parents went through with the unwanted incident). Another name, like Seymeze, given to a wedlock child means "Let's see"; in the same way, a wedlock child might be given the name Semeya, which means "Let's talk" (field data collected from NDI Loveline in 2015). These children most often bear their maternal grandparents' names rather than their biological mother's name, on their birth certificates and other official documents. (My own case is evidence: I am referred to using both my maternal grandmother's and grandfather's names on my official documents and not my biological mother's name.) Sometimes the father's name is omitted from the birth certificate.

Marriage of a Wedlock Child

Unlike any other marriage ceremony, the marriage of a wedlock child is gender-different. Although ordinary marriages ceremonies are gendered, depending on whether a family is welcoming a wife for their boy child or giving their girl child out for marriage. Besides the normal procedures that are followed in the traditional weddings in the Mbu community, that is, meeting with the biological parents for a formal expression of the intention of the groom, following the directives on the other family members to contact next as directed by the bride's parents, the case of the wedlock girl child is more complicated. This is due to the complications arising between the rightful owners of the child—the maternal grandparents and uncles, according to tradition—and some greedy persons who may appear at the last moment in the name of the biological parents. This situation has often caused problems in families, especially when the groom is wealthy. The scramble to confirm the rightful representative of the bride's family becomes more complicated if the bride's maternal grandfather is no longer living. The biological father of the bride may use his role as head of the family in this patriarchal community to dominate the bride's grandmother. It is taboo for a woman to stand and collect a bride price in this community or to stand as a family head in official and important circumstances, of which marriage is a key example.

There is usually a conflict about who should be considered the father's representative since the wedlock girl child is raised by many hands. In some cases, the biological father of a wedlock girl appears to claim the role of father when the child has grown to maturity. In this case, he is expecting part of the bride price as his legal right for his last-minute contribution in bringing the girl to life. As the customs and traditions stipulate, the maternal grandparents have the full right to collect the bride price for these children that they suffered for. To reduce future conflicts, some families decide to raise the bride price package in order to share with the biological parents as a symbol of recognition for their contribution in bringing the child into the world. In contrast, the wedlock boy needs only to mobilize resources that enable him to invite his friends or any goodwill relation to accompany him to his bride's place. The rituals of the marriage ceremony symbolize the union of separate kinship groups through the exchange of gifts, and the public nature of the marriage signifies the couple's responsibilities to their society. The negotiation process for the female wedlock child's marriage involves many persons, making the bride price package heavier, which can be discouraging. Some of these wedlock girls end up not getting married because three different people, or groups of people, claim ownership to the right to receive the bride price: the social or adoptive parents, the biological father, and the maternal grandparents.

Right to Inheritance of a Wedlock Child

The right to inheritance of a wedlock child is also differentiated by gender in traditional Africa. Given the diversity of the positions held by these children in their various families—the maternal family, the adoptive father's family, and the biological father's family—their right to inheritance is conditioned by the goodwill of the aforementioned families. They do not have an absolute right, as does a child born within marriage. If it happens that any of their parents die without giving them their share of the wealth, there is a high possibility of conflicts of ownership arising between the legitimate children and the adopted wedlock children of the same family. Most often, the part of the wealth to be offered by parents to male wedlock children are given when these parents are still alive. This is true only for the male wedlock child, because the girls are believed to be their future husband's property and have no right to inheritance from their home (field data collected by NDI Loveline, 2015). Conflicts arising from inheritance issues are traumatic for wedlock children when they are reminded that they are issues of sexual mistakes. Therefore, the part of the wealth that will be given to this category of children is decided upon by their adoptive parents.

Funeral Arrangements of Wedlock Children

Just as the marriage of a wedlock child is gendered, so are such an individual's funeral arrangements. It is more serious in the case where these children are still dependent and single. Conflicts may arise during funeral arrangements for wedlock children, especially when many people are weighing in on where and when to bury them. In this community, burial rites are very important and play an important role in the social and cultural life of the people. Even with the advent of Christianity and modern laws, tradition still rules, and members are afraid to transgress. The wedlock girl often stands in contested ownership between the maternal grandparents, the biological father, and the adoptive father, who may be the husband to the mother; this dynamic complicates the issue of who has to claim her corpse. The same question may arise for a wedlock boy child, if he is still under the jurisdiction of his parents.

Wedlock Children and the Challenges of Modernization

Among the child's rights as stated by the United Nations' 1989 *Convention on the Rights of the Child* is the right to be named and officially be recognized by a biological father. For example, a child without a father's name on the official documents is violated. This official recognition opposes the African customs and traditions regarding children born out of wedlock and results in certain conflicts and confusion between and within families. Many wedlock children end up frustrated in terms of their wishes to be recognized by their biological parents. At the same time, they are afraid of being punished by those adhering to the customs and traditions (field data collected by NDI Loveline, 2015). This clash in values has not only affected but also jeopardizes the social stability of wedlock children in this community.

In an African traditional community, children are regarded as contributors to increase the family size and consequently as a support to the labor force, especially in the case of male children. During the preindustrial society, for example, foster parents preferred older boys for their labor value. African traditions and customary beliefs still hamper persons who try to disrespect the rules governing the paternity of wedlock children with serious sanctions awaiting those persons who try to break this rule by searching for their biological fathers without the permission of their maternal grandparents.

CONCLUSION

This chapter explained the origin of some gender challenges encountered by single girls/women in raising children born out of wedlock in the context of Africa, and of Cameroon in particular, where the patriarchal system gives more power to men than to women. The chapter is focused on gender roles and societal expectations of wedlock children based on the patriarchal construction and framing of women's place in the traditional African community. It offers an illustration of how the issue of gender is manifested in African patriarchal societies. The socially constructed beliefs regarding the responsibilities of the mother in childrearing originated from biological functions and are gendered inclined. African patriarchy is at the root of some gender challenges that are encountered by single girl/women mothers with the issue of wedlock children, because this society lays all the blame on the girls and often denies them certain opportunities under traditional gender roles. Tracing the fact that gender advocacy has failed to protect every child and proclaims equal rights for every child, it becomes apparent that the same legislation disfavors girl children in many domains, such as in the case of wedlock children.

REFERENCES

Hess, Beth, B., Elizabeth Warren Markson, and Peter J. Stein. 1988. *Sociology*, 3rd edition. New York: Macmillan.

Oyeronke, O. 1997. "Conceptualizing Gender: The Eurocentric Foundations of Feminist Concepts and the Challenge of African Epistemologies." *Jenda: A Journal of Culture and African Women Studies* 2 (1). https://pdfs.semanticscholar .org/af57/1563763fd8f5ad20a21ee6b64c69906282c1.pdf.

Pressly, Linda. 1995. "Challenging Nigeria's Sexual Taboos." *BBC World Service*. http://news.bbc.co.uk/2/hi/africa/4220038.stm.

United Nations. 1989. *Convention on the Rights of the Child*. https://www.ohchr.org /en/professionalinterest/pages/crc.aspx.

Chapter 5

Widow Inheritance in Northern Uganda

Patriarchy or Parenting?

Charles Amone

The discourse on widow inheritance in Africa has been dominated by the concepts of patriarchy, male chauvinism, and oppression of women (Nyanzi et al. 2009; Beswick 200; Afisi 2010). "In many areas," writes Bulkachuwa (1996, 15), "women are still regarded as chattels to be inherited." Feminists and women rights' activists perceive widow inheritance not only as discriminatory and inhuman but also as one of the few relics of barbarism (Sigman 2006). Thus, since the 1980s, leading international organizations have appealed to the Acholi to abandon cultural practices that such organizations deem abhorrent and oppressive to women, including widow inheritance (Mujuzi 2012).

This chapter provides an alternative view to illustrate that among the Acholi, widow inheritance has little to do with patriarchy, pleasure, and hegemony; rather, it is a cultural mandate for men to provide for the family of their dead brother or close relative.

Widow inheritance refers to a cultural practice where a male relative of a deceased man takes over the responsibility of the widow for sexual fulfillment as well as for social, ritual, economic, and emotional support (Gwako 1998; Obwa et al. 2018). It is a common traditional and cultural practice among the Lwo peoples of eastern and north-eastern Africa and among other ethnic groups in different parts of Africa (Oluoch 2013).

Using qualitative research methods and design, participant reflection, literature review, and documentary analysis were conducted to unpack widow inheritance as a popular cultural practice among the Acholi people. The documents analyzed included verdicts of clan courts and clan meeting minutes of Acholi clans in the Gulu, Kitgum, Amuru, and Pader Districts. These are the oldest of the eight Acholi districts. The clan meetings were chaired by traditional Acholi chiefs known locally as *Rwodi Moo*. The meetings discussed issues of widow inheritance and included inherited widows, widow inheritors, and chiefs' palace officials.

The available literature on widow inheritance (Dvora 2004; Asiimwe and Owen 2011, Beswick 2001) reveals that the practice has been in existence since biblical days, when the Jews encouraged it for widows who had never borne a male child with their deceased husband (Dvora 2004; Eryl 1991). Today, although it is practiced in many parts of Africa and Asia, widow inheritance is on the wane—but not among the Acholi, who regard it as an important element of cultural identity whose primary aim is to provide social and economic support to a widow and her children upon the death of the woman's husband.

To understand widow inheritance and get to the bottom of its persistence, it is necessary to start with a discussion about the institution of marriage as perceived by the Acholi. This chapter has six sections besides the introduction and conclusion, the topics of which are: the institution of marriage among the Acholi, widow inheritance and traditional Acholi religion, widow inheritance and child care, the clan system and widow inheritance, misconceptions about widow inheritance, and the Acholi traditional process of widow inheritance.

THE INSTITUTION OF MARRIAGE AMONG THE ACHOLI

To the Lwo group, marriage is intended to be an everlasting contract whose purpose and function extends beyond the physical death of one or both spouses (Oluoch 2013). *Min ot* (mother of the home) or *won ot* (father of the home) are the names Acholi people use for married couples. *OT* denotes the homestead and not just the house. When the father or the mother dies, the homestead remains. This homestead has to be supported by kinship in the interest of the living partner and the children. Polygyny ensures that if the wife dies, the co-wife continues to uphold her responsibilities. However, in the case of a monogamous marriage, the clan will support the widower in remarrying. Widow inheritance is treasured in this same spirit (Odoki 1997).

The care for children also justifies widow inheritance. Acholi marriage is not just for companionship. Marriage is meant more importantly for procreation, because children ensure continuity of the family, lineage, and clan. Children are also important for labor, defense, and pride. This is why even if a child is a product of adultery committed by a married woman, that child is still considered the progeny of the man to whom the woman is married.

In the Acholi tradition, a married Acholi woman is not only a wife to the husband but also a wife of the household, the homestead, and the clan. Feminists may not agree with this perspective, although culture always has a social and economic base from which it has to be viewed. An Acholi marriage is established through the payment of bride price. According to Mugyenyi et al. (2007), bride price plays an important role in cementing the marital relationship in Africa. Traditionally, bride price is collected by members of the family or clan, an indication that marriage is not just a husband-and-wife affair but one of the entire extended family. Death of a spouse does not dissolve marriage (Oluoch 2013), which is why the inheritor has to be the brother of the deceased or a member of his clan. Today, widow inheritance takes place more commonly in rural than in urban Acholiland because the clan system is stronger among rural dwellers.

Traditionally, Acholi marriage takes a long time (Grove 1919), as does its dissolution. Courtship involves the brothers, sisters, parents, and close relatives of both the bride and the groom. Because the culture is patrilocal, every family or clan member engaged in Acholi marriage is concerned about the personality of the bride soon to join their unit. The features that attracted the entire family or clan of the groom to the bride remain even when the groom dies, and these have to be utilized for the benefit of the clan. To date, clan meetings are still frequently announced over all the radio in Acholiland.

WIDOW INHERITANCE IN TRADITIONAL ACHOLI RELIGION

Among the Acholi and the Lwo people generally, a person physically dead is still considered alive, present, and capable of influencing the living (Oluoch 2013). The Acholi overwhelmingly believe that the ghost of a dead person can come back to haunt relatives (Awuor 2013). The dead regularly appear in dreams to their close relatives to express anger about the conduct of the living. In rare cases, the spirits of the dead also appear during the day but are seen by only one person. When the spirits of the dead appear, elders gather immediately to analyze the cause of the dead person's displeasure. For departed men, it is always the dire conditions in which their children and wife are living.

The dead are also believed to sympathize with the living when the latter are in distress. When a child is unhappy, the child's departed father or mother is also unhappy. It is the responsibility of the living to make sure that all children, including orphans, are happy. Acholi people believe that when a dead man sees his children going hungry, he returns to afflict the living with diseases and misfortunes. Acholi men inherit their late brother's wives to make the dead brother happy by ensuring that his wife and children are provided for. This is what Odoki (1997) calls "Cen." *Cen* is the dead person's spirit that torments the living when provoked. One well-known way of provoking *Cen* is failing to provide for the dead person's children.

Related to the concept of *Cen* is the belief in *Ayweya*—the spirits that live in forests, on mountains, and in rivers and lakes. When someone cries without justifiable reason, they invite *ayweya* to their home. The Acholi cry only when in physical pain or to mourn the dead. There is a prescribed period for mourning; one should not cry months after losing a loved one. Widow inheritance is one way of making the children and widow happy so they don't grieve the dead for too long, lest they invite *ayweya* that will afflict the entire family or clan with disasters like measles, childlessness, or famine (Okebiro 2016).

In the days before formal education and urbanism gained grounds in Acholiland, every Acholi home had an *abila* (a shrine) where departed ancestors were honored and consulted about problems afflicting their living kin. Gendered roles are adhered to in the context of the abila. The man builds it, but the role of maintaining it rests with women. During incantations, certain words are said by a woman, and others are muttered by a man. The only way to maintain the *abila*, therefore, is to have a man and a woman in every homestead (Girling 1960).

Acholi men, like most elderly African men, tend to speak in parables. An old man who wants to encourage his son to inherit the wife of his dead brother will exhort him: "*Cet i gwok abila pa omeru,*" which is "go and take care of your brother's *abila*." In fact, the word *laku* (wife inheritance) is rarely used by old people. In most cases, they use phrases like *anga ma obitingo kwot pa omeru?* (Who will carry your brother's shield?), *anga ma obigwoko gang pa omeru?* (Who will provide for your brother's household?) (as contained in the meeting minutes of Palabek kal Chiefdom). Both expressions point to religious, social, and economic responsibilities.

WIDOW INHERITANCE AND CHILDCARE

To the Acholi, a child is any person who has not yet reached puberty. Children are provided for by adults, including parents, elder siblings, and close relatives. The segregation of duties and the gendered roles that define the Acholi and most pre-colonial African societies dictate that the greatest support to children comes from their parents; the form that support takes depends on the sex of the parent. Every woman is anxious about her children's welfare, including shelter, nutritional provision, and education (Kudo 2017). Widows whose children are grown don't care about inheritance, but those with young children need to be inherited, because they must, for example, secure shelter for themselves and their children when their husbands die.

In the olden days and in rural Acholiland today, a typical home tends to have at least two huts: one for sleeping, the other, a kitchen. With time, the number of huts will increase, with two more huts, one for boys and one for girls. The task of building the huts rests with the husband. An unmarried woman or a widow will therefore lack shelter, since she has no husband (Obwa et al. 2018). Gwako (1998) interviewed a lady in western Kenya who said, "Perhaps I would not be having this house if I had declined to be inherited by him. My decision has so far paid generously, and I have no regrets whatsoever" (p. 183).

Before the advent of missionaries and the eventual European colonization of Africa, informal education was what prepared a child for adult life. Today, both informal and Western educations are pursued. Acholi indigenous education provides life skills to a child. Women provide these skills to the girls and men to boys, and this is done on a daily basis until the child becomes an adult. A child raised by a single mother or father is expected to miss out on some crucial life skills, including hunting, fishing, farming, construction, self-defense, and manners. Modern researchers have confirmed that the early days of a child are important for their education, as is reported here:

> Studies have confirmed that the early years of life are critical for the acquisition of the life concepts, skills and attitudes that lay the foundation for lifelong learning. Once a child fails to acquire sufficient educational stimulation from those responsible for her or him in the vital early years, the lost ground is hard to recover. (Awuor 2013)

One purpose of widow inheritance is to ensure that male children acquire these life skills, including hunting, carpentry, farming, construction, and courtship, that only men provide.

Men are expected to prevent adolescent girls from flirting with boys of undesirable character, including sorcerers and night dancers. Every family requires some kind of protection from this category of people. *Ot ma otoo* (which literally means "a dead home") is the phrase commonly used for a home without a father. Girls from such a home are vulnerable to sexual abuse. It is for this reason that widow inheritance is regarded as a social obligation to ensure care for the widow and the children (Mabumba et al. 2007). This practice is not in any way meant to downplay the roles of women in the Acholi society; if a man is unmarried, he too is considered as not having a home. An unmarried man suffers as much scolding and stigma as an unmarried woman.

THE CLAN SYSTEM AND WIDOW INHERITANCE

Among the Acholi, the question of bride price, as explained earlier, means the bride is married to the clan, and death does not terminate that marriage. The widow is expected to remarry, but within the clan, and that second marriage takes the form of widow inheritance because the clan cannot pay the bride price twice for the same woman. To oppose the concept of widow inheritance, it may be best to begin by rejecting the concept of bride price.

Widow inheritance among the Acholi, according to court verdicts scrutinized, is not a form of male chauvinism—it is a traditional cultural practice that formalizes the mandate that men are to guarantee lineage progression. Every Acholi clan is concerned with the extension of its genes. A widow inherited by a man from another clan will extend, through childbirth, the genes of another clan. That eventuality is considered worse if the two clans are rivals.

Early visitors to the Acholi were impressed by the clan system. Acholi households are close to each other under the clan arrangement (Girling 1960). The current clan names, such as *Pamwa, Pauma,* and *Patanga*, refer to the clans of *Mwa, Uma,* and *Atanga,* respectively. They tell the name of the founder of the clan. Each of the clans is known for something specific: hunting, farming, medicine, dance, music, pottery, ironwork, artisanship. These skills are taken as their niches. Within the clan there are also lineages known for specific fields. Some of these are evil, such as sorcery and witchcraft; others are congenital, such as *apoya* (mental sickness), *yom* (shortened prepuce), and *racu* (ugliness). Widow inheritance is intra-clan, intended, first, to avoid bad genes from other clans, and second, to ensure that the inheritor teaches the values, traditions, and niches for which the clan of the dead man is known. In brief, the goal is continuity.

For these reasons, Okech (2019, 2) argues that "what happens amongst the Lwo is not 'inheritance,' but a leviratic union" in which tradition requires that a *levir* (which means a husband's brother, although the meaning expands to include any male relative who is from the husband's clan) is "required by tradition to take on the brother's widow to provide support and protection (Ocholla-Ayayo 1980; Ogot 1967; Ogutu 2001, 12)." Such support can normally come only from a brother or a close relative.

This argument takes us back to the theme of the introductory section of this chapter: Widow inheritance is in the interest of women and children, not of men. It is Acholi society's means of administering social justice or of securing human dignity for all its members. The Acholi society has from time immemorial lost a disproportionate number of its men. In pre-colonial times, the Acholi were constantly at war, either with neighbors or among different clans (Girling 1960). Large numbers of men died in those wars.

Under British colonial rule, the Acholi comprised much of the army, and many died in the two world wars, while others became migrant workers in the southern half of Uganda (Postlethwaite 1947). The high mortality of men that arose from wars, traditional hunts, and the role of providing security for the family, for example, by fighting wild animals, necessitated that widow inheritance be established to cater to the needs of children and widows.

Given that today HIV/AIDs can be a risk factor in widow inheritance, the Acholi should consider expunging the sexual component of widow inheritance if the relevant widow so desires. In this way, widow inheritance will serve only the economic and cultural needs of the children and the widow.

When independence was attained, Idi Amin killed many Acholi from 1971 to 1979 because of their support for deposed leader Milton Obote (Finnström 2006). The Ugandan civil wars in Luwero Triangle and West Nile from 1979 to 1986 killed a good number of Acholi men because they were prominent in the national army. In both places, government soldiers were called Acholi soldiers (Mutibwa 1992). Then from 1986 onward, Acholi men perished in successive rebel movements, including in the Lord's Resistance Army (Finnström 2006). Thus, the Acholi society has always been demographically imbalanced in favor of women, but this is a disadvantage when it comes to finding a marriage partner.

Acholi culture emphasizes marrying young girls, and virgins for that matter (Beswick 2001, 50). A man who marries an old woman with children is scolded by peers and seen as a failure. For this reason, a widow with children has limited chances of finding a marriage partner in the traditional Acholi society. Widow inheritance is the Acholi's traditional way of overcoming the stigma associated with marrying a widow, in that taking care of the woman is the man's formalized responsibility.

Without the practice of widow inheritance, in a typical rural setting, it is hard for widows to get partners and produce children—and again, procreation, rather than companionship, is seen as the goal of marriage. It would be hard for a widow to get a suitable monogamous partner, even if the culture were more supportive or their doing so, without wife inheritance. Therefore, the clan has to intervene to get her an inheritor, who, besides caring for children, will meet her sexual needs.

Another important factor is property inheritance. Inheritance is one of the ways by which women accumulate wealth (Deere 2006). In traditional Acholi society, the property of a man includes his spear (*tong*), hoe (*kweri*), shield (*kwot*), head gear (*kono*), domestic animals, and the plot of land on which he farms or grazes his animals. He owns these in the trust of the clan. The person to inherit them after his death ought to be a clan member. The *kono, kwot*, and so forth are tied to clan identity. If a widow were to surrender them to another clan, it could cause inter-clan warfare. Widow inheritance minimized inter-clan wars over widows and the property left by the dead man.

MISCONCEPTIONS ABOUT WIDOW INHERITANCE

This section is intended to shed light on the institution of widow inheritance and to debunk the misconceptions that result in some groups and individuals' calling for the practice to be criminalized (Afisi 2010; Nyongkah 2018). Every society has unique features, including the socio-political and economic challenges that give rise to peculiar cultural practices. There are many prominent people in Acholiland today who were raised by the stepfathers who inherited their mothers. Such people, and the women who successfully brought up their children with the support of inheritors, attest to the value of widow inheritance.

Although Uganda adopted an open policy toward AIDS in the early 1980s (Mabumba et al. 2007), feminists still regard widow inheritance as one of the avenues for the spread of HIV/AIDS (Conroy 2011; Kudo 2017). They argue that widow inheritance, like other forms of marriage, should take place only after thorough voluntary counseling and testing of the widow and the inheritor who are opting for an inheritance union. When Uganda's HIV/AIDS policy is followed, widow inheritance cannot be an avenue for the spread of the scourge. Therefore, to condemn widow inheritance for spreading HIV/ AIDS is to condemn all forms of marriage. One reason elderly women counsel the widow before her choice of the *lavir* (widow inheritor) is to reveal, among other things, the health status of the potential inheritors. Alternatively, an HIV test can sort out this issue.

There is also the containment argument that has been advanced in favor of widow inheritance vis-à-vis the spread of HIV/AIDS (Okech 2019). Two widows who refused to be inherited appeared in the court of Labigiryang Chiefdom. According to the Labigiryang Chiefdom Court's file, as seen by the Author on July 3, 2018, in Palabek Kal sub-County, Lamwo District, Uganda, both widows admitted to having had many sexual partners since the deaths of their respective husbands. Given the high level of promiscuity in urban Uganda, there is reason to believe that the HIV-positive woman married to one partner may spread the virus to fewer people than the woman who remains unmarried for long.

Another misconception has been that under widow inheritance, the inheritor is imposed on the widow (Conroy 2011). Among the Acholi, this is untrue because the widow has to consent to the man. In many cases, the widow proposes to the man. This assertion has been confirmed by Nalubega (2018, para. 6), who quotes an Acholi traditional chief (*Rwot*) as follows:

I told them that she will only get married to their son if she consents to the marriage. I also reminded them that if they forced her out of her property or into marriage, then they would face the law stipulated by the clan committee leaders.

Furthermore:

If the family did any of the two, they would face a fine of UGX 50,000 [and] 50 strokes of the cane for each, and [they would have to] organize a feast during which they would return the stolen property or set the widow free from a forced marriage to one of them. (Nalubega 2018, para. 7)

The statements above were made in defense of a woman named Angwech who refused to be inherited. The *Rwot* made it clear, first, that widow inheritance is not forceful; second, that the widow is not denied her husband's property when she declines inheritance; and third, that there is a by-law for sorting out disputes arising from cases of widow inheritance.

There has also been some argument that widow inheritance is a show of patriarchy and male hegemony over women (Nyanzi et al. 2009). All Lwo traditions are considerate of women (Okebiro 2016). The fact is that in the days before capitalism gained roots in northern Uganda, the energies of men and women were complementary such that it was hard for anyone to run a home alone. Marriage being mainly for procreation, it was hard for aged widows to get spouses for marriage, which explains why men had to force their sons to inherit the widows of their brothers (Grove 1919). Here is the plea of one South Sudanese woman who could not get an inheritor: "In the old days the parents solved the problems of brothers-in-laws and forced them to take responsibility. But now they do not. It is chaos. The system is not benefiting us. . . . Men do not give a care about the women" (Beswick 2001, 48).

This Dinka woman (the Dinka are Lwo like the Acholi) was frustrated by the burden of caring for children without the help of a man. The brothers-in-law never accepted the responsibility of inheritance, and the father-in-law could not exercise his authority over this matter, as he would have done in the olden days.

Some scholars, including Bulkachuwa (1996), have stated that widows cannot inherit or own property of their late husbands. In Uganda, the deceased person's property may be distributed according to either the deceased person's will (testate succession) or a prescribed set of laws for property division if the person died without leaving a will (intestate succession) (Mujuzi 2012). Acholi men always leave a verbal will that guides the family to share property, and this will cannot deviate from the known cultural norms. If the man dies intestate, the known procedures are followed to the letter in the awareness that the dead man's spirit (*Cen*) can haunt the family and clan if his property is squandered.

Conroy (2011)'s claim that inherited widows have no right over the children they bear or to participate fully in public life and in the decision-making process within their immediate community is debatable. One of the reasons for inheritance is that, under its auspices, widows are heard. Among the Acholi, clan meetings are for men, and the women are heard through their husbands. But women also have their forum, in which men are heard through their wives. That is why wherever there is a *Rwot* (traditional chief), there is also a *Rwot Okoro* (the head of women in the chiefdom). The reasons for having separate meetings for men and women are the same as those for conducting separate focus group discussions (FGDs) for men and women in modern anthropological research.

Do inherited widows make up the bulk of domestic violence victims? Not according to the court cases handled in the Palabek Chiefdoms Courts in 2018. Acholi wives are treated equally irrespective of how they are acquired. True, domestic violence has been reported many times in Acholiland, but the cases are not restricted to inherited widows (Okello and Hovil 2007). There are known ways of resolving conflict in family, lineage, and clan. Likewise, the taboos associated with wife battering benefit all married women.

THE ACHOLI TRADITIONAL PROCESS OF WIDOW INHERITANCE

The duration of widowhood rites varies from one African society to another, but it depends primarily on the cause of death of the husband (Sossou 2002; Nyongkah 2018). Among the Acholi, if the husband dies of natural causes and at home (*too pyen*), all the ceremonies are performed within one week and end with the last funeral rites. If, on the other hand, the man dies away from home, his spirit will have to be invited home to live among the other departed ancestors. The Acholi believe that a dead person's spirit remains where the body was buried. In all cases, widow inheritance commences after the last funeral rites.

Whereas Nyanzi et al. (2009) have stated that among the Baganda, the *omukuza* (widow inheritor) is chosen at night during a meeting that the widow does not attend because the widow is not a clan member, the Acholi choose theirs in the early morning (*anyango*) and the widow is offered the opportunity to choose from among the gathered clan members. This takes place on the day after the last funeral rites. According to Laker of Palabek Chiefdom, "All the potential inheritors assembled early in the morning and after a discussion which involved counseling and warning from elders to those who will not be chosen, I was summoned at 10:00 o'clock and introduced to them seated in a row and facing the homestead" (Chiefdom document of Palabek kal, seen by the author on July 3, 2018).

During the time when elders were counseling the potential lavirs, Laker was engaged by her mother-in-law and other women of Lamwo Clan, who discussed in low tones all the men seated, revealing to her what she had not known about some of them. She had already been approached by three of the men seated and had already made a choice. Laker told the mother-in-law which people had approached her, and all the women decided that she should take one called Ojara. When she was invited to the arena to make a choice, she had already made up her mind with the guidance of the elderly women and the mother-in-law (Description given in Palabek Chiefdom court). The inheritor is chosen publicly to ensure harmony among brothers and to protect the widow from the unwanted sexual advances of other men.

As can be seen, the choice of widow inheritor was not imposed on Laker, although her choice was restricted to clan members. The following account offers evidence that contradicts what has been reported about Uganda in reference to widow inheritance:

> A woman has lost her husband to AIDS. She has children. She owns little or nothing in her own name. . . . If she lives in Uganda, she will likely be "inherited"—forced to have sex with her late husband's male relatives—until she becomes little more than a concubine to one. (Conroy 2011, 706)

In the case of Laker, she was not forced to have sex with her male relatives prior to inheritance; neither was the inheritor imposed on her. Had she objected to inheritance, she would have remained in her homestead to look after her children but would not be culturally permitted to have children with a man from another clan. Widow inheritance mainly involves widows of childbearing age (Mabumba et al. 2007).

Inherited widows of the Acholi are never taken as concubines. It is unclear in which part of Uganda Conroy, quoted above, conducted her fieldwork, but among the Acholi, there are many inherited widows who are treated like other wives. Since the purpose of widow inheritance is to provide for the widow and her children, it follows that women who are economically secure are more likely to resist it (Gwako 1998). This explains why widow inheritance is less common in urban centers and is almost unheard of among the educated elite.

CONCLUSION

Although the African cultures have been viciously blamed for promoting discrimination against women by men (Mujuzi 2012; Ayodele 2016; Conroy

2011), this research indicates that widow inheritance is not a show of patriarchy, but rather an additional responsibility that men undertake on behalf of their departed brothers to ensure continuity of the family and the clan. Seen from this perspective, widow inheritance is not a privilege for men but a responsibility, and those who never inherit their brother's widows and therefore allow them to get married to a "stranger" are mocked and loathed.

Widow inheritance should, therefore, not be proscribed; it should instead be modified to suit current socioeconomic conditions. The advantages of Western education today mean that people no longer depend on physical energy as they did in the past. Many women today can care for their children without the support of an inheritor. These women reside mostly in the urban centers. As is true of the widows who chose inheritance, those who did not should never face discrimination.

Although human rights instruments such as the Convention on the Elimination of all Forms of Discrimination Against Women (CEDAW) privilege an independent, free woman (Fox 1998), their application should take place in a context of awareness of a people's unique traditions. Traditional cultural practices "reflect values and beliefs held by members of a community for periods often spanning generations" (Oluoch 2013) and should be respected. Therefore, when designing an intervention for widow inheritance, it is important to consider the cultural values underlying the practice instead of criminalizing a custom that has developed over centuries (Mabumba et al. 2007).

Synonymous with a levirate marriage among the Jews, widow inheritance in the Acholi culture is meant to serve as protection for the widow and her children by ensuring that they have a male provider and protector. The reality that sometimes the practice can be enacted abusively should not obscure the positive purpose for which widow inheritance was born and persists. Rather than being proscribed, this cultural practice should be modernized to cater to the interests of the modern, educated, and financially stable widows who are able to provide for their children. One way of improving widow inheritance is to remove the sexual rights element from it while maintaining the other protections for the children and the widow. There are widows today in Acholiland who want to be inherited. Such widows may not be loud and bold like some of their educated counterparts, but their interests too should be taken into account, because widow inheritance among the Acholi can benefit the widows and their children.

REFERENCES

Afisi, Taiwo Oseni. 2010. "Power and Womanhood in Africa: An Introductory Evaluation." *Journal of Pan African Studies* 3 (6): 229–38.

Asiimwe Florence, Akiiki, and Owen Crankshaw. 2011. "The Impact of Customary Laws on Inheritance: A Case Study of Widows in Urban Uganda." *Journal of Law and Conflict Resolution* 3 (1): 7–13. doi:10.5897/JLCR.

Awuor, Keya Seline. 2013. "Effects of Widow Inheritance on Children's Right to Early Childhood Education in Ugenya District–Siaya County, Kenya." M.A. Education Research Project, University of Nairobi.

Ayodele, Johnson Oluwole. 2016. "Widows and Inheritance Hijacking Practices in Ilara Mokin, Ondo State, Nigeria." *African Journal of Criminology and Justice Studies: AJCJS* 9 (1): 116–39.

Beswick, Stephanie. 2001. "'We Are Bought Like Clothes': The War over Polygyny and Levirate Marriage in South Sudan." Special Issue, Dimensions of Gender in the Sudan, *Northeast African Studies*, New Series 8 (2): 35–61. doi:10.1353/nas.2005.0023.

Bulkachuwa, Zainab. 1996. "The Nigerian Woman: Her Rights and Obligations." *Women Herald* (8): 15–17.

Conroy, Sarah J. 2011. "Women's Inheritance and Conditionality in the Fight against Aids." *Wisconsin International Law Journal* 28 (4): 706–41.

Eryl, W. Davies. 1991. "Inheritance Rights and the Hebrew Levirate Marriage: Part 2." *VetusTestamentum* 31 (2): 138–44. doi:10.1163/156853381X00028.

Finnström, Sverker. 2006. "Wars of the Past and War in the Present: The Lord's Resistance Movement/Army in Uganda." *Africa* 76 (2): 200–20. doi:10.3366/afr.2006.76.2.200.

Fox, Diana J. 1998. "Women's Human Rights in Africa: Beyond the Debate over the Universality or Relativity of Human Rights." *African Studies Quarterly* 2 (3): 4–16. https://asq.africa.ufl.edu/fox_98/.

Girling, Frank K. 1960. *The Acholi of Uganda.* London: Her Majesty's Stationery Office.

Grove, E. T. N. 1919. "Customs of The Acholi." *Sudan Notes and Records* 2 (3):157–82. https://www.jstor.org/stable/41715820.

Gwako, Edwins Laban Moogi. 1998. "Widow Inheritance among the Maragoli of Western Kenya." *Journal of Anthropological Research* 54:173–98. https://www.jstor.org/stable/3631729?seq=1#metadata_info_tab_contents.

Kudo, Yuya. 2017. "Why Is the Practice of Levirate Marriage Disappearing in Africa? HIV/AIDS as an Agent of Institutional Change." Interim Report for Female Empowerment and Social Institution, IDE-JETRO.

Labigiryang Clan Court file-2018/003/2-Okello M, Palabek Gem Sub-county-Lamwo District, 2018.

Mabumba, E. D., P. Mugyenyi, V. Batwala, E. M. Mulogo, J. Mirembe, F. A. Khan, and J. Liljestrand. 2007. "Widow Inheritance and HIV/AIDS in Rural Uganda." *Tropical Doctor* 37: 229–31. doi:10.1258/004947507782332955.

Mujuzi, Jamil Ddamulira. 2012."Widow Inheritance in Uganda." Pp. 393–403 in *The International Survey of Family Law*, edited by B. Atkin and F. Banda. Bristol: Jordan Publishing Limited.

Mutibwa, Phares Mukasa. 1992. *Uganda since Independence: A Story of Unfulfilled Hopes.* Kampala: Fountain.

Nalubega, S., and Lutheran World Federation. 2018. "Ending Widow Inheritance in Pader District." The Lutheran World Federation, Uganda program. info@lwf.or.ug.

Nyanzi, Stella, Margaret Emodu-Walakira, and Serwaniko Wilberforce. 2009. "The Widow, the Will, and Widow-Inheritance in Kampala: Revisiting Victimisation Arguments." *Canadian Journal of African Studies* 43 (1): 12–33. doi:10.1080/000 83968.2010.9707581.

Nyongkah, Rachel Tati. 2018. "Widowhood Rituals and Widow Inheritance in the Balikumbat, Cameroon." *International Journal of History and Cultural Studies (IJHCS)* 4 (1): 56–64. doi:10.20431/2454-7654.0401004.

Obwa, Florence Akinyi, Charles O. Oduke, Isaya Onjala, and Edward O. Okanda. 2018. "Socio-Economic Implications of Widow Inheritance Rituals." *Elixir Social Studies* 122: 51739–46. https://www.elixirpublishers.com/articles/1541243579 _ELIXIR2018086319E.pdf.

Ocan Odoki, S. 1997. *Death Rituals among the Lwos of Uganda: Their significance for the Theology of Death.* Gulu, Uganda: Gulu Catholic Press.

Okebiro, Gilbert. 2016. "Wife Inheritance and Ethics among the Abagusii of Southern Western Region in Kenya." Available at SSRN: https://ssrn.com/abstract=2869113 or doi:10.2139/ssrn.2869113.

Okech, Awino. 2019. *Widow Inheritance and Contested Citizenship in Kenya.* London: Routledge.

Okello, Moses Chrispus, and Lucy Hovil. 2007. "Confronting the Reality of Gender-based Violence in Northern Uganda." *International Journal of Transitional Justice* 1: 433–43. doi:10.1093/ijtj/ijm036.

Oluoch, Elizabeth Asewe, and Wesonga Justus Nyongesa. 2013. "Perception of the Rural Luo Community on Widow Inheritance and HIV/AIDs in Kenya: Towards Developing Risk Communication Messages." *International Journal of Business and Social Science* 4 (1). http://www.ijbssnet.com/journals/Vol_4_No_1_January _2013/24.pdf.

Postlethwaite, John Rutherford Parker. 1947. *I Look Back.* London and New York: T. V. Boardman and Company Ltd.

Sigman, Shayna M. 2006. "Everything Lawyers Know about Polygamy Is Wrong." *Cornell Journal of Law and Public Policy* 16 (1): 103–29. https://scholarship.law .cornell.edu/cgi/viewcontent.cgi?article=1105&context=cjlpp.

Sossou, Marie-Antoinette. 2002. "Widowhood Practices in West Africa: The Silent Victims." *International Journal of Social Welfare* 11: 201–09. doi:10.1111/1468-2397.00217.

Weisberg, Dvora E. 2004. "The Widow of Our Discontent: Levirate Marriage in the Bible and Ancient Israel." *Journal for the Study of the Old Testament* 28 (4): 403–29. doi:10.1177/030908920402800402.

Chapter 6

Patriarchal and Traditional Gender Roles in Pre- and Post-Independent Eritrea

A Sociopolitical Analysis

Valentina Fusari and Venkatanarayanan S

Patriarchy "tends to be deployed as an overarching concept to signify a fundamental power differential between men and women in which women are invariably the victims and men the unnamed perpetrators of gender wrongs" (Greenhalgh 2012, 130–31). Such power disparity affects every socio-economic and political institution since patriarchy creates conditions for unequal relations in every sphere by marginalizing women (Makama 2013). The politics of patriarchy can be understood clearly by examining the contradiction between nature and culture in all social institutions. As patriarchal notions and practices encompass wider realms of human affairs, they end up being a useful descriptive tool for discussing social patterns. Although patriarchal societies and their traditions have evolved through different stages, they still glorify the specialization of reproductive labor for women to maximize fertility and protect their sexuality as a demographic dividend in grooming future generations.

The chapter investigates the long-term changes in the perception and agency of the Eritrean female population in carrying or countering the patriarchal values against the backdrop of changing mortality and migration rates within the Eritrean population. This changing demographic scenario has resulted in women having greater responsibility than the traditionally assigned role provides. Indeed, by positioning gender at the center and factoring voices from the margins, as was theoretically suggested by bell hooks (hooks 2000a, b), we examined the prevalent discourse about the slackening of the patriarchal system, looking at the emergence of new patterns of domination and subordination in post-liberation Eritrea.

Colonialism, liberation struggle, and migration involve a reworking of traditional power relations, but the patriarchal notions and practices have not been completely eroded. Furthermore, colonialism and liberation struggle have already been studied from a gender perspective; hence, we deserve more attention to geographical and social mobility and to their impact on Eritrean patriarchal society. Therefore, we consider two emblematic reference periods in order to underline differences and continuities that shape a new gender role system.

The first period covers around thirty years (1961–1991). Women joining the Eritrean liberation struggle, embracing gunfire as well as enforcing nationalist propaganda, thereby creating a new female figure within the Eritrean society (the *tagadalit*, female liberation fighter), characterized it. The second period covers the following almost three decades (1991–2019), that is, Eritrea after independence. It has been explored in terms of security, sociopolitical stability, and forced migration, but it gives scope for understanding how gender roles have responded to direct and indirect policies of the government. We draw particularly on discussions conducted during the fieldwork carried in Eritrea between 2012 and 2014, as well as on extensive desk research of published and unpublished materials. Demographic guesstimates rely on the National Statistics Office of Eritrea, which outlines the increase in female-headed households, arising from male migration and the dislocation of the male population within the country following the introduction of the National Service and the Warsay Yikealo Development Campaign (WYDC).[1] Thus, our aim is to assess whether the change in the patriarchal system is due to historical events and gender equality policies or whether it is the residual effect of migration related to the sociopolitical situation in Eritrea.

After a brief presentation of Eritrea's patriarchal tradition and of the changes arising from colonialism, we analyze women's participation in liberation struggle and the struggle's consequent implications for gender relations. Then, we provide an overview of how the Eritrean People's Liberation Front (EPLF) sought to implement gender equality after independence and of the difficulty of translating EPLF's model of gender equality in the field to civilian life on a national scale. Finally, we critically evaluate the relation between migration and the patriarchal system, as well as the impact of the recent peace between Eritrea and Ethiopia.

GENDER ROLES IN THE LIGHT OF TRADITION AND COLONIALISM

Eritrean society is by tradition highly conservative with regard to women's bodies and sexuality, and migrant Semitic groups, which multiplied their lineage by mingling with the local matriarchal populations and imposed patriarchy (EPLF 1985; Pollera 1922), probably influenced their cultural positioning.

In Eritrea, patriarchy is culturally entrenched in the majority of ethnic groups[2] through customary laws and is reinforced by religion (Christianity and Islam) in spite of the presence of matrilineal groups (i.e., the Nara and Kunama) (Tucci 1950) as well as tutelary provisions for married women and their offspring. Thus, the cultural diversity among groups results in multiple patriarchal models rather than a single one (Kibreab 2008). However, despite their difference, they limit equity, access to (im)material resources, and entitlement for women, while different forms of subordination and domination are institutionalized in the realms of family, law, and education (Cowan 1983). Socialization, as presented by formal and informal institutions, prescribes to members of different Eritrean cultural groups specific gender roles, which most people consider the correct and appropriate way to behave. As a result, the roles played by men are highly valued, whereas female roles are often perceived as less important to the livelihoods or survival of households and of society; therefore, girls are socialized from earliest childhood to be submissive, passive, meek, and quiet (Bahta 2004). However, women are invariably deemed to be the protectors of family virtue; in other words, their sexuality is controlled by norms and rules defined by men (Favali and Pateman 2003).

Members of cultures that have a history of strong traditions resist any changes in perceived appropriate gender roles, deeming them unacceptable and therefore untenable in many situations. Those who embrace traditional beliefs and patriarchal patterns profoundly militate against gender equality and agency. Furthermore, women are imbued with the importance of obedience to their reproductive and wifely roles, and the job market is segregated into male and female sectors, forcing women into the role of both protectors and socializers of traditional mores, an understanding that is professed by the main religions in the area and reinforced by feudalism (Kibreab 2008).

The colonization of Eritrea changed the people's political, economic, and cultural ties with neighboring areas. It divided ethnicities, histories, kin groups, and authority structures and reshaped regional economies (Woldemikael 2013). The Italian presence, and the subsequent British administration, produced a fundamental and transformative long-term effect on Eritrean society by opening new opportunities for women (Tseggai 1990). Indeed, as men joined the colonial army, women managed their households, especially during long-lasting and faraway military campaigns (e.g., in Libya, Somalia, and Ethiopia). Moreover, mainly in urban areas, women entered the salaried labor market, for example, in the light industry or as house cleaners (NUEW 1985), but they also managed to run their own business (e.g., *suwa* houses). When

Italy lost its colonial control over Eritrea in 1941, women hired by Italian families had the opportunity to follow their employers to Italy, thereby pioneering the Eritrean female migration to Europe, anticipating the well-known trajectory towards the Gulf countries (Kifleyesus 2012; Ramos 2017) as well as creating transnational families (Fusari 2011; Marchetti 2011).

JOINING THE LIBERATION FRONT: LOST (IN) GENERATION

The ever-increasing participation of women in conflicts across Africa and elsewhere demonstrated that war is not an exclusively masculine endeavor and that women are not always peaceful, victims, spectators, or prizes. Indeed, the common wisdom suggests that women's engagement with violence is unnatural, abnormal, and perverse or distorted, because of their caretaker role (Shekhawat 2015).

Eritrea offers an example of women becoming indispensable for non-state armed groups in waging their wars against states. They comprised almost one-third of the troops at the front and 13 percent of front-line fighters during the liberation struggle (1961–1991). Women played their socially ascribed gender role and even assumed new responsibilities performing different activities ranging from military to caring deeds. Indeed, they experienced a strong nationalist sentiment and identified with the Front's ideology (Pool 1997).

Initially, the Eritrean Liberation Front (ELF), founded in 1960, started demanding independence from Ethiopia; but it was the Eritrean People's Liberation Front (EPLF), a splinter group from ELF, formed in 1971, that won the country's independence in 1991. EPLF was "a syncretistic, independent Marxist-oriented guerrilla movement—a secular, multi-ethnic vanguard party" (Pool 2001, 156)—whose members used to transcend gender roles, as performed the same tasks as well as live "communally as comrades in mixed units" (Bernal 2001, 129). From a gender perspective, the EPLF wanted "to expand the notions of what women could do, and to break down gender barriers that had kept women out of certain kinds of work" (Bernal 2001, 134). The EPLF's approach to gender equality was grounded in Marxist ideas, and policies regarding gender were conceived and implemented initially by male leadership as no women sat on the EPLF's governing council until 1987. When women were elected to the Central Committee in March 1987, EPLF General Secretary Isaias Afewerki demanded that the six new female members would approach their new role "not as women" (Akinola 2007) because EPLF also resorted to the erasure of the feminine to promote gender equality. Thus, many female combatants adopted masculine attitudes and values to fit in a new empowered role: therefore, a woman fighter with her characteristic unisex dress and unkempt hairstyle personified an image of progress, a rupture with the past, and liberation from oppressive traditions (Weber 2011). At first, the women fighters came from an urban, educated background. Later these women fighters were successful in mobilizing women from rural and all ethnic backgrounds. Mainly, previous colonial *askari* (soldiers) and peasants who had endured oppression by landed gentry as well as women resisting male domination flocked to EPLF, as their primary goal was to destroy the feudal form of labor relations in order to enable and secure social and ideological transformations (Jameson 1988; Wilson 1991).

Like in other liberation struggles, female *tegadelti* combatants experienced momentary emancipation from patriarchy. Nevertheless, they confronted gender-based discrimination with varying intensity and they could not totally relieve from patriarchal control, as it was deeply embedded in society. The incessant reinforcement of discriminatory patriarchal values ensured the superior position of men before, during, and after conflict (i.e., in liberation front and in the following ruling party). Consequently, patriarchy continued surreptitiously, even when equality was a projected goal of the movement, and women suffered in gender-specific ways, including experiences of sexual violence (Kibreab 2017a).

During the liberation struggle, in the liberated areas, EPLF issued laws and policies aimed at promoting women's equality and enhancing women's rights. Indeed, it tried to dismantle customary practices perceived and perpetrated as the key locus of women's subordination. For example, the marriage law (1977) fostered a new idea of marriage as the partnership of a man and a woman free to exercise their choice. It was a radical departure from the traditional marriage, understood as an agreement between lineages, which subjugated the marrying couple (Silkin 1989). The EPLF tried to revolutionize the subjugated social position of women by imitating women in men's image and by virtually eliminating the family as a social institution within its ranks. At the same time, many civilian women had to assume traditionally male responsibilities for managing households, properties, and businesses in the absence of their brothers and husbands who were involved in liberation struggle as fighters or who migrated as exiles or refugees. Nevertheless, once they came back to Eritrea, they reasserted their claims to family resources and authority.

The extent of women's integration into the liberation front appeared as "a new kind of national integration for women once Eritrea gained independence and the EPLF assumed the control of the state" (Bernal 2000, 129).

INDEPENDENT ERITREA

The aim of newly independent Eritrea was toward development, leaving aside vast gender inequalities and securing economic and political rights of women, which were denied in the traditional patriarchal society (Connell 1998).

Patriarchal ideology was partially diluted during the liberation struggle, but it reemerged as soon as violence decreased and political dialogue initiated between Eritreans and Ethiopians. By excluding women from the peace process and undermining the gender aspects, the traditional patriarchal notions got strengthened and legitimized. The contradiction between women's visibility in wartime and their sudden invisibility in peacetime disclosed the subordinate and week position of women in the Eritrean society. Despite its aim to promote an egalitarian society avoiding any form of gender discrimination, the EPLF was unable to break entirely with tradition or with the past. It echoed the gender role system as rooted within the wider Eritrean society (Gruber and Garcetti 1998). Thus, former female *tegadelti* become "the victims of selective amnesia" (Shekhawat 2015), in which the role they played in wartime did not allow them to be considered as equal stakeholders in peace-making processes.

The resurgence of domestic relations as well as the transformation from the relationship a liberation movement has to its members to the one of the government to its citizens prevented women to translate their gains in front in peacetime opportunities.

In 1994, the EPLF became the ruling party People's Front for Democracy and Justice (PFDJ), and the government continued to support gender equality under the law, even taking affirmative action measures.[3] According to Macmillan, Shofia, and Sigle (2018), women's presence in national legislatures above a threshold of around 30 percent is associated with significant declines in childhood and maternal mortality, even after controlling for other features of women's status like education and labor force participation. This association is particularly strong where economic and social development is low and democracy weak as in Eritrea. In spite of assured adequate political representation, Eritrean women seemed to be disadvantaged as citizens of the new nation as social circumstances reverted to traditional mode. Indeed, women who spent much of their adult life fighting at the front faced challenges in reintegrating into civilian life. In the aftermath of the war, some 30,000 female ex-combatants began new civilian life in Eritrea, but only 14 percent had readily employable skills, and many did not have a home or a family to whom they could return (Hains, Ijumba, and Nicholls 1994; Kidan 2019). Thus, opportunities for employment became crucial once they had to reintegrate into civilian life and were no longer guaranteed subsistence by the EPLF. The glorification of women as the backbone of the liberation front and their accidental empowerment were replaced by neglect, apathy, and stigmatization.

Since 1991, the EPLF ex-fighters returning back to their civilian life accepted and encouraged the resurgence of traditional domestic values, which created different situations for men and women. Women ex-fighters remained trapped between the revolutionary aspirations they learned in the *mieda* (battlefield) and the cultural gender inequalities persisting within the Eritrean civil society: the qualities that made them good fighters and the masculinization they underwent now make them stigmatized and unmarriageable women. Besides, marital status regained importance as a significant factor granting women's socio-economic well-being. Furthermore, fertility problems were common among ex-combatants due to war wounds or post-traumatic stress disease affecting women's identities as wives and mothers, and redefining their worth in terms of their contribution to the family, kinship as well as to national development (Rock 1999).

To protect the gender equality gains of liberation struggle, the National Union of Eritrean Women's (NUEW)[4] acted with an objective to advocate the protection and development of those rights achieved by women during the struggle (NUEW 1994). Nevertheless, this is an arduous task because of the entrenchment of male-centered, patriarchal structures, the resilience of traditional gender roles, and male pre-eminence in the new government. Despite the presence of female ministers , women struggle to reconcile the gender disparity they face since their own struggle for independence. Furthermore, the newly independent Eritrea's focus on economic consolidation overshadowed all other social issues.

Parallel to the shift from the front to the government, the shift from the nationalist project to one of development was on the way. Though women's labor played a significant role during liberation struggle, after independence the ensuing capitalist political economy called for gendered skills and assets, and rewarded women differentially, pushing them into feminized labor sectors, characterized by low growth perspectives (Weldemichael 1996). The transformation from wartime situation to peacetime has not provided deserving positions for ex-female fighters in the new nation, as the traditional patriarchal norms took center stage after the liberation struggle (Muller 2005). The skills and the expertise of ex-women combatants had less acceptability and marketability in the traditional Eritrean society (Gebremedhin 2001). Therefore, working as a barmaid or prostitute became the stereotype of the demobilized female independence fighters. Prostitution as a survival strategy in post-war societies is rather common because of cultural obstacles to reintegration resulting in ex-combatants' marginalization. Thus, they had to rely exclusively on their ability to generate an income (Coulter, Persson, and Utas 2008).

The newly formed government introduced progressive post-war policies aimed at strengthening gender equity, like Family Law and Proclamation of Land Tenure 58/1994. Nevertheless, within the Eritrean society, patriarchal notions survived the liberation struggle and fortified in the post-conflict situ-ation. The dismantling of the patriarchal order in wartime was limited, since women did not benefit from a reordering of the social structure in peacetime. In such an environment, the NUEW's mission aimed at ensuring that "all Eritrean women confidently stand for their rights, and equally participate in the political, economic, social and cultural spheres of the country, and share the benefits" (UNDP 2014, 4). To achieve such goal, NUEW fights against several factors that continue to inhibit women's progress, like early socializa-tion equating femininity with weakness, and other traditional barriers rooted in a patriarchal culture, both of which undermine women's acceptance of gender education and willingness to enter political life. Other factors, such as women's lower socio-economic status, the so-called transitional political situation, limited institutional capacity, as well as the lack of public dia-logue about women's issues hinder efforts to increase women's political participation.

Despite difficulties in translating declared policies for gender equality in implemented actions, the day-to-day living experience of women countering patriarchal notions empowered women at the familial level. Since 1994, the Eritrean National Service and the following WYDC, introduced after the last border conflict against Ethiopia (1998–2000), intensified the pressure among the Eritrean youth (Kibreab 2017b). In 2002, the military National Service has been tied to the WYDC in which the youth are required to per-form their national service as forced labor for an indefinite time (Kibreab 2009), worsening the position of women that frequently experience sexual harassment and labor exploitation in the training centers like Sawa (Human Rights Watch 2019). Young men fled the country to avoid the compulsory Nation Service and the WYDC, whereas— at the initial stage—families pushed young women to get married and got pregnant to avoid or interrupt their service. Therefore, men migrated to find better economic prospects, but women became head of their households, as demonstrated by the two Eritrean Demographic and Health Surveys (1995 and 2002) and the follow-ing Eritrean Population and Health Survey (2010). Indeed, the proportion of female-headed households increased from 31 percent in 1995 to 47 percent in 2002, and to 47.2 percent in 2010. However, there is a difference between rural and urban areas: in urban areas, the trend is much more evident, as the female-headed households were 44.2 percent in 1995, 52.2 percent in 2002, and 53 percent in 2010 (NSO 1995, 2003, 2013). Cumulative factors led to this increase: the male death toll due to the liberation struggle and border conflict, male displacement within the nation as civilian or army servants, and male international migration.

The national service commitment for all adult men and women that have not been demobilized *en masse* since 2001 resulted in a high employment level (78.7%), but the over-15 employed population are classified as "working poor" with a purchasing power parity of $2 per day (UNDP 2015), becoming another main driver of international migration (Bozzini 2011). Besides, considering the high rate of inflation and the high cost of basic products in the country, wages are mostly insufficient for family survival. Eritrean families—as well as the nation itself—became increasingly dependent on remittances that boost further youth migration and diminish the likelihood of civil conflict within Eritrea where there is no route for individuals to express discontent.

MIGRATION AND RECONFIGURATION OF GENDER ROLES

Eritreans have fled the country in large numbers since the 1960s due to guerrilla war, poverty, and lack of freedom (GSDRC 2016, 1). As a result, in around thirty years, the independence war produced a diaspora of over a million people, mainly based in Sudan, the Middle East, Europe, and the United States, but few returned during the 1990s (Fusari 2017). Then, the border conflict with Ethiopia resulted in a further mass displacement.

The leader of the nation, Isaias Afewerki, used the crisis following the border conflict as a cover to exert control over society and state. The resulting policy, "designed to expand the sovereignty of the state over the population, is the immediate cause of the current economic, political, and citizenship crisis as well as the refugee crisis it has spawned" (Woldemikael 2013, viii). The more Eritrea enacted a severe policy to safeguard its national sovereignty and control the economic and political arena, the more it creates economic fragility, political tension, and social discontent that resulted in new forced migrants, who join the Eritrean diaspora communities around the world (Woldemikael 2018). Young Eritreans aged between 15 and 40 are most likely to leave to avoid National Service and in response to their perceived limited prospects within the country (O'Kane and Hepner 2009; Muller 2012). This figure might worsen because of the new desert locust invasion in the coastal region, where people risk facing starvation. The so-called militarization of the country has progressively led to family disintegration, as men are kept away from their families for long periods and to a general deterioration in the population's economic conditions (Hart and Mohammad 2013). Such conditions, in turn, make households increasingly dependent on remittances from abroad and motivate the young people to leave the country to earn for their families (Riggan 2013; Amahazion 2019). Then, young Eritreans consider leaving the country to be also a patriotic duty, as it was during the liberation struggle to make propaganda and collect money by working abroad.

Thus, because of biopolitics and forced migration, both female-headed households *de jure* (widowed or divorced) and *de facto* (where an adult male is absent) increased. There are key differences within the *de facto* category. For example, in case of male migration, *de facto* female-headed households may receive remittances from husbands or other related males and may maintain closer links with their husbands' wider kin group that can provide material and financial support[5] (RMMS 2015). Such assistance is not possible if the male partner is recruited in the WYDC, because his family does not separate him in order to earn more money abroad, but he is assigned elsewhere by the development program.

Eritrean mixed international migrants reach the Greater Horn of Africa and farther afield in North Africa and then Europe. Some forced migrants are even resettled in North America and Australia. Available data are scanty, but they suggest that up to 5,000 people used to leave the country every month before the peace with Ethiopia in summer 2018[6] (GSDRC 2016), when the border was open for a short time and a lot of women with their children fled into Ethiopia. At the end of 2015, the United Nations High Commissioner for Refugees estimated that more than 411,000 Eritreans were refugees or in refugee-like situations, but this is "likely an undercount, considering many do not register with authorities" (Horwood and Hooper 2016, 1). Many Eritreans cite conscription policy, poverty, and economic stagnation as reasons for migration. Migrants leaving Eritrea are mostly under-40 men, although the feminization of migration is increasing, also beyond the traditional destination, as the Gulf States (Kifleyesus 2012), and increasing the women's risk of violence, exploitation, and emotional suffering. Nevertheless, this mobility challenges traditional gender roles and raises questions for women remaining at home(land) about how to provide adequate support for their households when the patriarchal demographics crumble. Poorly educated or uneducated women usually enter the formal unskilled labor market or the informal sector, however increasing their autonomy and decision-making power. Women are also involved in managing remittances, estimated to be around one-third of national gross domestic product and a significant proportion of private household income, wherein they are used for their subsistence and other expenses like education and other necessities (Tewolde 2008).

CONCLUDING REMARKS

In Eritrea, a patriarchal family system continues to endanger women's status, although the government promoted, implemented, and sustained the development of gender equity and equality. Nevertheless, custom remained more important than law, as kinship and family are powerful institutions than the government.

Despite their effort and sacrifice during the liberation struggle, when women were mobilized ostensibly in the name of social change and gender equality, the primary objective of the liberation movement was to increase its fighting capability. Thus, what women gained during the liberation struggle did not automatically translate into a progressive public policy after the shooting stopped (Kibreab 2017a). Besides, the policy of expanding the control of the state over the population to maintain its security and sovereignty had the unintended consequence of large-scale migration of men, resulting in a large number of *de facto* and *de jure* female-headed households all around the country. Female participation and sacrifices during the liberation struggle do not yield the desired status to them in peacetime (Dore 2002). In Eritrea, only a party ruled after independence—and it is the only political party—and it confined women in its female wing (NUEW) without much independent agency in political decision-making. Furthermore, underdevelopment prioritized the focus toward economic development, resulting in reversing to old gender relations upholding patriarchal policies (Turshen 2010). In spite of progressive EPLF's ideology during the liberation struggle, based on gender equality, women and girls do still face vulnerabilities and exploitation. Therefore, whatever revolutionary changes occurred in gender roles in such situations, they are not static and most of the time reversed back to earlier patriarchal social setup (Rajivan and Senerathne 2010/11). Similarly, the Mozambican women participating in independence fight felt deceived after the struggle and relegated to their previous traditional roles, where men took advantage of the independence in establishing their dominance (Amfred 2010). The Angolan experience also shows that liberation time changes in gender relations did not last after independence, since they have to operate in traditional social norms and not wartime situation (Holness 2010). Immediately after independence, in Eritrea, men blocked the distribution of land to women reversing the progressive gains during the liberation struggle. Thus, the peacetime society gave a new challenge for the war-experienced women, as in spite of progressive policies by the government, they have to confront the regressive values of their own people (Connell 2010). Nevertheless, the side effect of Eritrean migration seems to be a weakening of the culture of patriarchy and subordination of women. Indeed, post-independence migration has opened up the space for women, but it is rather a forced situation than a real emancipation for them, as they have to face economic and social difficulties more than experiencing empowerment. Women liberation is an ongoing process that involves both men and women belonging to different generations and backgrounds. They have to keep engaging to fight against patriarchy, which is entrenched in society for a long time. The transformation of gender roles in Eritrean society needs to be contextualized within the huge migration registered in the last two decades to understand the nuances of this transformation. Moreover, the recent peace with Ethiopia opened a new era for female geographical and social mobility, involving above all young women and leaving home the elderly that used to be more closed to patriarchal values.

NOTES

1. The Warsay Yikealo Development Campaign (WYDC) was implemented in Eritrea two years after the end of 1998—2000 border conflict with Ethiopia. The campaign extended indefinitely the 18-month compulsory National Service (Gaim Kibreab 2013).

2. There are nine recognized ethnic groups in Eritrea: Tigrinya, Tigre, Saho, Kunama, Rashaida, Bilen, Afar, Beni Amir, Nara. For the sake of space, we refer to specific readings for a detailed description and analysis of the Eritrean ethnic and language composition. See: Pollera 1935; Gebre-Medhin 1989; Favali and Pateman 2003; Miran 2009; Bereketeab 2010; Connell 2019.

3. In national and regional assemblies, 30 percent of seats are reserved for women. Women compete against each other for the votes of both men and women. Women also run against men for the remaining 70 percent of seats. Consequently, the percentage share of seats held by women in the *Hagerawi Baito* (National Assembly) was equal to 22 percent in 2017, wherein at least 11 seats out of 150 must be women.

4. In 1979, it was established as one of the mass organizations of the EPLF, but now it is an "autonomous non-governmental organization" dedicated to improving the status of Eritrean women. During the liberation struggle, it succeeded in organizing and encouraging women's participation in the war effort. Since independence, NUEW enhances the role of women by raising their political consciousness through literacy campaigns, credit programs, English language lessons, and other skills training (NUEW 1994)

5. However, it is important to underline that Eritreans face huge risks during their journeys, because of traffickers' activities along the borders, the dangers associated with smugglers' services and states' border control activities. But not only routes within Africa are risky, as journeys from Libya to Italy are often undertaken on overcrowded makeshift boats, with a mortality rate across all journeys of 2 percent (RMMS 2015).

6. Figures on Eritrean migrants are limited in quantity and quality because of the difficult in registering the ongoing flow leaving the country. Moreover, there are no clear statistics about the Eritrean diaspora's size, formed by migrants, refugees, asylum seekers, and individuals resettled, together with previous generations of migrants and their children. This is mainly due to the difficulty in assessing a continuously oscillating flow of migrants, who are sometimes recorded as asylum seekers and at other times as labor migrants (GSDRC 2016).

REFERENCES

Akinola, Olufemi A. 2007. "Politics and Identity Construction in Eritrean Studies 1970–1991: The Making of Voix Eeythree." *African Study Monographs*, 47–85. http://jambo.africa.kyoto-u.ac.jp/kiroku/asm_normal/abstracts/pdf/28-2/28-2 -AKINOLA.pdf.

Amahazion, Frikrejesus. 2019. "Understanding Remittances in Eritrea: An Exploratory Study." *International Journal of African Development* 5 (2): 5–23. https://scholar works.wmich.edu/cgi/viewcontent.cgi?article=1092&context=ijad.

Arnfred, Signe. 2010. "Women in Mozambique: Gender Struggles and Gender Politics." Pp. 113–28 in *African Women: A Political Economy*, edited by Meredith Turshen. New York: Palgrave Macmillan.

Bahta, Senait. 2004. "Women's Folklore: Eritrea." Pp. 512–14 in *African Folklore: An Encyclopedia*, edited by Philip M. Peek. New York: Routledge.

Bereketeab, Redie. 2010. "The Politics of Language in Eritrea: Equality of Languages vs. Bilingual Official Language Policy." *African and Asian Studies* 9 (1–2): 149–90. doi:10.1163/156921010X491308.

Bernal, Victoria. 2000. "Equality to Die for? Women Guerilla Fighters and Eritrea's Cultural Revolution." *Political and Legal Anthropological Review* 23 (2): 61–76. doi:10.1525/pol.2000.23.2.61.

Bernal, Victoria. 2001. "From Warriors to Wives: Contradictions of Liberation and Development in Eritrea." *Northeast African Studies* 8 (3): 129–54. doi:10.1353/ nas.2006.0001.

Bozzini, David M. 2011. "Low-tech Surveillance and the Despotic State of Eritrea." *Surveillance & Society* 9 (1–2): 93–113. doi:10.24908/ss.v9i1/2.4102.

Connell, Dan. 1998. "Strategies for Change: Women and Politics in Eritrea and South Africa." *Review of African Political Economy* 25 (76): 189–206. doi:10.1080/03056249808704309.

Connell, Dan. 2010. "Strategies for Change: Women and Politics in Eritrea and South Africa." Pp. 137–54 in *African Women: A Political Economy*, edited by Meredith Turshen. New York: Palgrave Macmillan.

Connell, Dan. 2019. *Historical Dictionary of Eritrea*, 3rd edition. Lanham, MD: Rowman & Littlefield.

Coulter, Chris, Mariam Persson, and Mats Utas. 2008. *Young Female Combatants in African Wars. Conflict and Its Consequences*. Uppsala: Nordik Afrikan Institute.

Cowan, Nicole Anne. 1983. "Women in Eritrea: An Eye-Witness Account." *Review of African Political Economy* 10 (27–28): 143–52. doi:10.1080/03056248308703555.

Dore, Giovanni. 2002. "Donne del Fronte eritreo: sessualità e gestione del corpo dalla guerra al rientro nella società civile." *La Ricerca Folklorica* 46: 73–82.

EPLF. 1985. *Females in Eritrean Society*. Unpublished typewritten document. Asmara, Eritrea.

Favali, Lyda, and Roy Pateman. 2003. *Blood, Land and Sex: Legal and Political Pluralism in Eritrea*. Indiana: Indiana University Press.

Fusari, Valentina. 2011. *Dinamiche etnodemografiche all'interno dello spazio geopolitico eritreo*. Siena, Italy: Libreria Scientifica.

Fusari, Valentina. 2017. "Un'opportunità per chi? Peculiarità e ambiguità delle migrazioni di ritorno in Eritrea." *Africa e Mediterraneo* 86: 35–38.

Gebre-Medhin, Jordan. 1989. *Peasants and Nationalism in Eritrea: A Critique of Ethiopian Studies*. Trenton, NJ: Red Sea Press.

Gebremedhin, Tesfa G. 2001. *Women, Tradition and Development in Africa: The Eritrean Case*. Trenton, NJ: Red Sea Press.

Greenhalgh, Susan. 2012. "Patriarchal Demographics? China's Sex Ratio Reconsidered." *Population and Development Review* 38 (Supplement): 130–49. https://onlinelibrary.wiley.com/doi/pdf/10.1111/j.1728-4457.2013.00556.x.

Gruber, Janet, and Eric Garcetti. 1998, November. "'He gave me Permission to go.' Gender in Post-War Eritrea." Paper presented at the *African Studies Association Annual Meeting*. Chicago, IL, October 29–November 1, 1998. https://assets.publi shing.service.gov.uk/media/57a08da6e5274a31e0001998/R6836ASA_US_1998.p df.

GSDRC. 2016. *Rapid Fragility and Migration Assessment for Eritrea—Rapid Literature Review*. Birmingham: University of Birmingham.

Hains, B., P. Ijumba, and P. Nicholls. 1994. *Gender and Development Strategy*. Asmara: World Vision Eritrea.

Hart, Nicole, and Abdulkader Saleh Mohammed. 2013. "Dreams Don't Come True in Eritrea: Anomie and Family Disintegration Due to Structural Militarisation of Society." *Journal of Modern African Studies* 51 (1): 139–68. doi:10.1017/ S0022278X12000572.

Holness, Marga. 2010. "Angolan Women's Congress." Pp. 129–35 in *African Women: A Political Economy*, edited by Meredith Turshen. New York: Palgrave Macmillan.

hooks, bell. 2000a. *Feminism Is for Everybody: Passionate Politics*. London, UK: Pluto Press.

hooks, bell. 2000b. *Feminist Theory: From Margin to Center*. London, UK: Pluto Press.

Horwood, Christopher, and Kate Hooper. 2016. *Protection on the Move: Eritrean Refugee Flows through the Greater Horn of Africa*. https://www.migrationpoli cy.org/research/protection-move-eritrean-refugee-flows-through-greater-horn-afri ca.

Human Rights Watch. 2019. *"They Are Making Us into Slaves, Not Educating Us". How Indefinite Conscription Restricts Young People's Rights, Access to Education in Eritrea*. https://www.hrw.org/report/2019/08/08/they-are-making-us-slaves-not -educating-us/how-indefinite-conscription-restricts.

Jameson, J. 1988. "Eritrean Women: Fighters and Peasants." *Eritrea Information* 10 (4): 6–12.

Kibreab, Gaim. 2008. "Gender Relations in the Eritrean Society." Pp. 229–62 in *Traditions of Eritrea: Linking the Past to the Future*, edited by Tesfa G. Gebremedhin and Gebre Hiwet Tesfagiorgis. Trenton, NJ: Red Sea Press.

Kibreab, Gaim. 2009. *Eritrea: A Dream Deferred*. Melton: James Currey.

Kibreab, Gaim. 2013. "The national service/Warsai-Yikealo Development Campaign and forced migration in post-independence Eritrea." *Journal of Eastern Africa Studies* 7 (4): 630–49. doi:10.1080/17531055.2013.843965.

Kibreab, Gaim. 2017a. "Sexual Violence in the Eritrean National Service." *African Studies Review* 60 (1): 123–43. doi:10.1017/asr.2017.5.

Kibreab, Gaim. 2017b. *The Eritrean National Service: Servitude for "the Common Good" and the Youth Exodus.* Suffolk: Boydell & Brewer.

Kidan, Helen. 2019. "From Empowerment During War, Eritrean Women Must Fight Gender Discrimination in a New Peace". Inter Press Agency, http://www.ipsnews.n et/2019/04/161175/?utm_source=rss&utm_medium=rss&utm_campaign=161175.

Kifleyesus, Abebe. 2012. "Women Who Migrate, Men Who Wait: Eritrean Labor Migration to the Arab Near East." *Northeast African Studies* 12 (1): 95–127. doi:10.1353/nas.2012.0028.

Macmillan, Ross, Naila Shofia, and Wendy Sigle. 2018. "Gender and the Politics of Death: Female Representation, Political and Developmental Context, and Population Health in a Cross–National Panel." *Demography* 55 (5): 1905–34. doi:10.1007/s13524-018-0697-0.

Makama, Godiya Allanana. 2013. "Patriarchy and Gender Inequality in Nigeria: The Way Forward." *European Scientific Journal* 9 (17): 115–44. doi:10.19044/ esj.2013.v9n17p%p.

Marchetti, Sabrina. 2011. *Le ragazze di Asmara. Lavoro domestico e migrazione postcoloniale.* Roma, Italia: Ediesse.

Miran, Jonathan. 2009. *Red Sea Citizens: Cosmopolitan Society and Cultural Change in Massawa.* Bloomington and Indianapolis: Indiana University Press.

Muller, Tanja R. 2005. *The Making of Elite Women: Revolution and Nationa Building in Eritrea.* Leiden, The Netherlands: Brill.

Muller, Tanja R. 2012. "Beyond the Siege State—Tracing Hybridity during a Recent Visit to Eritrea." *Review of African Political Economy* 39 (133): 451–64. doi:10.1 080/03056244.2012.710839.

NSO. 1995. *Eritrea Demographic and Health Survey 1995.* Calverton: National Statistics Office & Macro International Inc.

NSO. 2003. *Eritrea Demographic and Health Survey 2002.* Calverton: National Statistics Office and ORC Macro.

NSO. 2013. *Eritrea Population and Health Survey 2010.* Asmara: National Statistics Office & Fafo Institute for Applied International Studies.

NUEW. 1985. "The Position of Women in Colonial Eritrea." *International Conference on Eritrean Women.* Bergen, Norway.

NUEW. 1994. "The National Union of Eritrean Women: History of Development and Programming." Unpublished typewritten document. Asmara, Eritrea.

NUEW, UNDP. 2014. *10 Years Women in Eritrea.* NEUW-UNDP: Asmara.

O'Kane, David, and Tricia Redeker Hepner. 2009. *Biopolitics, Militarism and Development: Eritrea in the Twenty-First Century.* New York: Berghahn.

Pollera, Alberto. 1922. *La donna in Etiopia.* Roma, Italia: S.A.I. Industrie Grafiche.

Pollera, Alberto. 1935. *Le popolazioni indigene dell'Eritrea.* Bologna, Italia: Cappelli Editore.

Pool, David. 1997. *Eritrea: Towards Unity in Diversity.* London: Minority Rights Group International.

Pool, David. 2001. *From Guerillas to Government: Eritrean People's Liberation Front.* Athens: Ohio University Press.

Rajivan, Anuradha K., and Ruwanthi Senarathne. 2010/11. *Women in Armed Conflicts: Inclusion and Exclusion.* Asia-Pacific Human Development Report.

Ramos, Manuel J. 2017. "'Sponsorshipped': Reflections on Temporary Female Migration from the Horn of Africa to the Gulf and Lebanon." Pp. 81–101 in *Fluid Networks and Hegemonic Powers in the Western Indian Ocean*, edited by Ian Walker, Manuel J. Ramos, and Preben Kaarshlom. Lisboa: Centro de Estudos Internacionais.

Riggan, Jennifer. 2013. "Imagining Emigration: Debating National Duty in Eritrean Classrooms." *Africa Today* 60 (2): 84–106. https://muse.jhu.edu/article/536443.

RMMS. 2015. *A Certian Catalyst: An Overview of the (Mixed) Migration and Development Debate with Special Focus on the Horn of Africa Region.* Nairobi: Regional Mixed Migration Secretariat.

Rock, June. 1999. "Relief and Rehabilitation in Eritrea: Lessons and Issues." *Third World Quarterly* 20 (1): 129–42.

Shekhawat, Seema. 2015. "Conflict, Peace and Patriarchy: Female Combatants in Africa and Elsewhere." *Conflict Trends* 2015 (4): 3–10. https://www.accord.org.za/conflict-trends/conflict-peace-and-patriarchy/.

Silkin, T. 1989. "'Women can only be free when the power of kin groups is smashed': New Marriage Laws and Social Change in the Liberated Zones of Eritrea." *International Journal of the Sociology of Law* 172: 147–63.

Tewolde, Brahne. 2008. *A Socio-Economic Analysis of Migration and Remittances in Eritrea.* Roma: GAN.

Tseggai, Araia. 1990. "Eritrean Women and Italian Soldiers: Status of Eritrean Women under Italian Rule." *Journal of Eritrean Studies* 4 (1–2): 7-12.

Tucci, Giovanni. 1950. *I Baria e i Cunama: e il problema del loro matriarcato.* Napoli, Italy: Tipografia Lorenzo Barca.

Turshen, Meredith. 2010. *African Women: A Political Economy.* New York: Palgrave Macmillan.

UNDP. 2015. *Human Development Report 'Eritrea'.* New York: UNDP.

Weber, A. 2011. "Women without Arms: Gendered Fighters Constructions in Eritrea and Southern Sudan". *International Journal of Conflict and Violence* 5 (2): 357–70.

Weldemichael, A. 1996. "Women's barriers for top managerial positions: case study in Asmara area." Unpublished typewritten document. Asmara, Eritrea.

Wilson, Amrit. 1991. *The Challenge Road: Women and the Eritrean Revolution.* London: Earthscan.

Woldemikael, Tekle M. 2013. "Introduction." *Africa Today. Special Issue: Postliberation Eritrea* 60 (2): v–xix. doi:10.2979/africatoday.60.2.v.

Woldemikael, Tekle M. (ed.). 2018. *Postliberation Eritrea.* Bloomington: Indiana University Press. doi:10.2979/postliberationeritrea.0.0.01.

Chapter 7

Equal Spaces or Patriarchy?

*Examining Women's Participation
in Tax Rulemaking*

Bernadette Malunga

One of the crucial issues in the gender equality and nondiscrimination discourse is the exclusion of women from participation in public affairs and governance of their countries (Ebeku 2005). Ebeku (2005) reports that in Africa women are deliberately excluded from participating in public affairs because of customary and traditional views of women as perpetual minors and inferior to men. The concept of participation has become important for women's international human rights discourse and is often employed as a measure of equity and fairness (Ebeku 2005). Participation increases the chances of incorporating the needs and interests of those involved. However, women's participation in tax rulemaking processes has hardly been discussed and interrogated in Malawi, even though women face many challenges related to the content and application of taxes in Malawi.

THEORETICAL FRAMEWORK

The chapter is based on a human rights approach to tax rulemaking. The human rights approach demands that attention be given to the experiences of different groups that are being marginalized and/or having their rights violated (Hellum, Kameri-Mbote, and van Koppen 2015). The human rights framework in tax rulemaking is supported by a number of multilateral, regional, and bilateral human rights agreements that prohibit discrimination and promote equality (Tran-Nguyen 2004). For example, paragraph 58b of the Beijing Platform for Action 1995 calls for governments to analyze, from a gender perspective, policies, and programs—including those related to macroeconomic stability, structural adjustment, external debt problems, taxation, and all relevant sectors of the economy with respect to their impact on poverty, on inequality, and particularly on women. Furthermore, the Convention on the Elimination of all forms of Discrimination against Women (CEDAW) refers to sex as prohibited grounds for discrimination. The principle of nondiscrimination is stated quite broadly in CEDAW and includes discriminatory purpose and effects. A broad interpretation of the nondiscriminatory principle "indicates a human rights approach to combating discrimination as opposed to a formal legal approach in which a (symmetrical) sex equality or equal treatment norm prevails" (Holtmaat 2013, p99). Discrimination, according to CEDAW, includes "hidden or indirect forms of sex discrimination" (Holtmaat 2013, p100). It also includes "structural or systematic gender stereotypes and gendered structures that are deeply rooted in religion, culture, or tradition of a particular society as well as in its laws and public policies" (Holtmaat 2013, p100). It is not sufficient simply to extend rights to women, if the gender-specific factors causing women's disadvantage are to be addressed fully. Rights must be infused with substantive gender equality. This means that states have to "move away from a concept of equality that simply demands that women be treated in the same way as men" (Fredman 2013, p223). Such a formal conception of equality expects women to conform to patriarchal-oriented social structures. It does nothing to challenge the structures themselves. Furthermore, formal equality "assumes that the aim is to treat everyone on their merits, regardless of their gender" (Fredman 2013, p224). However, "treating gender as irrelevant merely ignores the ongoing disadvantage experienced by women," thereby entrenching the disadvantage (Fredman 2013, p224). This means that equality may demand not identical treatment but very different treatment (Sen 1992).

METHODOLOGY

This chapter uses data that was collected in Malawi between 2016 and 2017. The data was collected as part of the author's doctoral studies at the University of Nairobi in Kenya. The research aimed at assessing the nature of women's participation in customs clearance rulemaking in Malawi. During the study, the methods of customs clearance rulemaking, the type of women's participation in rulemaking, and how the rulemaking methods assist in the incorporation of women trade-related gender needs were carefully interrogated. Employing a qualitative methodological design, fifty-six cross-border traders (thirty women and twenty-six men) were interviewed. Key informant interviews were also conducted with tax officials and other relevant stakeholders. For the duration of the data collection, participant observations on how customs rulemaking is conducted were also carried out.

CONCEPTUALIZING PATRIARCHY

Patriarchy is a system of social structures and practice in which men dominate, oppress, and exploit women in private and public spaces (Johannsdottir 2009). Patriarchy implies that men hold power in all the important institutions of society and that women are deprived of access to such power (ibid). Private space patriarchy is based upon household production, with a patriarch controlling women individually and directly in the relatively private spheres of the home. Public space patriarchy, on the other hand, is based on structures other than the household where institutions conventionally regarded as part of the public domain are central in the maintenance of patriarchy (Kambarami 2006). Patriarchy is composed of a number of structures, including the patriarchal mode of production, patriarchal relations in work, patriarchal relations in the state, and patriarchal relations in cultural institutions. This chapter focuses on patriarchal relations in the state, which refers to the fact that the state is patriarchal, racist, and capitalist and has a bias toward patriarchal interests (Johannsdottir 2009). The chapter discusses the manifestations and institutionalization of patriarchy in tax rulemaking and how the same can be countered.

Women Challenges with the Contents and Application of Tax Rules

There are a number of customs clearance rules that apply to women cross-border traders. The study focused on two procedures for customs clearance: First, customs clearance procedures for small-scale traders who use form 49 under the Customs and Excise Act. Under these rules, traders ("traders" will be used in this chapter as a collective term for cross-border traders of both sexes and women traders or men traders will be used to identify the specific sex) have to show that their goods do not exceed a prescribed amount of MK 500, 000 (USD 700). The traders are also required to pay a processing fee of MK 10,000 (USD 12), import duty at 30 percent, VAT at 16.5 percent (Malawi Revenue Authority 2018) and excise duty for some goods at 10–20 percent (Malawi Revenue Authority Customs officers (2), personal communication, June 2016).

Second, customs clearance procedures under the Simplified Trade Regime (STR) also apply to small-scale traders. The STR is an initiative which aims at assisting small-scale traders by reducing costs of exporting and importing goods in the Common Market for Eastern and Southern Africa (COMESA) region (Malawi Revenue Authority 2018). There are a number of rules under STR that were mentioned as follows; first, the traders have to show upon reaching the borders that the goods imported are from the COMESA region. Second, the traders have to import goods of not more than USD 1,000. Third, the traders have to import goods specified under a common list (Malawi Revenue Authority 2018).

Small-scale traders, in general, and women, in particular, encounter a number of challenges with the customs/tax rules themselves as well as the application of the rules. The tax rules are mostly not favorable to women's trade, which results in a number of negative consequences.

High Tax/ Customs Duty Rates

Among the many challenges against women cross-border traders, the rules pertaining to taxes were the most complained about. Every trader inter-viewed complained that the tax rates in the clearing of goods are very high, and as such, they work against the promotion of women's trading activities. Furthermore, the imported goods also attract a lot of taxes on the same goods, namely import duty, VAT, and excise duty for some goods (Malawi Revenue Authority 2018). The customs officials at the borders confirmed that Malawi has high taxes as compared to other countries, in that in most cases the taxes are equivalent or come near to the cost of buying the goods (Malawi Revenue Authority Customs Officer at Mchinji border, personal communication, July 2016). It was noted that the high taxes have a greater negative impact on women's trading activities as compared to men's trading activities. This is due to the fact that women do trade at a small scale because their capital is smaller, meaning that the taxes imposed on their goods consume a significant portion of their business capital. The business capital of women cross-border traders starts as low as MK 30,000 (USD 41) (focus group discussions with women and men cross-border traders in Mchinji, personal communication, July 2016).

Second, the goods which most women trade in (e.g., cosmetics) attract high taxes because they are considered as luxuries (Malawi Revenue Authority 2018). Third, women, as compared to men, have no knowledge of tax rates, goods exempted in tax, and how tax is calculated, which makes them vulnerable to discrimination and can be taken advantage of. In addition, apart from the high taxes, women pay other expenses relating to travel, accommodation (bathroom facilities), food, pieceworkers, debts, and bribes, which is paid from the same small business capital (Women cross-border traders at Songwe border, personal communication, November 2017).

Arbitrary Application of Customs Clearance Rules

Related to the high taxes is the manner of application of the taxes. Most of the women cross-border traders are not aware of the rates on which tax is calculated, nor are they given any explanation of how tax is calculated, neither are they involved in the calculation of the taxes. The customs officers unilaterally impose the tax; as a result, their calculations are treated as suspicious. The traders complained about huge variations of taxes on the same type of goods with the same quantity for different traders (focus group discussion with women cross-border traders in Lilongwe, personal communication, July 2016).

Furthermore, customs officials usually ignore cross-border traders' documentation on the goods imported and use their own system of valuation (focus group discussion with women cross-border traders in Rumphi, August 2016.) It was observed that the cross-border traders were not asked for receipts or invoices of their goods, but tax was still computed and imposed on their goods. In addition, the unilateral calculation and imposition of taxes by customs officers as well as the high tax rates fuelled corruption among the officers (Male cross-border trader in Blantyre, July 2016). The high taxes results in women cross-border traders negotiating reductions, which according to customs officials, is not allowed.

Small quantity of goods attracts high taxes and they ask us to give that amount and an extra for their own personal use. So, for example, the tax will be MK 30,000 (USD 41); they will write a receipt of MK 10, 000 (USD 14) and we pay MK 20, 000 (USD 27), the other MK 10,000 (USD 14) becomes theirs (male cross-border trader in Lilongwe, personal communication, June 2016).

Lack of Knowledge of Customs Clearance Rules

There is a high level of lack of knowledge of customs clearance rules among traders. This challenge is more pronounced on the female traders as compared to the male traders. For example, most of the women have no information about what goods are taxable and what goods are exempted from tax or general knowledge on tax rates. As compared to the women traders, the majority of male traders stated that they have access to customs clearance information. The men get information from customs books, media outlets, and the internet (women and men cross-border traders (15) in Lilongwe and Mchinji, personal communication, June–July 2016). The lack of knowledge by women traders is attributed to a number of factors, such as a lack of transparency in the administration of customs clearance. For example, in the two borders visited, there was no customs official acting as a desk officer to inform the traders about customs clearance rules before and after importation of goods.

The borders hardly have documentation to help traders make a wise decision before importing goods. Women traders mostly get information from seasoned and experienced traders. The lack of knowledge also results from the constant change of customs clearance rules and the traders are not involved in the formulation or modifications of such changes (officer in the Ministry of Finance, personal communication, August 2016.) For instance, the taxes often change every year, but there is no established channel of communication to appraise traders on the same (women cross-border traders in Blantyre and Lilongwe, personal communication, June 2016). In addition, most women traders have low education, which contributes to the lack of knowledge of clearance rules as the clearance rules are mostly in documents that are in English, difficult to read, and understand even for those who are more literate (focus group discussion with women and men cross-border traders in Lilongwe, personal communication, August 2016).

The problem of lack of knowledge of customs clearance rules by women is compounded by their lack of negotiation skills. The women traders, unlike male traders, are less vocal and often do not demand a justification of the application of the rules such as tax computations. Most women traders were reported as resorting to tears while the men negotiate their way through and have their taxes justified and sometimes reduced (customs officer at Mchinji border, personal communication, July 2016).

Unfavorable Simplified Trade Regime Customs Clearance Rules

The Simplified Trade Regime (STR) customs rules are a Common Market for Eastern and Southern Africa (COMESA) initiative that were introduced to assist small-scale traders by exempting them from the payment of some taxes such as import and excise duties. However, the STR rules have certain features that do not agree with women's trading behavior. First, traders are only allowed to import or export goods listed under a common list. The list is not comprehensive enough as it excludes goods that are mostly imported by women (women cross-border traders in Mchinji, personal communication, July 2016). Most women who get goods from COMESA import goods (e.g., wrappers/ Zitenje, cosmetics, and accessories) which are not on the list. In addition, the traders are limited to import goods up to USD 1,000 when in other countries, such as Zambia, traders can import goods worth USD 2,000 (Simplified Regime Desk officer at the Mwamwi/Mchinji border post, personal communication, July 2016).

Second, the STR facility is limited in its application. The goods that are cleared subject to the STR clearance rules must come from the COMESA region (Malawi Revenue Authority 2018). Albeit, most women traders get their goods both from COMESA region and other countries outside COMESA, including Tanzania and South Africa. Furthermore, most women traders do not understand this limitation, as long as they have got the goods from a COMESA country, such as Zambia, they assume that STR clearance rules will apply (customs officer at Mchinji border, personal communication, July 2016). Notwithstanding, the traders have to show that their goods were manufactured in Zambia and Zimbabwe, which invokes some level of animosity between the traders and customs officers. The traders think that the officers are unnecessarily refusing to let them import goods that are allowed under common list (focus group discussion with men and women cross-border traders in Mchinji, personal communication, July 2016).

Third, there is uncertainty regarding what goods are allowed under the STR. The traders are sometimes denied the ability to clear goods through STR even though the goods are covered under the common list. For example, there is juice commodity under STR but the officials refuse to clear certain types of juices. The list also includes sugar as an acceptable imported good, but the traders have since been denied to clear sugar pursuant to the STR clearance rules. The uncertainty of what goods are permitted under STR creates confusion among traders as they are not sure when approaching the borders if their goods would pass under the STR or not (focus group discussion with male cross-border traders in Mchinji, personal communication, July 2016).

Lastly, there is a general lack of knowledge among women traders about the operations of STR. To this end, some of the women traders (six out of the thirty interviewed) are not using the facility even where it could have helped their businesses.

WHY WOMEN'S PARTICIPATION IN TAX RULEMAKING IS RELEVANT

From the discussion above, it is clear that women meet a lot of challenges with the content and application of tax rules. As such, it becomes imperative for women to be involved in the formulation of the tax rules. The chapter contends that women should have a voice in tax rulemaking not only to achieve gender parity but also to transform the agenda, values, and processes of tax rulemaking in Malawi (Verma 2004). The women traders stated a number of reasons justifying the need for their participation in tax rulemaking. First, the women traders said that their involvement in tax rulemaking is essential because it would ensure their right to do business and would protect their businesses from collapsing. They also said that their non-involvement in the formulation of the tax rules brings about rules that are unfavorable (e.g., the imposition of high customs rates on their goods).

These unfavorable rules often work against women traders' right to do business and force them into illegal trade practices or push them out of trade. Second, women traders stated that they would want to be involved in tax rulemaking because it is through their trade that the country is being financed (female cross-border trader in Blantyre, personal communication, July 2016). The traders were of the view that the government is surviving on the money that the women traders pay at the borders and they need to be involved when making rules. Small-scale traders who frequently cross the borders than the large-scale traders claim that they pay more taxes to the government as compared to large-scale traders (women cross-border traders in Rumphi, personal communication, August 2016).

Third, the traders stated that it is important for the women traders to own the rules and participation in tax rulemaking is the only way to ensure their ownership. They suggested that if the women own the rules, there will be a reduction in corruption and the smuggling of goods. This argument was supported by some duty bearers that for proper implementation of the tax rules, women traders need to be involved (senior state advocate in the Ministry of Justice, personal communication, August 2016).

> Over the years we have seen that when we let people know about what is happening, they do accept the changes without giving much problems. Mostly our programs with the people are about informing them about what we are doing and not necessarily seeking their views on whether to introduce programs or not. Where we have not engaged the people, we have seen resistance coming in various forms e.g., through court. (Marketing officer at Malawi Revenue Authority Head office, personal communication, August 2016)

Fourth, women involvement in tax rulemaking is considered essential as it acts as a channel of communication about how the tax system should work effectively. Out of the thirty women traders interviewed, twenty-three women traders stated that they do not have adequate information about how the system works as they are not in touch with the officials, have no access to the customs rules, and only get information from other experienced traders (women cross-border traders in Lilongwe, Rumphi, Mchinji and Blantyre, personal communication, June to August 2016).

Lastly, women involvement in tax rulemaking is considered essential by some duty bearers arguing that the women traders have the hands-on experience with the tax rules so that they would be in a better position to point out what works and to suggest possible solutions to the challenges women traders' face when doing cross-border trading (Policy planners (3) at Malawi Revenue Authority Head office, personal communication, August 2016).

TRENDS OF PATRIARCHY IN TAX
RULEMAKING IN MALAWI

The research found that women have limited access to tax rulemaking and, as a result, women hardly participate in the process. The minimal participation of women is brought by the patriarchal nature of the rulemaking process that fails to structure public participation in a way that allows effective women's participation. Some of the concerns about the patriarchal nature of public participation are discussed below.

Lack of Information

The field research noted that women are mostly not aware that tax rulemaking happens and that they can participate, partly due to the means in which the state disperses information about the occurrence of tax rulemaking. The communication means are patriarchal in nature and not women friendly. The research found that public consultations notifications are inadequate to incorporate women's participation in tax rulemaking. The notifications to consultation meetings are initiated by the Ministry of Finance, which issues public calls to the tax consultation meetings. The public calls go through national radios, television, as well as local newspapers. The majority of the women traders stated that they have never heard of calls to tax rulemaking. However, most of the men traders were aware of these calls saying that they get the information through radio adverts. The women traders indicated that there is a need to work on ensuring that the public consultation meetings are communicated effectively and timely. In Mchinji District, for example, women suggested the use of community radios, which seems accessible to most of the women traders. This agrees with previous studies that have found that women mostly access community Radio in Malawi (Mhangama 2015). Mhagama (2015) states that community radio can empower women by providing them with access to information, which is a scarce resource in rural areas. Women traders at Blantyre and Lilongwe markets suggested that the state should give letters to market officials or committees of cross-border associations inviting the traders to rulemaking processes. The current notification procedures are not accessible to women traders as such they work to exclude them from participating in the rulemaking process. Innovative and traditional ways of disseminating information that goes beyond the common media outlets are necessary to reach out to women traders. This is also in line with previous research in Malawi, which has shown that in general men have more access to the most common three types of media (radio, newspaper, and television) than women (National Statistical Office 2004). The Malawi Demographic Health Survey (MDHS) recorded that 12 percent of men have access to all three types of media as compared to women, who were at 5 percent.

Cost of Participation

The field data shows that the current nature of participation in tax rulemaking is too costly for most women. The system only allows bureaucrats and at the minimum the well-to-do in society (who are mostly male) to access and effectively influence the process. The research found that public consultation meetings are done in one central district in each of the four regions of Malawi. The meetings take place at upscale hotels and usually last for half a day. The consultation meetings are open to everyone, including institutions and associations. However, it was reported and observed that the public, especially women, do not patronize these consultation meetings. The women traders reported that even if they were aware of these consultation meetings, they would not go due to logistical challenges. The first challenge is the lack of resources to enable the women traders to attend consultation meetings. Participants to consultation meetings need funds for transportation, meals, and accommodation. The majority of women in Malawi are poor, with no adequate resources to enable them to engage in processes that affect their lives (van Klaveren 2009). Effective participation requires money, time, organization, and expertise (Lenny 1976). The lack of women's participation in tax rulemaking is likely to continue as long as cost, time, and effort to make a contribution continues to be relatively high and the government's failure to reimburse incurred expenditures (Coglianese 2008).

Conceptualization of Tax Rules

The patriarchal nature of tax rulemaking is also evidenced in the way the tax rule makers conceptualize a "rule" in tax rulemaking. There is an erroneous understanding by the rule makers and implementers in the tax agency of how tax rules should be conceptualized and applied. The understanding is that rules are supposed to be gender-neutral as regards content and application. The rule makers and implementers in the tax agency were of the view that for fairness purposes, rules are not supposed to give unequal treatment and favor one group as opposed to the other.

"Laws and regulations are not supposed to differentiate in content and application. An importer is an importer and the law is supposed to apply the same across the board and not favour one particular group" (customs officer at Malawi Revenue Authority Head office, personal communication, June 2016).

When drafting the rules, there are no specific gender guidelines to help incorporate and mainstream women's and men's needs in the rules as required by international conventions that Malawi is party to. For instance, the Convention on the Elimination of all forms of Discrimination against Women (CEDAW) mandates state parties to ensure the right of women to participate in the formulation and implementation of government policy. Article 4 of CEDAW allows positive discrimination in favor of women for the purpose of achieving de facto equality. In particular, CEDAW in article 14(1) mandates state parties to take into account particular problems faced by rural women in the economic survival of their families. Paragraph 2 of the article 14 obliges state parties to ensure that women are participating and benefiting from rural development, particularly in the elaboration and implementation of development planning at all levels.

The lack of a gender focus in tax rulemaking has brought about unfriendly and discriminatory rules that have managed to push women into illegal activities such as the smuggling of goods. Individual traders and some customs officials also noted that women are more disadvantaged with the application of the customs clearance rules. This is due to the fact that women trade on a small scale as they have a small capital base as compared to men. For instance, in Mchinji District, the capital of the businesses of eleven women respondents was from a minimum of MK 40,000 (USD 55) to a maximum of MK 500,000 (USD 699). Furthermore, women have no access and are not knowledgeable of customs rules contributed by low education as well as by non-participation in the formulation of the rules.

The chapter argues that the current concept of a "rule" in tax rulemaking is based on the ideology of liberalism which has no capacity to challenge patriarchal institutions. This ideology focuses on individuals while considering the individual as the most important basic unit of society (Beetman 1995). Beetman (1995) states that liberalism emphasizes equality of opportunities and that people should be given equal opportunities in the affairs of the state (ibid). Furthermore, it is assumed that the state should have minimal power in controlling the affairs of individuals. He adds that liberalism is based on an economic aspect of capitalism that leaves the individual to fight in the free market (ibid). A liberal state is therefore more or less a society of "survival of the fittest" because it does not allow the intervention of the state in the enjoyment of rights (ibid). In liberal societies, laws and their regulations are based on the concept of rule of law, which says that no one is above the law but that all are equal before the law (ibid). Such a view-point entails that under a liberal law, special arrangements for any person or any group of people is denied. All people are supposed to be subject to the same law. Therefore, the principles of equal individual rights and majority rule provide the theoretical basis of liberal democratic nations. However, the individualistic, egalitarian form of liberal law in ethnically plural and patriarchal societies may lead to the violation of the human rights of members of minority collectives, including girls and women (ibid).

The liberalist view of what the law and its regulations should be is evident in the tax rules that apply to cross-border traders. The tax rules are individualistic and egalitarian in content and application despite the glaring differences among women and men cross-border traders. The Liberalist view is articulated, as the best, by almost all customs officials who are involved in the formulation and implementation of the tax rules. "However, when we are making the rules, the general principle is that we have to be blind on how they affect one group as compared to the other. The rules have to be the same for everyone and should not favour one group" (Officer in the Ministry of Trade, personal communication, July 2016).

Consequently, gender is not treated as an issue in tax rulemaking. The tax rules are not analyzed from a gender perspective to assess how they impact on men and women. The lack of attention to gender issues perpetuates the disadvantaged position of women in cross-border trade in Malawi. Despite the fact that section 13 of the Constitution of the Republic of Malawi mandates all government agencies to take into account gender equality in national policy, responses from key informants in this study indicate otherwise. That is, the gender equality clause of the Malawian Constitution clause is being violated.

The study shows that on the surface, the tax rules do not discriminate against women. The discrimination comes through the impact and effect of the trade rules on women. It was reported that many women, as opposed to men, are the ones involve in informal cross-border trade due to the hostile tax rules at the borders. Some women also reported to have stopped engaging in cross-border trade as they were not comfortable with using the informal routes, thereby denying them their right to earn a living (ex-woman cross-border trader in Mchinji, personal communication, July 2016).

Though men and women face almost the same problems with the content and application of the tax rules, it was reported that men in most cases are able to work around the rules when crossing the borders through negotiation due to their knowledge of the rules. Men were able to state that they have ever seen the tax books which contain the clearance rules or that they have read about the customs rules on the internet. Most men, as compared to women, had a good educational background. All twenty-six men interviewed had a high school certificate, except two who only had a junior high school education. As compared to the women traders, five had done primary education, nineteen had a junior high school certificate, six had a high school certificate, and two had done tertiary education.

Noteworthy, it was mentioned during the interviews that the differential impact of the customs rules on men and women has been previously recognized by the government mainly through presidential directives. For example, it was reported that some presidents decreed the exemption of import taxes on women traders. However, such decrees were not backed by laws or regulations and were sometimes met with resistance from the rule makers or implementers (Kamuzu International Airport customs officer, personal communication July 2016). It is against this backdrop that the chapter emphasizes that gender considerations need to be factored in when conceptualizing and formulating the rules to avoid indirect discrimination when implementing the tax rules.

CONCLUSION

The chapter has shown that in Malawi there is minimal involvement of women in tax rulemaking. The theoretical and situational analysis discussed shows that the current tax rulemaking system is patriarchal in nature and thus not an enabling institution to facilitate effective women's participation. The chapter shows that the tax rulemaking processes prefer male as opposed to female contribution. As a result of this disadvantage, a number of women have gone into illegal trade, which is not conducive to the development of their trading activities. The chapter has further shown that women's participation in tax rulemaking is also a matter of rights and therefore an entitlement that is not negotiable. A number of commitments have been made by Malawi in international conventions, promoting women's participation in public affairs or governance. Observance of participation rights is therefore critical to good governance in a country as it ensures that vulnerable groups such as women are given priority.

REFERENCES

Beetman, D., et al. 1995. *Politics and Human Rights.* Oxford: Blackwell Publishers.

Coglianese, C. 2009. "Transparency and Public Participation in the Rule Making Process". The George Washington Law Review 77: 924–972.

Ebeku, K. 2005. "African Women and Participation in Public Life and Governance: Relevant Laws and Overview of Recent Experience." Law and Politics in Africa, Asia and Latin America38(1): 56–77.

Fredman, S. 2013. "Engendering Socio-Economic Rights." In Hellum, A. and Aasen, H.S., eds. *Women's Human Rights; CEDAW in International, Regional and National Law.* United Kingdom, Cambridge University Press 217–241

Hellum, A., Kameri-Mbote, P., and van Koppen, B. 2015. *Water Is Life: Women's Human Rights in National and Local Water Governance in Southern and Eastern Africa.* Harare: Weaver Press.

Holtmaat, R. 2001. "Gender, the Analytical Concept that Tackles the Hidden Structural Bias of Law." RechtRichtung Frauen: BeitragezurfeministischemRecht swisschenschaft, Lachen/St Gallen: Dike Verlag. 124–157

Holtmaat, R. 2013. "The CEDAW: A Holistic Approach to Women's Equality and Freedoms." In Hellum, A. and Aasen, H. eds. *Women's Human Rights: CEDAW in International, Regional and National Law*. Cambridge: University Press. 124–157

Johannsdottir, N. 2009. "Patriarchy and the Subordination of Women; from a Radical Feminist Point of View." Haskoli Isalnds. https://skemman.is/bitstream/1946/3017/1/Nina_Katrin_Johannasdottir_fixed.pdf.

Kambarami, M. 2006. "Femininity, Sexuality and Culture: Patriarchy and Female Subordination in Zimbabwe." University of Fort Hare. http://www.arsrc.org/down loads/uhsss/kmabarami.pdf.

Lenny, D. 1976. "The Case for Funding Citizen Participation in the Administrative Process." *Administrative Law Review* 28(3): 483–509.

Malawi Revenue Authority. 2018. "Common Market for Eastern and Southern Africa COMESA Simplified Trade Regime STR." https://www.mra.mw/custom-and-excise/common-market-for-eastern-and-southern-africa.

Malunga, B. 2018. "Participation in Customs Clearance Rulemaking: A Case of Women Informal Cross Border Traders in Malawi." Doctoral Thesis, University of Nairobi, Kenya.

Mhagama, P. 2015. "Harnessing the Potential of Community Radio in Empowering Rural Women in Malawi." *Sociology Study*, 5(2): 91–102. Malawi National Statistical Office, 2004. Malawi Demographic and Health Survey.

Sen, A. 1992. *Inequality Re-examined*. Clarendon Press: Oxford.

Tran-Nguyen, A., et al. 2004. *Trade and Gender: Opportunities and Challenges for Developing Countries*. United Nations, UNCTAD: NewYork and Geneva.

Van Klaveren, M., et al. 2009. "An Overview of Women's Work and Employment in Malawi." Amsterdam Institute for Advanced Labour Studies, AIAS.

Verma, V. 2004. "Engendering Development: Limits of Feminist Theories and Justice." *Economic and Political Weekly*, 39: 49.

Chapter 8

Zambia's Prison Laws and Allied Legislation

The Plight of Women Prisoners Accompanied by Children

Ellah TM Siangándu

Zambia has a total of eighty-eight prisons: fifty-four standard prisons and thirty-four open-air prison farms, one of which is exclusively for juveniles (Prison Walls 2018). There are three main female prisons: the Livingstone, Mukobeko, and Kamfinsa Female State Prisons. As of May 2017, women constitute approximately 3 percent of Zambia's total prison population of 25,000 (World Prison Brief Data 2018). A lack of information means that it is not clear how many inmates are currently imprisoned with children. The prison laws and allied legislation have not always served women imprisoned with children well. The phrase *prison laws* is used to refer to all legislation relevant to women imprisoned with children. Allied or related legislation refers to any other legislation applicable to women incarcerated with children in Zambia, apart from the Prisons Act and Regulations. The law does not recognize the multiple roles of women incarcerated with children as carers and as convicted offenders. This is the case even though in Zambia women are the primary caregivers responsible for raising children (UNODC and WHO 2009). The children of women in prison are commonly referred to as circumstantial children. There are children that are in prison on account of their imprisoned mother (Nkole 2018). They are either born to incarcerated women or admitted into prison with their mother in accordance with Section 56 of the Prisons Act and Regulations.

This chapter aims to identify the gender gaps in Zambia's prison laws and allied legislation by interrogating its gender sensitivity to ascertain the extent to which it accounts for the plight of women incarcerated with children. The object of the chapter is to highlight the gender gaps, in addition to the opportunities for law and policy reforms in Zambia relevant to women imprisoned with children. It adopts the fundamental principles of equality and nondiscrimination as the basis for identification of the gender gaps in the prison laws. The concept of substantive equality as a tool to gender main-streaming is then considered. The contention is that substantial gender equality can be achieved only by implementing the principles of nondiscrimination and equality. Finally, the concept of substantive equality is employed as a basis for the critique of Zambia's Prison laws and allied legislation.

The legal doctrine aspect of the Women's Law methodology is adopted to interrogate Zambian laws applicable to women incarcerated with children. The Women's Law approach explores women's experiences from their perspective by questioning and investigating the law (Bentzon et al. 1998). Doing so is vital to uncover the flaws in what seem to be gender-neutral laws and regulations, which are in fact gendered and negatively impact women incarcerated with children. The doctrinal analysis of the prison laws and relevant legislation is adopted in order to identify the gender gaps in the law. It further uses the descriptive and analytical approach to the relevant legislation, regulations, case law, and international and regional human rights instruments and literature applicable to women incarcerated with children.

Following the adoption of the Convention on the Elimination of all Forms of Discrimination against Women (CEDAW) in 1979 and its entry into force in 1981, feminist discourses have emphasized substantive equality, which is the equality of outcome, in contrast to the equal treatment of women and men alone. Substantive equality, that is equal opportunities, means players who have equal prospects, equal means, and an absence of hindrances to the prospect of enjoying opportunities (Kinyanjui and Kameri-Mbote 2018). According to Fredman (2016), the focus should not be only on equal treatment of individuals but also on ensuring that individuals enjoy equal opportunities. Women incarcerated with children have a duty to care for their children and to transform into responsible individuals as convicted offenders.

To enable women imprisoned with children to efficiently undertake their roles of mother and convicted offender while in correctional facilities, the prison laws must address their specific needs. Incarcerated women's responsibility of caring for their infants in correctional facilities should not constitute a hindrance to the women's participation in various activities or programs intended to transform them into more law-abiding citizens upon their release from the correctional facilities. Proponents of the substantive equality approach, such as Rosenfeld (1986), stress that although in certain situations availing formal equality suffices, at other times it is necessary to introduce positive action to enable individuals to enjoy equal opportunities. Fredman and Goldblatt (2015) summarize substantive equality as encompassing four features: the need to address social and material disadvantage experienced by women, the acceptability of differential treatment of women in situations where it is necessary, social change, and the notion that substantive equality focuses on individuals. The four features are addressed in depth below.

First is the need to address the social and material disadvantage experienced by women serving sentences with children because of the gendered nature of prison. The prison system must operate in such a way that it ensures that women incarcerated with children enjoy opportunities available to other women and men. This proposition substantiates the need to have affirmative action intended to improve the life situation of women incarcerated with children. This is vital in efforts to empower them to overcome the challenges that they face in correctional facilities by leveling the playing field for all female inmates. Associated with this is the second feature of substantive equality, which is the acceptability of differential treatment of women in situations where it is necessary, such as correctional facilities, to facilitate equality as an outcome. The third part focuses on social change. It involves transformation of institutions such as correctional facilities such that they operate in a manner that takes into account the gender differences among inmates, for example by not requiring women incarcerated with children to adapt to socially acceptable male standards or those of other imprisoned women. Fourth, contrary to formal equality, which is based on uniformity of treatment, substantive equality focuses on individuals (Fredman 2009; Barnard and Hepple 2000). With reference to this chapter, it refers to women imprisoned with children as a category of inmates.

The contention is that imprisoning women with children negatively disadvantages them because it violates the fundamental legal principles of nondiscrimination and equality guaranteed under national and international human rights law. Munalula (2018) notes that inequality as a social construction can be deconstructed and reconstructed to achieve equity. Equity is defined as "just and fair distribution of benefits, rewards and opportunities between" individuals including women incarcerated with children (Gender Equity and Equality [GEE] 2015, Article 2). Failure to address the gender-specific needs of women imprisoned with children constitutes discrimination against them contrary to Article 266 of the Constitution of Zambia (The Constitution, Amendment Act 2016). It defines discrimination as "directly or indirectly treating a person differently on the basis of that person's birth, race, sex, origin, colour, age, disability, religion, conscience, belief, culture, language, tribe, pregnancy, health, marital, ethnic, social or economic status." Discrimination is therefore the distinction, marginalization, or restriction made based on any of the above-mentioned grounds.

Women incarcerated with children are negatively impacted because discrimination has an effect of "impairing or nullifying the dignity of a person or the recognition, enjoyment or exercise by a person of that person's rights and freedoms as specified in the Constitution or any other law" (GEE 2015, Article 2). The principles of nondiscrimination and equality are further addressed in the *Protocol to the African Charter on the Rights of Women* of 2003 (Maputo Protocol) and in the *Southern Africa Development Community Gender Protocol* of 2008 (SADC Gender Protocol), which Zambia has signed and ratified. For instance, Article 2 of the Maputo Protocol provides for the elimination of discrimination against women. To that purpose, it imposes an obligation on states parties to combat all form of discrimination against women through legislative, institutional, and other measures. Accordingly,

> States must include in their constitutions and other legislation the principle of equality between women and men; prohibition of harmful cultural practices that can endanger health and general well-being of women; to integrate a gender perspective in all policy decision; legislation, programmes as all other activities of life; take corrective and positive action in those areas where discrimination against women in law and in fact continues to exist.

Article 24 of the Maputo Protocol provides for special protection of women in distress. It states that the states parties, such as Zambia, shall "ensure the protection of poor women and women" generally. This includes women from marginalized population groups who must be provided with an environment suitable to their condition and their special physical, economic, and social needs; and that they shall "ensure the right of pregnant or nursing women or women in detention by providing them with an environment which is suitable to their condition and the right to be treated with dignity."

Article 30 of the African Union's (n.d.) African Charter on the Rights and Welfare of the Child (ACRWC) provides a special provision that aims to protect children of imprisoned mothers and the unborn children of pregnant imprisoned mothers. In fact, Chirwa (2002) and Gose (2002) both describe this as a unique feature of the ACRWC that is not found in other international conventions on the Rights of the Child. This provision has especially been incorporated in the Charter because a mother, within the African context, is regarded as the primary caretaker of children (Gose 2002). Zambia is no exception, as alluded to above in the introduction section. Article 30 provides that

> [s]tates Parties to the present Charter shall undertake to provide special treatment to expectant mothers and to mothers of infants and young children who have been accused or found guilty of infringing the penal law and shall in particular: (a) ensure that non-custodial sentence shall always be first considered when sentencing such mothers; (b) establish and promote measures alternative

to institutional confinement for the treatment of such mothers; (c) ensure that a mother shall not be imprisoned with her child; (d) ensure that death sentences shall not be imposed on such mothers; (e) the essential aim of the penitentiary system will be the reformation, the integration of the mother to the family and social rehabilitation.

Apart from the international and regional human rights treaties, soft law can also be used as a tool for the identification of the gender gaps. Thus, the commonly accepted standards for incarceration of women with children as provided by the United Nations Rules for the Treatment of Women Prisoners and Non-Custodial Measures for Women Offenders (the Bangkok Rules) are considered.

Bangkok Rule 1 clearly provides that regarding implementation of the principle of nondiscrimination with reference to the treatment of prisoners, "account shall be taken of the distinctive needs of women prisoners in the application of the Rules." This measure is vital in efforts to achieve substantial gender equality. Additionally, Bangkok Rule 40 provides that "[p]rison administrators shall develop and implement classification methods addressing the gender specific needs and circumstances of women prisoners to ensure appropriate and individualised planning and implementation towards those prisoners' early rehabilitation, treatment and reintegration into society." Bangkok Rule 42 further states that imprisoned women must have, first, "access to a balanced and comprehensive programme of activities, which take account of gender-appropriate needs"; second, "the regime of the prison shall be flexible enough to respond to the needs of nursing mothers and women with children; childcare facilities or arrangements shall be provided in prisons in order to enable women prisoners to participate in prison activities"; third, "particular efforts shall be made to provide appropriate programmes for . . . nursing mothers and women with children in prison." Mainstreaming gender in the prison law thus implies that the law must account for the perspectives of women incarcerated with children.

Rule 48 of the Bangkok Rules especially makes reference to breastfeeding mothers and mothers with children in prison and provides a minimum standard for their treatment in prison. Accordingly, "adequate and timely food . . . shall be provided free of charge for pregnant women, babies, children and breastfeeding mothers." Rule 49 of the Bangkok Rules states that "[d]ecisions to allow children to stay with their mothers in prison shall be based on the best interests of the children." Children in prison with their mothers shall never be treated as prisoners. Furthermore, Rule 50 states that "[w]omen prisoners whose children are in prison with them shall be provided with the maximum possible opportunities to spend time with their children." Regarding children living with their mothers in prison, Rule 51 of the Bangkok Rules provides that the children must be provided with an environment that is "as close as possible to that of a child outside prison."

Finally, Rule 52 provides that "[t]he removal of the child from prison shall be undertaken with sensitivity, only when alternative care arrangements for the child have been identified and, in the case of foreign-national prisoners, in consultation with consular official." It further provides that once children are "separated from their mothers and placed with family or relatives or in other alternative care, women prisoners shall be given the maximum possible opportunity and facilities to meet with their children, when it is in the best interests of the children and when public safety is not compromised." The Bangkok Rules are comprehensive and can play a fundamental role in enabling the gender mainstreaming of Zambia's prison laws and related legislation. The Bangkok Rules constitute "soft law," meaning they are not binding by virtue of having been adopted by the United Nations General Assembly (Resolution A/RES/65/229), which had the capacity to make only nonbinding decisions, except for those regarding financial matters. But soft law contributes significantly to the creation of customary international law, which is an acceptable source of international law (Article 38 of the Statute of International Court of Justice).

Having considered the relevant international human rights provisions intended to protect women incarcerated with children, the question that arises concerns the effect of these provisions on Zambia's legal system. Zambia is a landlocked country located in southern Africa. It gained independence from Great Britain in 1964. Consequently, the Zambian legal system is based on English common law. In terms of the relationship between national and international law, Zambia is a dualist system. International treaties once signed and ratified by Zambia are not automatically considered part of domestic law (Redson 2014). This is the case because international treaties are not self-executing; they need to be domesticated into national law in order to become enforceable in the Zambian courts. Domestication is the act of integrating provisions of international treaties and instruments into national law to allow for enforcement. Section 2 of the Ratification of International Agreements Act of 2016 (RIA) provides for the ratification of international agreements and the procedure for the domestication process. Section 12(2) of the RIA Act further clarifies that it is the process of domestication that grants an international agreement legal effect through the adoption of legislation or any other enforceable means. Therefore, if the provisions of the treaties are to guarantee protection and promotion of rights of women incarcerated with children, they must be integrated into the national law. On this basis, the next section identifies the gender gaps in the constitutional, statutory, and policy framework relevant to the incarceration of women with children.

CONSTITUTIONAL, STATUTORY, AND POLICY FRAMEWORK FOR MAINSTREAMING THE PRISON LAWS IN ZAMBIA

This section considers the extent to which the law recognizes that female inmates with circumstantial children have specific needs by virtue of their roles as convicted offenders in need of reformation and as mothers bestowed with the responsibility of caregivers. It does so by identifying the gender gaps in the Constitution, the Prisons Act, and other legislation relevant to the incarceration of women with children. The intention is to advance a critical understanding of the gender gaps and challenges faced by women incarcerated with children.

The Penal Code Chapter 87 of the Laws of Zambia

Sections 24 and 26 of the Penal Code Chapter 87 of the Laws of Zambia (Penal Code) provide for imprisonment as a mode of punishment in Zambia. Section 26 states:

> (1) All imprisonment shall be with or without hard labour in the discretion of the court, unless the imposition of imprisonment only without hard labour is expressly prescribed by law; (2) a person liable to imprisonment for life or any other period may be sentenced for any shorter term; (3) a person convicted of a felony, other than manslaughter, may be sentenced to pay a fine in addition to imprisonment; provided that, where such person is a corporation, the corporation may be sentenced to a fine instead of imprisonment; [and] (4) a person convicted of manslaughter or a misdemeanour may be sentenced to pay a fine in addition to or instead of imprisonment.

The above provision applies to both women and men. It is crafted in a gender-neutral manner that assumes that the impact of the law on women and on men is the same. The provision fails to acknowledge specific circumstances of women, such as the responsibility to care for children. Neither are there specific sentencing principles that are considered during the sentencing of pregnant women or mothers with caretaking responsibility. The law focuses on the offender alone; thus, it does not take into account the context in which it is applied. The provisions of the Penal Code therefore contradict Article 30 of the ACRWC, which imposes an obligation on state parties, such as Zambia, to provide special treatment to convicted mothers of infants and young children by ensuring that a noncustodial sentence is considered a priority when sentencing such mothers. The law must recognize that its impact will be different depending on whom it is applied to.

The Constitution of Zambia, Chapter 1 of the Laws of Zambia

Following the 2016 amendment of the Constitution, the Zambia Prisons Services (ZPS) was renamed Zambia Correctional Services (ZCS) pursuant to Article 193(1) C. The ZCS is responsible for the management, regulation, and security of prisons and correctional centers and for performing other functions as prescribed in Article 193 (4) of the Constitution. The renaming of the ZPS to the ZCS implies that prisons should no longer be viewed as a black hole but viewed as a place where convicts are sent in order to transform and eventually return to society to make a positive contribution. The fact that offenders are incarcerated is considered sufficient punishment. This thinking is in line with Article 30 (e) of the ACRWC, which provides that the crucial aim of the "penitentiary system must be reformation, the integration of the mother to the family and social rehabilitation." It is crucial that the domestic laws be aligned with international and regional human rights instruments to enhance the protection of female inmates with children. However, the law reforms must also be relevant to the plight of women incarcerated with children.

The Preamble of the Constitution of Zambia upholds the human rights and fundamental freedoms of every person and confirms the equal worth of women and men, thereby reaffirming the idea of gender equality. Article 1 of the Constitution provides that the Constitution is the supreme law of the Republic of Zambia and that any other written law, customary law, and customary practice that is inconsistent with its provisions is void to the extent of the inconsistency. Article 7 of the Constitution provides for the sources of laws in Zambia. However, the provision is silent on international treaties or instruments that Zambia is a party to.

Furthermore, Article 8 provides for the national values and principles that include "human dignity, equity, social justice, equality and non-discrimination." Article 8 (b) and (c) of the Constitution specify that national values and principles shall apply to the "enactment and interpretation of the law as well as the development and implementation of state policy." The Constitution in Article 266 entrenches the concept of gender, which is defined as "female or male and the role individuals play in society as a result of their sex or status." However, gender has not been mainstreamed in the Bill of Rights (Articles 11–32 of the Constitution). This section of the Constitution protects the fundamental rights and freedoms of all persons in Zambia. Female prisoners with children, like any other convicts, retain certain fundamental rights and freedoms, with the exception of those restrictions that are necessary for the purposes of the sentence. For instance, women incarcerated with children have a right to life (Article 12). Article 15 of the Constitution provides for protection from inhuman treatment, and Article 23 guarantees protection from discrimination.

However, the Constitution is silent on women's rights; neither does it make reference to women serving sentences with children. It does not address the unique needs of women incarcerated with children, such as access to food, right to raise children in an acceptable and suitable environment, and access to suitable correctional facilities cells, among other necessities. The Constitution is silent on social and economic rights that are essential for women incarcerated with children. As a result, they are negatively impacted by the law as they fail to effectively undertake their mothering responsibilities while in prison. The Constitution furthermore does not recognize the right to equality or to the protection of women from discrimination (Munalula 2018).

The Prisons Act, Chapter 97 of the Laws of Zambia

The Prisons Act, chapter 97 of the laws of Zambia (Prisons Act), makes minimal reference to women incarcerated with children; in the absence of empirical research it is difficult to ascertain how they are impacted by the law. The Prisons Act was enacted in 1966, two years after Zambia gained its independence from Great Britain. The Prisons Act and Regulations (considered below as subsidiary sources of law) are the main instruments governing imprisonment in Zambia. Article 2 of the Prisons Act defines a prisoner as "any person, whether convicted or not, under detention in any prison." The Act makes few references to women prisoners generally. For instance, section 7, which focuses on women prison officers and women prisoners, provides that "in every prison in which women prisoners are imprisoned there shall be women prison officers who shall have the care and the superintendence of the women prisoners, and who shall be responsible for their discipline." This provision is positive, in that it recognizes that female inmates can be vulnerable and in need of protection. According to Rule 33 of the Bangkok Rules,

All staff assigned to work with women prisoners shall receive training relating to the gender specific needs and human rights of women prisoners; Basic training shall be provided for prison staff working in women's prisons; Where children are allowed to stay with their mothers in prison, awareness-raising on child development and basic training on the health care of children shall also be provided to prison staff, in order for them to respond appropriately in times of need and emergencies.

Section 56 of the Prisons Act is the only provision that refers to women imprisoned with children. It states:

Subject to such conditions as may be specified by the Commissioner, the infant child of a woman prisoner may be received into the prison with its mother and may be supplied with clothing and necessaries at the public expense: Provided that, when the child has attained the age of four years, the officer in charge, on being satisfied that there are relatives or friends of the child able and willing to support it, shall cause the child to be handed over to the relatives or friends, or, if he is not satisfied, shall, subject to any other written law, hand the child over to the care of such welfare authority as may be approved for the purpose by the Commissioner.

This provision makes attempts to promote the rights of both the woman prisoner and the child to enjoy their entitlements without being discriminated against. It does so by providing the State with a twofold obligation to formulate and implement policies aimed at ensuring that the specific needs of incarcerated women and their children are provided for. Although the Act permits children to be admitted to prison with their mothers, it fails to offer further mandates necessary to protect and uphold the rights of both children and their imprisoned mothers.

For instance, upon admission to prison with a parent, the Act does not impose an obligation to acquire personal details of the child, such as name, age, details about parents, and home address, to be recorded. Section 57 is restricted to the convicted offender only. In contrast, Rule 2 of the Bangkok Rules provides that "adequate attention must be paid to the admission procedures for women and children, due to their particular vulnerability at this time." Contrary to the Zambian Prison Laws, the Bangkok Rule number 3 requires both the female inmate and the child to register their number and personal details prior to being admitted to prison. Accordingly, the "records shall include . . . at least the names of the children, their ages and, if not accompanying the mother, their location and custody or guardianship status." It further provides that "all information relating to the children's identity shall be kept confidential, and the use of such information shall always comply with the requirement to take into account the best interests of the children." Mandating that information be recorded can enhance protection of both the child and the parent. Rule 29 of the Nelson Mandela Rules (UN GA A/RES/70/175) also provides that "a decision to allow a child to stay with his or her parent in prison shall be based on the best interests of the child concerned." However, the law does not adequately address women incarcerated with children.

On the contrary, the Prisons Act imposes discretion on a Commissioner to decide whether to admit a child into prison; this discretion implies that the treatment and conditions for the incarceration of female prisoners with children will vary from one correctional facility to another. Section 56 of the Prisons Act falls short of establishing a positive obligation on the state to provide the basic needs, such as food, clothing, clean water, supplies of materials such as nappies, soap, health care, childcare facilities, access to programs, and activities. In reality, children imprisoned with their mother are denied access to adequate food, clean water, and supplies of materials, such as nappies, soap, and clothes (Ackermann 2015). The implementation of the law is poor. The law does not provide for proper measures to allow for section 56 of the Prisons Act to be implemented.

With reference to the accommodation of inmates, section 60 of the Prisons Act provides for the separation of inmates. Women serving sentences with infants are omitted from the list of prisoners capable of constituting a category within prison that requires separate accommodation. Section 60 of the Prisons Act provides for the separation of female and male prisoners, and it further categorizes this separation on the basis of young prisoners, adults, first offenders, prisoners with previous convictions, prisoners suspected or certified of being of unsound mind, and such other classes as the Commissioner may deem appropriate. This means that the most notable separation recognized by legislation is made, first, on the basis of sex. It is necessary for the law to go beyond sex and provide for separation on the basis of gender by providing women incarcerated with children with separate accommodation. Section 60(2)(f) of the Prisons Act makes provision for the creation of other categories of inmates that could be separated. Discretion is vested with the commission to establish a class as long as it is practical. The Act does not make reference to accommodation or facilities set up particularly for mothers with children. It is therefore not surprising that female inmates with children are forced to share cells with other female prisoners. These inmates are negatively impacted by the law, given that they are denied the option of engaging in other programs and activities within prison because of their role as mothers in prison. For instance, a lack of childcare facilities prevents women incarcerated with children from engaging in correctional activities and programs intended to transform their character.

Furthermore, the Act omits women incarcerated with children as a category of inmates that can be considered for issues related to remission of sentences or parole. Section 109 of the Prisons Act allows for the Commissioner to make recommendations for a convicted prisoner sentenced to imprisonment for more than a month to earn a remission of one-third of their sentence or entire sentence on the basis of commendable behavior. The extent to which women incarcerated with children are aware of the law, and the extent to which they are considered under the provisions, is not clear. The principles of equity and equality demand that all inmates must be accorded the opportunities to be subjects of the remission of a prison sentence.

With reference to parole, considered under sections 111 to 116 of the Prisons Act, there is no mention of women incarcerated with children. The Act fails to provide such women with the opportunity to be discharged from prison on the grounds of the best interest of the child. Parole is a conditional released of a convicted offender from a penal or correctional institution into the community, where the remainder of the sentence is served under supervision prisons. The fact that women incarcerated with children are not included on the list of eligible categories of prisoners implies that they are denied an opportunity to be released on parole. This means that women incarcerated with children are being treated unfairly, contrary to the principles of discrimination.

Section 146(1) Prisons Act confers enormous discretion upon the Minister of Home Affairs to make rules by the statutory instrument on issues that are critical to women imprisoned with infants. These issues include the classifications of prisoners into categories and their separation; matters relating to bedding, clothing, correction and training, provision of suitable diets and dietary scales, and penal and punishment diets. These are all significant issues concerning women incarcerated with children, yet discretion is vested with an individual, most likely a male person, who is vested with the powers of making the determination. Zambia has never had a female home affairs minister. Relying on a male person to make such vital decisions involving confined women with innocent children implies the continued violation of the fundamental rights of women.

The Prisons Rules: Subsidiary Legislation

Like the Prisons Act, the Prisons Rules make no reference to women serving sentences with children. Rule 16 of the Prison Regulations accords special care for certain prisoners, such as those that might be hospitalized but does not include women with children. Rule 66 of the Prisons Rules addresses issues relating to prisoners' clothing, bedding, and hair cutting, yet no reference is made to women with circumstantial children. It is thus unclear how the ZCS accounts for these children. In addition, the Prisons Rules are silent on the dietary scale for inmates with children. There is no reference to special care accorded to women incarcerated with children. Rule 17(1) of the Prisons Rules allows for an officer in charge to inquire into any complaints made by prisoners relating to rations. The Rule specifically articulates that prisoners are to be supplied with good quality rations and that every prisoner shall receive rations as provided for in the first schedule. The rule clearly illustrates how the system treats all prisoners the same regardless of sex and gender. The rule provides for one ration referred to as the ordinary diet. It is imposed on every prisoner without taking into account the specific needs of women imprisoned with children. The law not only treats women as a homogeneous group but also fails to acknowledge the unique needs of women serving sentences with their children.

It is interesting to note that Rule 206 of the Prisons Rules provides for prisoners under the sentence of death to be issued with special extras treats, such as tobacco, cigarettes, snuff, or any other luxuries as the Commissioner may direct. Yet there are no provisions with regard to female prisoners with children or any of their concerns. It is not clear what decisions about giving extravagant treats to prisoners who are sentenced to death are based on. However, it is vital that the law also recognize the needs of women incarcerated with children and ensure that these are mainstreamed through the Prisons Act and Regulations.

All prisoners, including women incarcerated with children, are entitled to engage in employment, in line with Section 75(1) of the Prisons Act. However, the general rule is that female prisoners can be employed only within the prison premises, in accordance with Section 75(2) of the Prisons Act. The matter relating to the employment of prisoners is further addressed under Rule 142(1) of the Prisons Rules, which empowers the Commissioner with the introduction of an earning scheme for prisoners. The work of caring for children undertaken by convicted imprisoned mothers is not recognized. Rule 142 must incorporate the work of caring and raising circumstantial children undertaken by women confined with children. Women incarcerated with children are precluded, by their role as parents, from engaging in employment, given that childcare facilities are unavailable in prison. The law therefore negatively impacts women incarcerated with children as they are deprived of an opportunity to earn money. The state must amend and adopt relevant legislation that recognizes this important role of mothers in prison. The first step toward recognition of the fundamental role undertaken by mothers would be by the laws incorporating their specific needs such as the provision of food, clothing, suitable activities. Recognizing their gender-specific needs will contribute toward the creation of equal opportunities among prisoners with reference to any activities, programs, or employment opportunity available in correctional facilities.

The Gender Equity and Equality Act 2015

The Gender Equity and Equality Act 2015 (GEE Act) recognizes the significance of mainstreaming gender equality in all areas of law, policy, and social relations. The GEE Act is significant to Zambia and for women generally because it domesticates the CEDAW, the Maputo Protocol, and the SADC Gender Protocol. The GEE Act defines gender equality as "the state of being equal in terms of enjoyment of rights, treatment, quantity or value, [and] access to opportunities" (Part I, section 2). However, the Act has yet to come into force; it awaits the amendment of the Bill of Rights section of the Constitution, which is amendable only by referendum. An attempt was made to amend the Bill of Rights in August 2016; however, it failed because of political factors.

CONCLUSION

The Zambia prison law is silent on women incarcerated with children. No special protection is afforded to them. For that reason, female prisoners accompanied by children continue to be marginalized by the system. The recognition of the concept of gender in the Constitution marks an important contribution in the quest for gender equity. The entrenchment of gender in the Constitution implies that it is crucial to mainstream it into the entire penal system to ensure equity among women incarcerated with children. To retain the provision of the law that allows mothers to be admitted to prison with children under the age of 4, it is necessary that interventions targeting poor conditions of incarceration be made to improve the experiences of mothers imprisoned with children. Measures must be put in place to ensure that the basic needs of these women are integrated into the penal laws, regulations, and practices. This chapter demonstrated how gender mainstreaming as a strategy is justified on the basis of the concept of substantive equality. This concept implies that the prison experiences of women accompanied by children can be enhanced by integrating gender perspectives into the prison laws and related legislation.

The Prisons Act must be amended and aligned with the Constitution. The law must reflect the specific gender needs of women incarcerated with children in line with international and regional standards and with best practices. As is illustrated in this chapter, the law is currently gender blind and does not adequately account for the responsibilities of women imprisoned with children. This category of prisoners is thus disadvantaged by the law. No specific treatment is accorded to them, despite their being expected to continue to undertake the role of caring for their children while in prison, at the cost of the reformation of their own characters and of opportunities for advancement. The law fails to acknowledge the need to protect the rights of these women and children. It is however necessary to conduct further empirical research to establish the specific needs of women incarcerated with children and their lived experiences. This is vital in efforts to ensure any proposed law reforms take into account their perspectives.

REFERENCES

Ackermann, Marlize. 2015. "Women in Pre-Trial Detention in Africa: A Review of the Literature." *Agenda* 29 (4): 80–91. doi:10.1080/10130950.2015.1122345.

Barnard, Catherine, and Bob Hepple. 2000. "Substantive Equality." *Cambridge Law Journal* 59 (3): 262–85. doi:10.1017/S0008197300000246.

Benzton, Agnete Weis, Anne Hellum, Julie E. Stewart, Welshman Ncube, and Torben Agersnap. 1998. *Pursuing Grounded Theory in Law: South-North Experiences in Developing Women's Law.* Oslo: Tano, Aschechoug.

Chirwa, D. 2002. "The Merits and Demerits of the African Charter on the Rights and Welfare of the Child." *International Journal of Children's Rights* 10 (4): 157–77. doi:10.1163/157181802401005421.

Const. of Zambia Act. 1991. Chapter one.

Fredman, Sandra. 2009. "Engendering Socio-Economic Rights." *South African Journal of Human Rights* 25 (3): 410–41. doi:10.1017/CBO9781139540841.011.

Fredman, Sandra. 2016. "Substantive Equality Revisited." *International Journal of Constitutional Law* 14 (3): 712–38. doi:10.1093/icon/mow043.

Fredman, Sandra, and Beth Goldblatt. 2015. *Discussion Paper: Gender Equality and Human Rights.* United Nations Women. https://www.unwomen.org/en/digital-libra ry/publications/2015/7/dps-gender-equality-and-human-rights.

Gender Equity and Equality Act, 2015. https://www.informea.org/en/legislation/ gender-equity-and-equality-act-2015-no-22-2015.

Gose, M. 2002. *The African Charter on the Rights and Welfare of the Child.* South Africa: University of Western Cape.

Kinyanjui, Sarah Muringa, and Patricia Kameri-Mbote. 2018. "The Constitutional Promise: Realising the Right to Gender Equality and Non-discrimination in Kenya." *East African Law Journal*: Special issue on gender (2019).

Munalula, Mulela Margaret. 2018. "'Engendering' the Curricula at the University of Zambia School of Law: Vision, Challenges, Successes." *East African Law Journal*: Special issue on gender (2019).

Nkole, Nkole. 2018, February 12. "Making Circumstantial Children Priority." *Zambia Daily Mail Limited.* http://www.daily-mail.co.zm/making-circumstantial-children-priority/.

Organization of African Unity. 1990. *African Charter on the Rights and Welfare of the Child.* https://www.refworld.org/docid/3ae6b38c18.html.

The Penal Code. Chapter 87 of the Laws of Zambia.

Prison Act and Regulations Chapter 97 of the Laws of Zambia.

Protocol to the African Charter on Human and Peoples' Rights on the Rights of Women in Africa (Maputo Protocol). 2003. https://www.un.org/en/africa/osaa/pdf /au/protocol_rights_women_africa_2003.pdf.

Ratification of International Agreements Act, 2016 (No. 34).

Redson, E. Kapindu. 2014, January. "The Relevance of International Law in Judicial Decision-making in Malawi." Pp. 74–84 in *Using the Courts to Protect Vulnerable People: Perspectives from the Judiciary and Legal Profession in Botswana, Malawi, and Zambia.* Southern African Litigation Centre. https://www.southern africalitigationcentre.org/wp-content/uploads/2017/08/Using-the-courts-WEB. pdf.

Rosenfeld, M. 1986. "Substantive Equality and Equal Opportunities: A Jurisprudential Appraisal." *California Law Review* 74 (5): 1687–712. doi:10.15779/Z380N07.

Southern African Development Cooperation Protocol on Gender Development. https ://www.sadc.int/files/8713/5292/8364/Protocol_on_Gender_and_Development _2008.pdf.

Statute of the International Court of Justice. https://www.icj-cij.org/en/statute.

United Nations Human Rights, Office of the High Commissioner. 1979. *The Convention on the Elimination of All Forms of Discrimination against Women.* https://www.ohchr.org/EN/ProfessionalInterest/Pages/CEDAW.aspx.

United Nations Rules for the Treatment of Women Prisoners and Non-Custodial Measures for Women Offenders (the Bangkok Rules). Resolution A/RES/65/229 (2010/16).

United Nations Standard Minimum Rules for the Treatment of Prisoners (the Nelson Mandela Rules). Resolution adopted by the United Nations General Assembly A/RES/70/175.

World Prison Brief. 2018. "World Prison Brief Data: Africa." http://www.prisonstudies.org/country/zambia.

Chapter 9

Challenging "Supernormal Patriarchy" in Artisanal and Small-Scale Mining Policies and Laws in Zambia

An Ecofeminist Perspective

Fatima Mandhu

At the international level, gender and natural resource extraction are addressed under goal number 5 of the United Nations (UN) Sustainable Development Goals (SDGs). The goal is to "achieve gender equality and empower all women and girls" (UN 2018a, headline). The progress of most African nations toward achieving goal number 5 was noted in the 2018 report, which acknowledged that "some forms of discrimination against women and girls are diminishing" (UN 2018b, para. 1). Yet, as the World Blind Union (WBU) noted,

> Gender inequality continues to hold women back and deprives them of basic rights and opportunities. Empowering women requires addressing structural issues such as unfair social norms and attitudes as well as developing progressive legal frameworks that promote equality between women and men. (WBU Statement n.d., para. 5)

It is clear that the development of a progressive policy and legal frameworks will promote gender equality for women engaged in mining. Natural resource extraction in most developing countries has the additional problem of the "resource curse" that poses many unique risks and challenges for men and for women. The term *natural resource curse* has been developed in international development theory to signify the alignment between natural resource abundance and poverty in resource-rich developing countries.

At the continental level, in Africa, about 3.7 million people are directly engaged in the Artisanal and Small-Scale Mining (ASM) sector, "and about 30 million depend on it for their livelihoods" (UN Economic Conditions for Africa 2016, para. 4). The mining industry in Africa has been identified as a key economic sector that has been driving and will continue to drive the development of the continent. The Africa Mining Vision (AMV) recognizes the contribution of ASM not only in promoting local economic development but also in promoting women's rights (African Union 2009). In terms of specific actions concerning ASM and gender equality in the mining sector, the AMV states that there should be initiatives to search for a new social contract regarding mining. The new social contract regarding mining would involve participation and sharing by the communities and the mining companies in the benefits of natural resource extraction. In addition, the vision stipulates that the Southern Africa Development Community (SADC) should harmonize mining policies, legislation, and regulatory frameworks for the region. This harmonization should prioritize social and gender issues, further "encourage linkages between communities and mineral development and uplift the role of women in mining" (African Union 2009, 46). For the purposes of this chapter, the focus is on the objective of the AMV that deals with the progress being made toward gender equality and the empowerment of women. I will also emphasize related action at the country level as proposed in the AMV, particularly regarding the integration of gender equality in mining policies and laws in relation to ASM. Even though there are several policies in Zambia that deal with mining as well as with land, water, and many other issues related to ASM, the focus of this chapter will be on the three major policies that directly govern ASM. These are the Mineral Resources Development Policy (MRDP 2013), the National Policy on Environment (NPE (Government of the Republic of Zambia [GRZ] 2007), and the National Gender Policy (NGP (GRZ 2014). The Constitution of Zambia is the supreme legislation that provides for the prohibition of all forms of discrimination under Article 23 (Constitution 1996, 2016). Article 23(3) defines discrimination:

> In this Article the expression "discriminatory" means, affording different treatment to different persons attributable, wholly or mainly to their respective descriptions by race, tribe, sex, place of origin, marital status, political opinions colour or creed whereby persons of one such description are subjected to disabilities or restrictions to which persons of another such description are not made subject or are accorded privileges or advantages which are not accorded to persons of another such description.

In spite of the nondiscriminatory provision in the Constitution, in reality, discrimination against women continues in all the sectors, including the mining sector, and at all levels (Intergovernmental Forum on Mining, Minerals, Metals and Sustainable Development [IGF], 2018).

The other pieces of substantive legislation dealing with mining include the Mines and Minerals Development Act (MMDA 2015), the Lands Act (LA 1995), and the Environmental Management Act (EMA 2011). The Mines and Minerals Development Act is mostly gender neutral, and it provides under section 29 that "a person who intends to carry on any artisanal mining, small-scale mining or large-scale mining shall apply for a mining licence under this Part" (MMDA 2015, 189). "A person" refers to both men and women. The LA is also mostly gender neutral, but it is subject to the Constitutional provision of nondiscrimination, like all other legislation. The EMA provides for the protection of the environment but makes no reference to gender in any of its provisions; hence, it is also mostly gender neutral.

In efforts to achieve gender equality in mining, the concept of patriarchy plays an important role, given that the mining sector primarily comprises men. ASM is often conducted in rural settings and is attracting a considerable number of women. Lahiri-Dutt argues that "new gendered geographies are being created as grinding rural poverty pushes large numbers of women into informal mining (also known as artisanal and small-scale mining or ASM)—a fundamentally different type of economic activity from the capitalised, industrialised mining operated by large corporations" (Lahiri-Dutt 2015, 523). The chapter will commence by defining *patriarchy*, followed by a discussion on patriarchy and supernormal patriarchy in ASM using the ecofeminist framework. Thereafter, the gender gaps in both the main policies and in the legislative framework will be identified, and finally a conclusion will be drawn.

DEFINING PATRIARCHY IN ASM

The origin of patriarchy can be traced to the ancient Greek civilization, where the term was used to mean "rule of fathers" (Meyers 2014). Hartmann defines patriarchy as the "set of social relations between men, which, though hierarchical, establish or create interdependence and solidarity among men that enable them to dominate women" (Hartmann 1981, 11). Bradshaw and colleagues concur, writing, "As patriarchal power operates at a hidden, subconscious level, as well as overtly, it leads women to internalise and accept their subordinate status to men as the natural order of things" (Bradshaw, Linneker, and Overton 2017, 441). In the context of extractive industries, the concept of patriarchy shifts to supernormal patriarchy arising from the exaggerated gender roles and supernormal profits. Patriarchy is defined as men having power over women creating male-dominated society. Under supernormal patriarchy that exists in countries whose wealth is linked to extractive industries, stronger patriarchal institutions exist at all levels of the society. Patriarchy has been heavily critiqued, in that it excludes other forms of oppression such as women-to-women and oppression of men by men, "both of which are central to maintaining patriarchal systems" (Bradshaw, Linneker, and Overton 2017). In addition, the concept of patriarchy failed to acknowledge the differences between diverse systems of gender oppression. A broader definition given to patriarchy by feminist writers, one that takes into account multifaceted dimensions, is:

> a set of social relations between men, which has a material base, and in which there are hierarchical relations between men and solidarity among them which enable them in turn to dominate women. The material base of patriarchy is men's control over women's labour power. That control is maintained by denying women access to necessary economically productive resources and by restricting women's sexuality. (Hartmann 1981, 14–15)

Apart from the issue of patriarchy, the involvement of women in ASM creates a relationship between women and nature. It is this relationship between women and nature that forms the nuanced arguments of the ecofeminist writers. Vandana Shiva (1988), an ecofeminist and activist, states that there is a close relationship between women and nature since both sustain life and that Western patriarchy has resulted in the domination of both women and nature (Shiva 1988). Linking patriarchy to natural resources, cultural ecofeminist approaches have blamed the patriarchal culture and the economic and political systems for global environmental degradation.

PATRIARCHY AND SUPERNORMAL PATRIARCHY IN ASM: THE ECOFEMINISM APPROACH

Grounded in developmental approaches, ecofeminism is more about change through social and political transformative struggles and practices viewed as a form of activism rather than a theoretical approach. This section of the chapter considers the challenges of patriarchy from an ecofeminist position—as caused by lack of gender equity in the laws and policies responsible for ASM.

Ecofeminist writers have identified at least eight different connections between women and nature. The one that relates to patriarchy is the conceptual connection that is structured on the domination of women and nature in value dualism based on the basic beliefs, values, attitudes, and assumptions that determine how one views oneself and others. When a conceptual framework maintains relations of subordination and dominance and explains and justifies these, it is said to be oppressive. An oppressive conceptual framework is called "patriarchal" when it explains and justifies the subordination of women by men (Ruether 1997). This oppression of women and nature is clearly visible in mining.

All levels of the mining sector, whether large-scale or small-scale, remain parts of a hypermasculine industry. Ruether elaborates: "As compared to the formal mining sector, the range of informal mining practices is characterised by the large number of women working as wage workers, diggers, panners, processors and traders of mineral commodities" (Ruether 1997 528). Under the discursive masculinity of mining, the ecofeminist view goes beyond the notion of the "death of nature" in mining to a gendered symbolism and the commodification of nature by the large corporate mines (Merchant 1990; Taussig 1980). Women and men in the mining industry experience the direct and indirect consequences of mining differently, and this was clearly noted in the Marikana mine workers' struggle (Benya 2015). The struggle was not only for men as mine workers—it also touched the core of women miners' lives. The fight involved providing decent living conditions for women, which could be achieved only if the men earned a living wage. Furthermore, the argument stated that women's unpaid labor in the homes as well as in the community, which sustains social life around the mines, goes unnoticed. A failure to notice work in the homes done by women is furthered by mining companies that encourage and pressure women to stay out of the professional life and to remain in their own domestic spaces. For example, on the copper belt in the mining towns of Northern Rhodesia, mineworkers were encouraged to live away from the mine site with their wives and family "to enhance the 'stability' of the labour force, while women vainly sought access to family income (Parpart 1986)" (Lahiri-Dutt 2015, 526).

Countries that have rich natural resources and wealth tend to display supernormal patriarchy at all levels of society. Defining patriarchy and super-patriarchy requires the policymakers, the government, and the legislators to understand the fact that women are not a homogeneous group but have differences. The differences between the women who perform different roles in the extractive industry "and the supernormal patriarchal relations that produce these differences" is what should be challenged (Bradshaw, Linneker, and Overton 2017, 447). To challenge the differences, the understanding of gendered relations as a multilayered fluid concept affecting different categories of women differently should be clearly stated as follows: "When an extractive industry develops and mines are opened, patriarchal relations shift in response to changing economic opportunities for men and women" (Bradshaw, Linneker, and Overton 2017, 443).

Though the women within the artisanal mining communities in Zambia are heterogeneous and unique, they tend to be engaged in specific roles.

Typically, they are laborers (e.g., panners, ore carriers, and processors) or providers of goods and services (e.g., cooks, shopkeepers). As compared to their
male colleagues, however, women typically do more marginal jobs and earn
less from mining. This is so because, first, women do not participate in large-
scale formal mining and therefore do not acquire the same skills as men who
find employment at large-scale mines, and second, women are tied to their
households through familial obligations. Women in Zambia act as mine owners and workers with regard to ASM but not to large-scale mining (IGF 2018).

Hinton and colleagues note that,

> despite their significance, women occupying roles not directly related to min-
> eral production have received minimal attention by researchers, development
> programmes and governments. In addition to their contribution to productivity,
> women in ASM communities are critical to community stability, cohesiveness,
> morale and general well-being, and act as primary agents in facilitating positive
> change. . . . Women who act as "cooks" are particularly significant, not only in
> terms of food preparation, but also with respect to managing food stocks and
> related financial reserves. (Hinton, Viega, and Beinhoff 2003, 8)

Both direct and indirect involvement of women in ASM is believed to be
on the rise in Zambia (IGF 2018). The rise in the involvement of women
both directly and indirectly in ASM can be attributed to a number of factors,
including "escalation of rural poverty from droughts and/or structural adjustment programmes resulting in a greater need to supplement incomes; outward
migration of skilled male miners from ASM development *or* in pursuit of
other opportunities in urban areas; evolving cultural norms with respect to
gender roles; [and] lack of employment in other sectors" (Hilson 2003, 160).

In other words, patriarchy should not be essentialized in the natural
resources industry. Women's work in the mining industry remains invisible
because of the status of the male miner; and, as Campbell notes:

> Miners are men's love object. . . . It is the nature of the work that produces a
> tendency among men to see it as essential and elemental, all those images of
> men down in the abdomen of earth, raiding its womb for the fuel that makes
> the world go round. The intestinal metaphors foster the cult of this work as dark
> and dangerous, an exotic oppression. . . . it constructs the miner as earth-man
> and earth-man is true man. And it completed the equation between some idea of
> elemental work and essential masculinity. (Campbell 1984 as cited in Macintyre
> 2016, 4)

This popular image of masculinity is what is represented in the corporate
mining world. However, to promote gender equality in the extraction of

natural resources, it is settled that not only for the large-scale mining but even for ASM, the redistribution of wealth should be prioritized to tackle the "resource curse" and the commodification of the earth's natural resources. Making gender consideration a priority in the policies and laws would result in bringing gender equity into the ASM sector in Zambia.

IDENTIFYING GENDER GAPS IN THE ASM POLICIES AND LAWS IN ZAMBIA

In Zambia, out of the total population of 14,375,601, the working-age population was 7,861,259; 75.9 percent of the working-age population (5,966,199) were in the labor force (i.e., economically active), and 24.1 percent were economically inactive. These statistics relate to the entire labor force in all sectors of the economy. Comparing genders among the economically active persons, 51.6 percent were female and 48.4 percent were male (Gender Statistics Report 2012). However, for the mining sector, in particular, there has been a surge in production, leading to an increase in employment (Ndulo and Chanda Services and Sustainable growth in Zambia 2016). According to the available statistics, the number of people currently working in the mining sector is 62,236 (Zambia Chamber of Mines 2020). However, women account for only 7.5 percent of the workers, compared with men at 92.5 percent (Gender Statistics Report 2010). Since women account for only 7.5 percent of the total labor force in the mining sector, it is obvious that women are not participating at a level comparable to that of men. More specifically, in ASM women are treated with more hostility than in other economic sectors, as was explained by the president of the Association of the Zambian Women Miners, who said: "We face a lot of rejection and we are not taken seriously by people in the field. There are a lot of traditional obstacles along the way. Chiefs feel undermined when they see women coming to mine in their areas. They are hostile" (Mining-Africa 1997). Furthermore, the male dominance or the superpatriarchal system prevalent in the mining industry hinders women from being accepted; according to Reinoud Boers, president of the Chamber of Mines in Zambia, "Negative attitudes to women in mining are an important constraint to women's effective integration in the industry. There is a great deal of male scepticism that needs to be tackled" (as quoted in Ranchod 2001, 14). The mining sector in Zambia has been a highly male-dominated industry, and women need to be included, especially in ASM.

The policies and laws regarding ASM are implemented by the Ministry of Mines and Minerals Development, and one of the hindrances faced by women is that most of the officials at the Ministry in charge of the implementation of the laws are male. "If you go to the Department of Mines of the Government," says Ranchod, "you find that geologists are men, engineers are men, metallurgists are men, surveyors are men and the people in charge of explosives are all men, so these are the imbalances we want to change. Women can actually do all the other works that men are doing" (Ranchod 2001, 14). These imbalances can be addressed to a certain extent by applying the ecofeminist drivers using organizations such as the Association of Zambian Women in Mining (AZWIM) to bring about changes in the attitudes of men who are behind the enactment and implementation of the policies and law that are mostly gender neutral. The MMDA (2015) which was enacted after the Mineral Resources Development Policy [MRDP] (GRZ 2013) had already been implemented. The Act has departed from the policy, given that its provisions are mostly gender neutral and the policy provided for mainstreaming gender by supporting gender equality through mining legislation (GRZ 2013). Additionally, the Act has not provided for equal opportunities for men and women to participate in mining.

Gender Gaps in the Policies Governing ASM

To achieve gender equity in ASM and increase the participation of women, gender considerations should be reflected in the policies. The MRDP is outdated, having been effected before the enactment of the new legislation. It advocates for equal opportunities for men and women to participate in mining but lacks in the provision of guidance as to how this balance can be achieved. Additionally, the policy lacks a system of information flow regarding ASM. Turning to the National Environmental Policy, it is clear that this policy needs revision urgently, since it was last updated in 2007. Even though the policy makes reference to the use of tools for mainstreaming gender in training in environmental and natural resource management, it does not specify what these tools are. The policy needs to take into consideration new and modern ecofeminist approaches to activism through associations such as AZWIM in mining and address the oppressive conceptual framework called "patriarchal." Finally, the Gender Policy is of a more general nature and provides for the revision of policies, programs, and legislation to include gender equality in its provisions. The Gender Policy needs to be coordinated with all the other policies in providing tools for the mainstreaming of gender in the policy and legislative frameworks for ASM. This approach will promote the participation of women in this sector and address the challenges of the "super patriarchy" from an ecofeminist perspective.

Gender Gaps in the Laws Regulating ASM

There are several Acts of Parliament that regulate ASM. One major Act (The Gender Equity and Equality Act 2013) has been omitted from this discussion because even though it has been enacted, it has not yet been brought into effect. The Act provides under section 1 that it will come into effect when the Ministry issues a statutory instrument indicating the date of commencement for the Act (Gender Equity and Equality Act 2015). The minister has not yet enacted the statutory instrument because the Bill of Rights has not been included in the Constitution because it was not allowed to be included unless it passed a referendum, which it did not do (United Nations 2017, 3). To date, the Gender Equity and Equality Act has not come into effect.

The Constitution of Zambia is the supreme legislation that prohibits all forms of discrimination, but in reality, discrimination against women continues in all the sectors and at all levels, including in the mining sector. The Constitution also provides for nonjusticiable principles on land policy, such as the polluter pay principle and other environmental principles. Cases relating to environmental issues are not decided as public interest litigation but are brought under the specific legislation, as in the issue of waste disposal in Zambia with regard to mining activity that was discussed in the case of *James Nyasulu and 2000 Others v Konkola Copper Mines Ltd, Environmental Council of Zambia and Chingola Municipal Council*, 2007.

In 2003, some 2,000 residents of Chingola in Zambia brought a class action suit against Konkola Copper Mines Ltd (KCM) in the High Court, arguing that the defendant had discharged mining effluent into the source of water for the community. On November 6, 2006, one of KCM's tailings pipelines ruptured, which led to effluent with high acidic content escaping into the Chingola and Mushishima streams, which feed into the Kafue River. The Environmental Council of Zambia had communicated to KCM, instructing them to cease operations of their tailings leach plant in view of the pollution of the Kafue River. The evidence brought before the court showed that some residents who drank water from the river suffered stomach pains, diarrhea, and chest pains. Others testified that when they attempted to boil the water, it produced bubbles that did not disappear when the water was cooled. In terms of the various uses of the water, it was clear that the water was used for bathing, cooking, and drinking. The trial judge's decision was that the second respondent in the case did not fail to perform their statutory duty. The judge went on to describe the duty of the mining company as follows: "to carry out inspection or supervise the pipes in question, regularly to meet the required acceptable standards and ensure that no leakage or spillage occurred" (*James Nyasulu and 2000 Others v Konkola Copper Mines Ltd, Environmental Council of Zambia and Chingola Municipal Council* 2007, J2). The judge found that the second defendant had not failed to do these things, but unfortunately did not cite a statute to support this finding. The court correctly found that the second respondent had done everything in its power to ensure that KCM complied with the law.

This judgment of the case was delivered in 2015 and has become an important finding for pollution caused by the mining companies in Zambia. The importance of this case is centered on environmental liability for multinational mining companies and breach of human rights in the natural resources extraction industry (Sambo 2019). Yet no explanation was given regarding the penalty for breach of noncompliance by the mining company.

This case involved large-scale mining where both men and women were affected by the polluted water; however, it was women and small children who bore the brunt more seriously in terms of health and provision of water for the family. The decision of this case was given in a gender-blind manner without reference to the adverse effects polluted water had on the lives of the women and children living in and around the mining community. The mining companies, as corporate giants, should be held accountable for both the environmental degradation and the health of the mining community that depends on the water sources.

Pieces of legislation other than the Constitution—the Mines and Minerals Development Act (MMDA), 2015 and the Environmental Management Act (EMA), 2011—were enacted very recently and therefore have not been subject to interpretation by the courts of law. The Mines and Minerals Development Act (No. 11 of 2015) is the substantive Act that regulates the mining sector. The MMDA is mostly gender neutral; it does not make reference to gender and ASM. The only section that refers to gender representation is section 6, which provides for Mining licenses committee and equitable gender representation when appointing the members of the Committee. The other specific provision under section 20 (1) of the MMDA (No. 11 of 2015) confers an obligation on holders of mining rights and provides that a holder of a mining right must give preference to products and services offered by Zambian companies. Section 20 of the MMDA encourages the empowerment of Zambian citizens, which includes both men and women. From section 20 of the MMDA, it can be argued that holders of a mineral right should employ Zambian citizens, preferably before considering persons from outside the country. In this respect, the MMDA confers liability on holders of a mining right that contravenes this provision. Arguably, the provisions of section 20 (2) of the MMDA are of a general nature, since they do not specify whether the ownership of the Zambian companies providing the products and services should be held by men or women or both. Nonetheless, section 20 of the MMDA remains silent on promoting gender equality in the companies that supply the products and services to the mining sector. Gender needs to be mainstreamed into the MMDA to promote the participation of women and empower them to benefit from ASM.

Ownership, access, and control of land play an important role in ASM. Zambia operates a dual land tenure system, with statutory land being governed under a statutory framework and customary tenure being regulated under customs. The Land Act of 1995 provides for leasehold ownership of land for up to 99 years by both men and women. Under customary tenure, most customs provide that men inherit most of the land. This dual legal structure of ownership makes it very difficult for women to own land in Zambia. It is accepted practice for women to get access to land through the permission of their spouses or other family members, because even if women technically have land ownership rights, men tend to control the land in reality. The Lands Act 1995 is gender neutral and does not address women's right to land ownership, access, and control with regard to the dual land tenure system (GRZ 2016). Environmental concerns in the mining sector are addressed under the Environmental Management Act, which is also mostly gender neutral. In particular, Sections 91, 92, 93, and 94 of the EMA provide for public participation, public hearings, and public reviews and regulations in the environmental and social impact assessments of projects, in general, and of mining projects, in particular. The EMA, on the other hand, does provide for decision-making powers of the community, but it lacks clarity about decision-making powers of affected members of the community, and these include women and men (GRZ 2016). The government notes, "The Act has no provisions on resettlement and compensation of communities affected by mining investments" (GRZ 2016, 11). However, there are no requirements under the EMA for mine developers to carry out a detailed human rights due diligence. Furthermore, environmental impact assessments generally focus more on environmental issues, with little or no attention paid in most cases to social and cultural impacts, as are provided for in the new initiatives under the AMV.

CONCLUSION

ASM is a very important sector for promoting economic development in Zambia. Several problems have been identified in the field, including the "resource curse"; however, the main problem is related to the lack of participation by women in this sector. Women have not been participating at the same level as men because of gender disparities caused by mostly gender-neutral policies and laws. The implementation of these gender-neutral policies and laws has resulted in unequal participation of women in ASM. To address the gender disparities and to increase the participation of women in ASM, the policies and laws should not only incorporate specific gender provisions but should also be interpreted and applied in a gender-sensitive manner. In addition, the laws should also address the issues of supernormal patriarchy in ASM. The ecofeminism activist approach should be harnessed to promote the inclusion of women in the male-dominated mining industry.

REFERENCES

African Union. 2009. "Africa Mining Vision." *Addis Ababa*. Accessed December 27, 2018. www.africaminingvision.org/amv_resources/.../Africa_Mining_Vision _English.pdf.

Benya, Asanda. 2015. "The Invisible Hands: Women in Marikana." *Review of African Political Economy* 42 (146): 545–60. https://doi.org/10.1080/03056244.20 15.1087394.

Bradshaw, Sarah, Brian Linneker, and Lisa Overton. 2017. "Extractive Industries as Sites of Supernormal Profits and Supernormal Patriarchy?" *Gender & Development* 25 (3): 443, 439–54. https://doi.org/10.1080/13552074.2017.1379780.

Campbell, Beatrix. 1984. *Wigan Pier Revisited: Poverty and Politics in the 80s*. London: Virago.

Constitution, Chapter 1 of the Laws of Zambia as amended by Act no. 2 of 2016. Accessed July 7, 2020. http://extwprlegs1.fao.org/docs/pdf/zam172703.pdf.

Environmental Management Act No. 12 of 2011. Accessed July 7, 2020. https:// www.ecolex.org/details/legislation/environmental-management-act-2011-no-12-of -2011-lex-faoc117523/.

Gender Equity and Equality Act N. 22 of 2015, laws of Zambia. Accessed July 7, 2020. https://www.informea.org/en/legislation/gender-equity-and-equality-act -2015-no-22-2015.

"Gender Statistics Report: 2010." Accessed December 31, 2018. https://www .zamstats.gov.zm/index.php/component/users/?view=login&return=aH R0cHM6Ly93d3cuemFtFtc3RhdHMuZ292LnptL2luZGV4LnBocC9wdWJssa WNhdGlvbnMvY2F0ZWdvcnkvNTQtZ2V uZGVyP2Rvd25sb2FkPTc 1MDpnZW5kZXItc3RhdGlzdGljcy1yZXBvcnQtYm9va2xldC0yMDEw& Itemid=101.

GRZ. 2007. "The National Policy on Environment." Accessed December 31, 2018. https://www.oneplanetnetwork.org/resource/national-policy-environment-2009-zambia.

GRZ. 2013. "Mineral Resources Development Policy." Accessed December 31, 2018. www.mmmd.gov.zm/?wpfb_dl=142.

GRZ. 2014, September. "National Gender Policy." *Ministry of Gender and Child Development*. Accessed December 31, 2018. extwprlegs1.fao.org/docs/pdf/z am152916.pdf.

GRZ. 2016. "Report of the Committee on Legal Affairs, Governance, Human Rights, Gender Matters and Child Affairs." *National Assembly of Zambia*. Accessed July 6, 2020. http://www.parliament.gov.zm/node/3943.

Hartmann, Heidi. 1981. "The Unhappy Marriage of Marxism and Feminism: Towards a More Progressive Union." Pp. 1–41 in *Women and Revolution: A Discussion of the Unhappy Marriage of Marxism and Feminism*, edited by Lydia Sargent. Boston: South End Press.

Hartmann, Heidi. 1996. "The Unhappy Marriage of Marxism and Feminism: Towards a More Progressive Union." Pp. 165–196 in *Radical Political Economy*, edited by Victor D. Lippitt. New York: Routledge.

Hinton, Jennifer J., Marcello M. Veiga, and Christian Beinhoff. 2003. "Women and Artisanal Mining: Gender Roles and the Road Ahead." Pp. 1–29 in *The Socio-Economic Impacts of Artisanal and Small-Scale Mining in Developing Countries*, edited by G. Hilson. The Netherlands: Swets Publishers.

Intergovernmental Forum on Mining, Minerals, Metals and Sustainable Development (IGF). 2018. *Women in Artisanal and Small-Scale Mining: Interventions for Greater Participation*. Winnipeg: IISD.

James Nyasulu and 2000 Others v Konkola Copper Mines Ltd, Environmental Council of Zambia and Chingola Municipal Council, 2007/HP/1286 [2011] ZMHC 86 (December 31, 2010).

Lahiri-Dutt, Kuntala. 2011. "The Megaproject of Mining: A Feminist Critique." Pp. 329–351 in *Engineering Earth*, edited by Stanley D. Brunn. Berlin, Germany: Springer Science+Business Media.

Lahiri-Dutt, Kuntala. 2015. "The Feminisation of Mining." *Geography Compass* 9 (9): 522–41.

Lands Act, Chapter 184 of the Laws of Zambia. Accessed July 7, 2020. https://za mbialaws.com/principal-legislation/chapter-184lands-act.

Macintyre, Martha, and Kuntala Lahiri-Dutt, eds. 2016. *Women Miners in Developing Countries: Pit Women and Others*. London: Routledge.

Machipisa, Lewis. 2020, July 7. "Mining-Africa: Rocky Path for Women Miners." *Inter Press Service*. Accessed December 31, 2018. https://www.ipsnews.net/1997 /12/mining-africa-rocky-path-for-women-miners/.

Merchant, Carolyn. 1990. *The Death of Nature: Women, Ecology and Scientific Revolution*. San Francisco: Harper.

Mines and Minerals Development Act No. 11 of 2015. Accessed July 6, 2020. http:/ /www.fao.org/faolex/results/details/en/c/LEX-FAOC191114/.

Ndulo, Manenga, and Josephine Chanda. 2016. *Services and Sustainable Growth in Zambia* Accessed July 7, 2020. http://saipar.org/wp-content/uploads/2016/10/ SAIPAR_Discussion-Paper-No-2-September-2016.pdf.

Ranchod, Sarita. 2001. "Mining, Minerals, Sustainable Development, Southern Africa: Gender and Mining Workplace." *African Institute of Corporate Citizenship Report* 21 (2): 23–35.

Ruether, Rosemary Radford. 1995. *New Woman/New Earth: Sexist Ideologies and Human Liberation*. New York: The Seabury Press.

Sambo, Pamela Towela. 2019. "Konkola Copper Mines PLC v Nyasulu and 2000 Others Appeal No. 1/2012." *South African Institute for Policy and Research Case Review* 2 (2): 1–7. https://scholarship.law.cornell.edu/scr/vol2/iss2/4.

Shiva, Vandana. 1988. *Staying Alive: Women, Ecology and Development*. New Delhi: Zed Books Ltd.

Taussig, Michael T. 1980. *The Devil and Commodity Fetishism in South America*. Chapel Hill: University of North Carolina Press.

UN Economic Conditions for Africa. 2016, May 15. "AMDC Helps Develop an Artisanal and Small Scale Mining Hub Knowledge." Accessed July 6, 2020. https ://www.uneca.org/stories/amdc-helps-develop-artisanal-and-small-scale-mining -knowledge-hub.

United Nations. 2018a. "Sustainable Development Goals." Accessed December 27, 2018. https://www.un.org/sustainabledevelopment/gender-equality/.

United Nations. 2018b. "Sustainable Development Goals: Progress and Info 2018." Accessed December 27, 2018. https://sustainabledevelopment.un.org/sdg5.

WBU. n.d. "WBU Statement on International Women's Day, 8 March 2019." http://www.worldblindunion.org/English/news/Pages/-WBU-Statement-on-International-Women%E2%80%99s-Day,-8-March-2019.aspx.

Zambia Chamber of Mines. 2020. "Employment Figures—Mining Companies." Accessed August 2, 2020. http://mines.org.zm/employment-figures/.

Chapter 10

Football Stadiums as Patriarchal Spaces

Experiences from Harare, Zimbabwe

Manase Kudzai Chiweshe

This chapter constructs a nuanced analysis of masculinized spaces to highlight the lived experiences of marginalization of women within football stadiums in Harare, Zimbabwe. The analysis examines how patriarchy pervades society and extends into all spaces, including recreational activities. The chapter is based on a qualitative research approach. The principal research methods for the study included ethnographic participant observation in football stadiums during twelve Premier Soccer League matches played in Harare. In-depth interviews were also conducted with purposively selected female and male football fans to provide a "thick" description of Zimbabwean football cultures. Findings indicate that the stadium has emerged as a neopatriarchal space in which specific forms of women marginalization and abuse are accepted and often promoted. The stadium has been constructed as a patriarchal cauldron through misogynistic elements that include songs, language, and actions, in which women who dare to "trespass" do so at their own peril. Women's harassment in stadiums is also practiced through specific forms of physical abuse, including fondling of breasts and buttocks and through unsolicited love and marriage proposals. The songs and chants provide narratives of masculine domination of an opponent, which is a vital part of watching and supporting football. The dominant gender regimes in football thus remain highly masculine. Fandom promotes an orthodox form of masculinity that promotes negative (e.g., sexist, misogynistic, and anti-female) attitudes toward women. In the end, I argue that the promotion of hegemonic masculinity leads to the marginalization of female fans and decreased attendance of women and children at football matches.

This research is based on stadium ethnographies in Harare, Zimbabwe, focusing on matches in the national premier league. It constructs the concepts of centered peripheries to highlight how stadiums are constructed as spaces in which the most overt and violent forms of patriarchy, which are in many ways frowned upon by society, become an accepted part and parcel of the football experiences. Heide (1978) argues that football stadiums are male-dominated spaces that are characterized by misogyny and thereby unconsciously entrench soccer as a patriarchal space. Patriarchy in the context of this chapter focuses on specific cultural norms and values that are embedded within the physical and social space of the stadium. Patriarchal views of women are played out in the game of football through songs and chants. Hegemonic masculinity is performed and reinforced within the stadiums. Vulgar and misogynistic language ensures that watching football in Zimbabwe remains a male activity. Therefore, it is within this context of an African football stadium that patriarchy and gender is examined.

WOMEN, FOOTBALL, AND EXCLUSION

There is a growing literature across the world focusing on women and football. Across these texts, the theme of exclusion of female fans is dominant but also female fans' agency and their responses to the processes of sexism in football. Pfister, Lenneis, and Mintert (2013) argue that football consumption provides an arena for playing out the gender in addition to doing gender and traditional forms of hegemonic masculinity in the community of male fans. Serrano Durá, Serrano-Durá, and Vladimir (2017) observe that although violence against women is rejected by Spanish society, violence-supportive attitudes are nevertheless present in football fandom. This study shows how football centers specific aspects that are shunned and placed at the periphery of the wider society. In their study, Serrano-Durá et al. (2017) show that depending on the context, misogynistic chants are normalized and excused by fans. According to Jones (2008), the use of sexist and homophobic language such as "playing like a girl" and "wuss" is viewed as a common part of the English game. In Zimbabwe, Ncube and Chawana (2018) focus on the construction of hegemonic masculinities in football fandom through popular football songs. Chiweshe (2017, 96) further asserts:

> Football stadiums provide an arena in which masculinity is constructed around
> a clear and distinct set of defining norms. Exaltation of manhood is part of foot-
> ball in Zimbabwe. The songs and chants tell a story of masculine domination

of an opponent which is feminized. The feminization of opposing teams is a vital part of watching and supporting football. The dominant gender regime in football thus remains highly masculine. Fandom promotes an orthodox form of masculinity that promotes socio negative (sexist, misogynistic, and anti-feminine) attitudes toward women.

What is clear from the above studies is that football cultures are inherently patriarchal. Anderson (2008) notes that as a highly segregated, homophobic, sexist, and misogynistic gender regime, sports fandom not only contributes to the gender order, but it also reproduces a conservative and stabilizing form of masculinity.

According to Connell (1990), sports and sports heroes are needed to ensure the cultural exaltation of patterns of masculinity. The stadium in the context of football becomes the space for this cultural exaltation. When women increasingly enter this space, they are viewed as intruders and unwelcome. King's study of Manchester United fans shows the resentment that working-class men have for female fans, mainly because they view football as a traditionally working-class men's sport of which they are the inheritors (King 2002). Women are not seen as authentic fans, whereupon they have to play into stadium masculinities to become what Chiweshe (2014) called "one of the boys." Several studies (Chiweshe 2014; Jones 2008; Toffoletti and Mewett 2012) outline how women in many cases have to deny their femininity within the stadium and play to hegemonic practices that include shouting at referees and singing vulgar and often misogynistic songs. Jones (2008, 516), for example, argues that "women sometimes downplay their gender identities to reinforce their fan identities," leading to both women and men playing out a fan identity that is shaped largely by a masculine and patriarchal construction of manhood. Women are in many ways forced into masculine identities, mainly because male fans tend to be highly critical of feminine traits. Such criticism is often accompanied by forms of derogatory and demeaning names. An example can be seen in ice hockey where female fans are labeled by male supporters as "puck bunnies," meaning that women are present at the games only to "lust" after the players (Crawford and Gosling 2004). Female references are also used to portray the opposing team and fans. The opposition is alluded to in derogatory sexual terms. For example, chanting among the Sydney Football Club Fans in Australia goes like this: "Your sister is your mother; your father is your brother; you all fuck one another" (Collingson 2009, 20). Denigration of women and women's bodies are thus part of the football stadiums, as is outlined in the cases from across the world cited above.

CONCEPTUALIZATION OF HETEROPATRIARCHY
AS CENTERED PERIPHERIES

Patriarchy within the context of this chapter is defined as a male-gendered power system: a network of social, political, and economic relationships through which men dominate and control female labor, reproduction, and sexuality, as well as define women's status, privileges, and rights in society (Chakona 2012). In the context of this study, the stadium is conceptualized as a space where a specific type of patriarchy operates in an institutionalized manner. This form of heteropatriarchy celebrates and valorizes heterosexual male sexual strength and prowess. Within the stadium, specific masculinities are privileged, and any diversion of these is frowned upon and, at times, met with violent resistance (Chiweshe 2017). Following Connell (1995), there are thus hegemonic masculinities that are practiced and that dominate stadiums; yet they are not overtly practiced in other spheres of life, such as the home, school, or church (Chiweshe 2014). In these spaces, they are practiced as "masked" forms of hegemonic masculinities. In the context of home, school, or church, hegemonic masculinity is often masked and institutionalized as normal or acceptable behavior. Hegemonic masculinity is thus in many ways covert, hidden, and masked at the periphery, yet within the context of the stadium is centered and celebrated. I utilize the concept of centered peripheries to highlight this unique nature of heteropatriarchy practiced in male-dominated spaces such as the football stadium. Glick and Fisk (2001) agree that heteropatriarchy, such as that practiced in stadiums, creates a male-dominated society based upon the cultural processes of sexism/heterosexism. In this chapter, I will show through an analysis of songs, chants, fan practices, and analysis of physical spaces how this sexism leads to the marginalization of women and feminine genders within the stadium. The analysis will highlight how the practices, such as vulgarity, that are often shunned in everyday polite societies are centered within stadium cultures in Zimbabwe. Gosling argues that sporting spaces such as stadiums provide an opportunity for the "legitimate expression of hypermasculinity" (2007, 253). Within such contexts, specific masculine expressions are encouraged and celebrated. To better convey how such marginal practices of masculinity are centered within stadiums, Connell's (2005) framework points to the fact that people *practice* masculinities and femininities rather than *having* or *being* them. This means that aspects of various masculinities can exist simultaneously in the same person, so that someone can engage in protest masculinity while appearing to be respectful to women (Connell 2005). Men thus understand how space and time shape the way they portray their masculinities. The men are able to act respectfully toward women outside the stadium but practice misogynistic acts at soccer matches. The stadium provides the context for the men to be overtly sexist and misogynistic. It is within the stadium that the peripheral ideas of masculinity are centered.

METHODOLOGICAL APPROACH

The study is based on an in-stadium ethnography that combined in-depth interviews, cyber ethnographies, and participant observation. The stadium provides an intimate social context in a closed physical space that offers an opportunity to understand how patriarchy operates even during leisure. For the study, stadium ethnographies included attending twelve matches played at Rufaro Stadium in Harare during the 2017 and 2018 period. The matches involved various teams that use the venue as their home ground. The researcher mainly observed various fan actions and cultures, including singing, chants, conversations, and physical activities of the fans. Stadium ethnographies allowed for immersion into the match practices of fans, the language and norms of the terraces. Ethnography was augmented by twenty in-depth interviews conducted before and sometimes after the matches. The interviews were conducted with ten women and ten men who supported different teams. The study also utilized cyberethnography throughout the 2017 and 2018 football seasons. The cyberethnography concentrated on official team websites and Facebook pages. It also concentrated on unofficial fan Facebook pages in an effort to understand how football fans have reconstructed stadium cultures on online platforms. In addition to the above study locations, newspaper reports and football magazines were also assessed in an attempt to understand how sports contents and information use, produce, and disseminate language that constructs football and, by extension, the stadium, as a men's world.

FINDINGS AND DISCUSSION

Discursive Analysis of Language and Gendered "Otherness" within the Stadium

It is important to first outline how language is used within the context of the stadium to recreate a patriarchial valorization of manhood. First, I sample lyrics from some of the songs from the terraces to highlight how the stadium has been constructed as a patriarchal space. In analyzing the songs, I provide four thematic areas that are dominant: the sexualization of woman, valorization of women's subordinate role, a celebration of male virility, and feminization of opponents. All the outlined categories of songs in many ways entrench patriarchy and police the stadium as a male-only space. Sexualization of women is seen in how some of the songs tend to portray women as sexual objects, for example, in the following:

1. *Matemai, Matemai, handichada kunzi Matemai, Ndoda kunzi Gumbura*
   ("I no longer want to be called *Matemai* but call me Gumbura"[1])
2. *Mwana uri wespare, ndinokuda ndakuona*
   ("You are my spare girlfriend, I only love you when I see you")
3. *Shinga muroora, wakauya wega kuzorohwa nyoro*
   (You should persevere daughter-in-law, you came on your own to be sexed")
4. *Mai mwana ndozvandisingade mumba mangu; Kana zvarema, tora tumapoto tora tuma radio*
   ("My wife, I do not want this kind of behavior in my house; better you leave with all the pots and radios")
5. *Hure riya ramatako mahombe, ratitadzisa kuuya kwedu kuDembare*
   ("The prostitute with bug buttocks stopped us from coming to watch my team, Dynamos")

All the above songs point to an underlying gender ideology that portrays women as sexual objects, weak, and available for male sexual pleasure at any time. This leads to a specific construction of heteronormative masculinity that valorizes male strength and demeans female presence within the stadium. The use of language in the songs provides an important base for the construction of patriarchal cultures in the terraces. The construction of women as sexual objects and the valorization of male sexual prowess is not the preserve of the stadium. It is a distinct feature of patriarchal societies. What is different within the stadium is the overt and misogynistic way in which these norms are celebrated and acted out. It is the centering of peripheries that provides an interesting juxtaposition of how specific spaces have been created in patriarchal societies to openly celebrate maleness. All the songs provide a central premise for the understanding of how stadium masculinities are constructed and viewed, which is why they are defined in opposition to weak femininity. This is particularly clear in the third and fourth songs, which construct women as nothing more than appendages of men who should know their place. Misogynistic utterances are a normal part of being a fan at the stadium. Armstrong and Young (2008) note that ritualized football singing can exclude as well as include, in songs that reflect and produce the self/other, insider/outsider binary to define football culture. In this instance, women mostly become the weakened, useless, and outside "other."

Embodied Experiences of Exclusion within Stadiums

Beyond the symbolic artifacts of gender exclusion, the stadium has visible physical barriers for women, as noted by participants in this research. First, the case study in Harare, the Rufaro Stadium, is an old, antiquated space that was created in colonial Rhodesia. As such, it remains an unfriendly space for fans who are forced to sit mainly in the sun on concrete terraces. One female participant noted:

> When the weather is hot the concrete is hot, and when the weather is cold the concrete is cold. It is not at all comfortable to sit on, but we endure. The most difficult thing for me is that it means that I am limited to jeans or long, thick skirts for the games. But with my body type, the jeans will lead to whistles from the men. Anyway, it is part of coming to the stadium.

In many ways, women normalize the limiting effects of the stadium's physical infrastructure. The concrete itself is a metaphor for strength and masculinity. It is a space that is physically demanding for those who do not occupy a masculine body. Another participant focuses on the sanitation system at the stadium and notes: "It is a mission to get into these toilets, especially for me." She continues:

> I do not know if they are cleaned from week to week, but it has to be an emergency that forces you in there. The toilets actually turn you into a man as they force you to pee from a standing position. For men, even when the toilets are not clean they can stand outside and pee against the wall. No one asks or looks. That is not possible for a woman.

The above quote shows that there are specific amenities, or lack thereof, related to public spaces that may in many ways exclude women from the stadiums. The stadium is a space where women face serious difficulties in relation to basic amenities. The sanitation problems are often compounded by the failure of the Harare City Council (owners of the stadium) to provide water.

The enclosed nature of stadiums built around imposing concrete structures provides a "masculine feel" to stadiums. The descriptions and nicknames given to stadiums also provide evidence of the masculinization of this space. At Rufaro Stadium, the stand opposite the VIP section has been nicknamed Vietnam. This is a direct reference to the Vietnam War, and the name portrays the often-violent acts of hooliganism, especially among the ultras of the country's most supported team, Dynamos. A female fan said this about the stand:

Vietnam ndeye vakashinga moyo. Kunotoda varume kana vari vakadzi vanoto-
fanirwa kuva nemweya wehurume. Kuno taurwa zvinyadzi ende hakuendwe
nevanyarikani. Sometimes unototya semukadzi kusvika ikoko [Vietnam is for
the strong at heart. It is for men, and women who go there should act like men.
They use vulgar language and you cannot go there with someone you respect.
Sometimes women are afraid of going there].

The area is thus an imposing space within this stadium, and anecdotal reports
show that, across the country, most stadiums have a similar place. Beyond
the imposing nature of such spaces is the fact that most sections of the stadiums in Harare provide no cover from the sun or rain, and this has led to the
nickname *madzvinyu* (lizards) for fans, because they are sitting in the sun on
hot days. In the hot weather, the concrete becomes very uncomfortable for
the fans; as one female fan noted, "If you are not careful, the concrete will
burn your buttocks off."

Physical Space, Patriarchal Norms, and Various Forms of
Sexual Violence

Interesting in the context of the above discussion on the exclusionary nature
of the physical spaces in the stadiums is the notion that football spaces, by
their nature, foster proximity of bodies, which can be problematic when it
leads to sexual violence. From the entrance into the stadium to the sitting
arrangements and the exit, the structure of the stadium makes it impossible
to maintain personal physical space. My experience at the games showed
that as a fan, you have to pick and choose spaces in the stadiums carefully if
you want to avoid physical contact. In some of the spaces, physical contact
with other bodies is unavoidable. The problem for girls and women is that
harassment of various types often arises in these spaces of close proximity.
I witnessed examples of women having their buttocks or breasts fondled at
the gates when the crowd is pressing to enter or leave the stadium. One of
the men I talked to admitted to harassing women, noting that "*ndipo patino-*
dyawo mahalf" (this is when we take advantage of girls without being seen).
The stadium is a space to perform manhood and affirm sexual virility. The
social and gender regimes of this space speak to and about women in specific
exclusionary terms that portray them as weak and as sexual objects. In this
study, I came across four specific ways in which the stadium is constructed
as a male domain in which women have to either act as males or accept abuse
of varying forms.

The physical act of sexual intercourse is often used to portray male power
and virility within the stadium. Sex is very much part of the football motif.
In Zimbabwe, generally, fans use sexual innuendo in reference to winning or
losing. One example from this research is that fans would describe beating

a rival team by referencing sexual intercourse. For example, fans would use concepts such as *tavaisa* or *tavakirwa* (we have sexed them). Losing and the sexual intercourse become synonymous. Sex is viewed as an act in which women lose and men gain. Even on the terraces, sex is often used as an instrument to conquer women, as can be seen in the chant "*tinodzikamisa mahure nenyoro*" (we discipline loose women with unprotected sex). Throughout, sex is constructed as a male pursuit in which men are winners and women are losers. Women's bodies are created as sexual objects for the enjoyment of men. This sexual othering of women normalizes the physical abuse perpetrated within the confines of the stadium.

No Place for "Proper" Women: Stadiums as Centered Peripheries

The stadium is constructed as a space that "proper" women should shun. Chiweshe (2017) argues that within the context of stadiums toxic masculinity pervades, which in many ways creates football fandom as a male-only pursuit. Ncube and Chawana (2018) show how in Zimbabwe, women who visit stadiums are largely seen as promiscuous or as rebels. The message is that no self-respecting or cultured girl can go into such spaces without tarnishing her reputation. Therefore, it is important to highlight how the stadium's toxic male ambiance helps us understand the wider social system of patriarchy and exclusion. Generally, the overtly sexual and vulgar behavior seen in stadiums represents the extreme forms of hegemonic masculinities steeped in patriarchal norms and values. The language and practices of the stadium are limited to this space and no other social spaces such as the home (except in the privacy of the bedroom), school, or church. This is the case because the vulgar and misogynistic nature of these practices is not welcome in everyday polite society. The everyday operation of patriarchy is institutionalized and gender inequalities are justified by a variety of cultural and religious ideologies. Even various forms of intimate partner and domestic violence are often practiced in hidden settings. In stadiums, however, the patriarchal practices at the periphery that include overt violence and misogyny are accepted as part of the space and become centered in defining football spaces as masculine. Responses from various female and male respondents highlighted the normalization and the acceptance of the male-dominant and misogynistic practices described above. When asked about their perceptions of misogynistic practices of men at the stadium during matches, participants provided varied responses, including the following:

1. *Ndezve kubhora.*
   (This is normal for football matches.)
2. *Asingade ngagare kumba.*

(If you do not like it, then stay away from the stadium.)
3. *Kutamba zvedu nekuseka. Kumba hati taure izvozvo.*
　　(We are just having fun. At home we do not say such things.)

The third quote above shows how sexist and misogynistic cultures are normalized and seen as confined to specific spaces yet shape how women are treated in wider society. The stadium in many ways mirrors the wider social system of patriarchy in which women are sexualized. Chiweshe (2014) shows how stadiums offer a space for male supporters to use vulgar language that they do not normally use in other public spaces. This is also true for female fans, because stadiums allow them to transcend the patriarchal demands of heteronormativity in which women are not supposed to be loud, vulgar, and outspoken. Some women participate and perpetuate heteropatriarchal practices within the stadium. They sing and chant misogynistic songs and call out players or even other male fans who are perceived to exhibit feminine traits. Women fans participate in promoting the same system of misogyny that undermines gender equality and defines women narrowly as sex objects. Through a process of dissociation, female fans actively participate in promoting processes that demean girls and women. Such female fans are in the habit of dismissing everything feminine as weak. Therefore, within the stadium, they dissociate themselves from women who are more likely to match the feminine stereotypes.

The construction of the stadium as a place primarily for men is also seen in the low numbers of women who watched matches in Harare. While there, although I could not acquire actual figures, my observation of the stands over the research period showed that there were by far more male than female fans. According to Pfister, Lenneis, and Mintert (2013), various studies in Denmark, Germany, and England indicate that football stadiums are predominantly occupied by men. The wider society view of large male attendance as an important way of dissuading women from inhabiting the stadium was noted by one of the respondents:

> My parents always tell me that no proper woman goes to a place where there are only men. It is a sign of being loose. They believe that stadiums are only dominated by men. They argue that male fans are rowdy and will harass me.

Another respondent also highlighted how many of her friends are actually afraid of going to the stadium, because there are a lot of men at the games. The overwhelming male presence within stadiums provides another disincentive for women to go to stadiums.

There are also some male football fans who label women who go to the stadium as promiscuous and immoral. Such sentiments were quite widespread among the male fans who I interacted within the stadiums. One male respondent in this study noted that *"kubhora kuno wanzouya mahure chete. Mukadzi kwaye haawanike munzvimbo dzakadai"* (it is mostly prostitutes that come to the stadiums. Stand-up women are not found in such places). Another respondent highlighted that *"ukaona murume auya nemukadzi kubhora ziva kuti ismall house. Hakuna murume anouya nemukadzi wemumba kubhora"* (when you see a man bring a woman to the stadium, know that it is his girlfriend and not his wife. No respectable man brings his wife to the stadium). Such views, however, were contradicted by some men who brought their wives to the matches. But such men usually sat in parts of the stadium that were sparsely populated.

In the stadium, women are reduced to their sexual body parts. In the stadium, I experienced instances where, when women walked past specific sections of the stadium, they were subjected to sexist chants focusing on their sexual parts and to cat whistles. One of the female respondents noted:

> You have to be strong-willed in some parts of the stadium—otherwise these men will eat you alive. They can smell fear, but if you show you do not fear, the abuse will not continue. It is not easy to be a woman in the stadium. You get love proposals all the time, and the most dangerous group is drunk males who can harass you.

The above narratives point toward a situation in which the stadium becomes an unfriendly space for women. Women who dare to enter such spaces are abused and labeled, making it clear to them that they are not welcome in this space.

MASCULINITIES, PHYSICAL VIOLENCE, AND THE STADIUM

Football has a gruesome past and present across the world that is related to fan violence, both within and without stadiums. Violence perpetrated by fans, players, and administrators has continually erupted in the context of Zimbabwean football venues. Violence remains a constant part of football in Zimbabwe and most other parts of the world. Frosdick and Marsh (2005, 5) argue that "the game of football has been associated with violent rivalry since its beginnings in thirteenth-century England. Medieval football matches involved hundreds of players, and were essentially pitched battles between the young men of rival villages and towns—often used as opportunities to settle old feuds, personal arguments, and land disputes." The past five years in Zimbabwe has seen increased reports of football-related violence (Mahlengwe 2015; Mataramutse

2015; Mhara 2016). Violence affects the growth of the game in the country and even its existence, because violence has economic consequences for football teams. First, violence leads to fewer people coming to games, because people fear injury and death. All teams in Zimbabwe are hugely dependent on money from gate takings given low sponsorship and the lack of commercialization of the game. Second, teams suffer financial losses through fines imposed by the authorities running the sport. Third, sponsors are reluctant to get involved with a sport that has a bad image. Fourth, and most important for the purposes of this chapter, violence keeps women away from the stadiums. The creation of the stadium as a war zone leads to the masculinization of this space and to the exclusion of women. Violence is constructed as a male pursuit; for that reason, it is believed that women, who are seen as fragile, should shun such spaces. As was highlighted earlier in the chapter, it is within the commotion at the stadium that male sexual abuse against girls and women is perpetrated.

CONCLUSION

This chapter examines how football stadiums construct patriarchal spaces that allow men to inflict violence and abuse on girls and women. The norms, actions, and culture of the stadium are steeped in a heteronormative patriarchal ideology that constructs anything female as weak, unwelcome, and out of place. I highlighted how the use of language, songs, and physical and symbolic abuse has led to multiple challenges for women within the stadiums. Football stadiums are physical embodiments of the construction of masculinity as strength and grit. They also provide a space in which specific forms of patriarchy can be practiced and encouraged without social sanctions. Women in such spaces are excluded, sexualized, and violated (both symbolically and physically). The chapter uses narratives of male and female fans to reveal how various aspects of the stadium environment are shaped to center, valorize, and celebrate heteronormative masculinities. It concludes that even with increased female spectatorship at the stadiums in Zimbabwe, there remains a bastion of patriarchy and a preserve for the acting out of hegemonic masculinities. Ultimately, the vision of women as the weaker, inferior sex portrayed in football imagery is not only a stadium phenomenon but one that young male fans grow up believing in and practicing, thereby entrenching toxic masculine behaviors within society.

NOTE

1. Robert Martin Gumbura is the founder of the Robert Martin Gumbura (RMG) Independent End Time Message Church of Zimbabwe. In February 2014, he was sent to jail for 50 years for raping four female members of his church.

REFERENCES

Armstrong, Gay, and Malcolm Young. 2008. "Fanatical Football Chants: Creating and Controlling the Carnival." *Sport in Society* 2 (3): 173–211. https://doi.org/10.1 080/14610989908721852.

Anderson, Eric. 2008. "'I Used to Think Women Were Weak': Orthodox Masculinity, Gender Segregation, and Sport." *Sociological Forum* 23 (2): 257–80. https://doi .org/10.1111/j.1573-7861.2008.00058.x.

Chakona, L. 2012. "The Impact of the Fast Track Land Reform Programme on Women in Goromonzi District, Zimbabwe." MA Thesis, Rhodes University, South Africa.

Chiweshe, Manase Kudzai. 2014. "One of the Boys: Female Fans' Responses to the Masculine and Phallocentric Nature of Football Stadiums in Zimbabwe." *Critical African Studies* 6 (2–3): 211–22. https://doi.org/10.1080/21681392.2014.940077.

———. 2017. *The People's Game: Football Fandom in Zimbabwe.* Bamenda: Langaa Press.

Collinson, I. 2009. "'Singing Songs, Making Places, Creating Selves': Football Songs & Fan Identity at Sydney FC." *Transforming Cultures eJournal* 4 (1): 1–13. https:// doi.org/10.5130/tfc.v4i1.1057.

Connell, R. 1990. "An Iron Man: The Body and Some Contradictions of Hegemonic Masculinity." Pp. 83–95 in *Sport, Men and the Gender Order: Critical Feminist Perspectives,* edited by Michael Messner and Don Sabo. Champaign, IL: Human Kinetics.

Connell, R. W. 2005. *Masculinities,* 2nd ed. Berkeley: University of California Press.

Connell, Raewyn. 1995. *Masculinities.* Berkeley, CA: University of California Press.

Crawford, Gary, and Victoria K. Gosling. 2004. "The Myth of the 'Puck Bunny': Female Fans and Men's Ice Hockey." *Sociology* 38 (3): 477–93. https://doi.org/10 .1177/0038038504043214.

Frosdick, Steve, and Peter E. Marsh. 2005. *Football Hooliganism.* Cullompton: Willan.

Glick, Peter, and Susan K. Fiske. 2001. "An Ambivalent Alliance: Hostile and Benevolent Sexism as Complementary Justifications for Gender Inequality." *American Psychologist* 56 (2): 109–18. https://doi.org/10.1037/0003-066X.56. 2.109.

Gosling, Victoria K. 2007. "Girls Allowed? The Marginalisation of Female Sports Fans." Pp. 250–60 in *Fandom: Identities and Communities in a Mediated World,* edited by Jonathan Gray, Cornel Sandvoss, and C. Lee Harrington. New York: New York University Press.

Heide, W. S. 1978. "Feminism for a Sporting Future." Pp. 195–202 in *Women and Sport: From Myth to Reality,* edited by Carole A. Oglesby. Philadelphia: Lea & Febiger.

Jones, KatherineW. 2008. "Female Fandom: Identity, Sexism, and Men's Professional Football in England. *Sociology of Sport Journal* 25 (4): 516–37. https://doi.org/10 .1123/ssj.25.4.516.

King, Anthony. 2002. *The End of the Terraces.* London: Leicester Univ. Press.

Mahlengwe, Bothwell. 2015. "Bold Words and Then What?" *Herald*, March 7, 2015. http://www.herald.co.zw/bold-words-and-then-what/.

Mataramutse, G. 2015. "Hooliganism: A Cancer Killing Our Game." *Daily News*, https://dailynews.co.zw/articles-2015-03-04-hooliganism-a-cancer-threatening-our -game/.

Mhara, Henry. 2016. "Govt raps Zifa for BF violence." *The Newsday*, August 16, 2016. https://www.newsday.co.zw/2016/08/16/govt-raps-zifa-bf-violence/.

Ncube, Lyton, and Fiona Chawana. 2018. "What Is in a Song? Constructions of Hegemonic Masculinity by Zimbabwean Football Fans." *Muziki* 15 (1): 68–88. https://doi.org/10.1080/18125980.2018.1503560.

Pfister, Gertrude, Verena Lenneis, and Svenja Mintert. 2013. "Female Fans of Men's Football—A Case Study in Denmark." *Soccer and Society* 14 (6): 850–71. https://doi.org/10.1080/14660970.2013.843923.

Serrano-Durá, José, Antonio Serrano-Durá, and Vladimir Essau Martínez-Bello. 2017. "Youth Perceptions of Violence against Women through a Sexist Chant in the Football Stadium: An Exploratory Analysis." *Soccer and Society* 20 (2): 252–70. https://doi.org/10.1080/14660970.2017.1302935.

Toffoletti, Kim, and Peter Mewett. 2012. *Sport and Its Female Fans*. New York: Routledge.

Chapter 11

Mame Diarra

A Case Study of a Senegalese Female Saint and Sufi

Cheikh Seye

This chapter is a case study of a female saint and Sufi aimed at exploring the mystical, spiritual, and social life of an outstanding African woman named Maryam Bousso, commonly known as Mame Diarra (1833–1866).[1] The chapter examines the ways in which Mame Diarra's life fits the mold of a female saint and a Sufi figure by addressing the following questions: What do Mame Diarra's spiritual identity and life story reveal about the female and sacredness in Islam, especially in Sufism? Does Mame Diarra's story proffer new ways of approaching women and gender in Sufism? Is it because of patriarchal and male chauvinistic interpretations that women are not foregrounded in the Islamic mystical tradition or granted a befitting depiction in matters related to sainthood and spirituality?

Sufism is a long-established Islamic mystical tradition that draws its doctrines and practices from the example of the early Muslim exemplars, called *al-Salaf al-Sāliḥīn* (The Righteous Predecessors). Although the Arabic word *taṣawwuf* (Sufism) was not part of the Islamic lexical repertoire during the time of the Prophet Muḥammad, its underlying reality was already practiced in the early Muslim community. Both Sufism and sainthood are distinct doctrines in Islam. Sainthood is part of the Islamic belief system and its discursive tradition. In *Realm of the Saint*, Vincent Cornell writes that "sainthood is a matter of discourse" (1998, 63). Cornell argues that in order to be recognized as a saint, "the prospective saint must manifest certain outward signs: exceptional piety, ecstatic states, intercession, evidentiary miracles, unusual modes of behavior, and the like" (63).

Mame Diarra was a saint and a Sufi in her own right despite, and not because of, her being the mother of Cheikh Ahmadou Bamba (1853–1927), the founder of the Mouridiyya Sufi order known as Mouridism. Mame Diarra was not just Cheikh Ahmadou Bamba's biological mother—she was also his early spiritual mentor. The mother initiated the son into the mystical path of Sufism at a very early age. Mame Diarra was instrumental in Cheikh Ahmadou Bamba's formative years leading up to his early Sufi connections and the foundation of his spiritual order (the Mouridiyya).

The contribution of female spirituality to male spirituality is insufficiently underscored in the sub-field of Islamic studies and in the field of religious studies in general. Rita Gross (1996, 19) castigates the androcentric approach in religious studies by arguing that "in androcentric thinking, any awareness of a distinction between maleness and humanity is clouded over, and female-ness is viewed as an exception to the norm." In Islamic studies, aside from the legendary female Sufi Rabi'a al-Adawiyya (d. 801 CE), few Sufi women have received due attention in the scholarly literature (as-Sulami 1999). In this chapter, I will articulate how Mame Diarra laid the social, spiritual, and mystical foundations for her son's development. Mame Diarra paved the Sufi Way for Cheikh Ahmadou Bamba and was thus instrumental in his later spiritual achievements.

SHORT BIOGRAPHY

No scholarly work has been devoted to Mame Diarra so far. The little infor-mation that is available about this legendary female figure stems mostly from oral sources. At least two reasons account for the systematic dearth of litera-ture on Mame Diarra. The first is that she had a very short life span (she lived for only 33 years). The second is that she lived in pre-colonial West Africa, which was characterized by the lack of substantive written sources on Muslim religious figures and the prevalence of oral literature. Hence, the Senegalese colonial archives do not provide any information on Mame Diarra.[2]

Mame Diarra Bousso was born in 1833 at Mbousôbé, in the Senegalese central province of Jolof, to parents who were teachers of the Qur'ān and Islamic studies. Her given name was Maryam as she was named after the Prophet 'Isā's mother in the Islamic tradition or Mary, Jesus Christ's mother, in the Christian tradition. In her youth, Mame Diarra learned the Qur'ān by heart and handwrote it entirely from memory. She was educated in Islamic studies by her own mother, Sokhna Astou ('Ā'isha) Walo Mbacké, who taught Islamic theology, jurisprudence, and exegesis of the Qur'ān.

According to oral tradition, Sokhna Astou Walo was a consummate peda-gogue and a social educator. She instilled in Mame Diarra the spiritual and social values for which she is usually commended in the Mourid tradition. Mame Diarra's father, Mouhammadou Bousso, was a scholar and an *imām* (prayer leader). He was, by all accounts, a *sharīf* or descendant of the Prophet Muḥammad. Mouhammadou Bousso traced his ancestry to Al-Ḥasan ibn Alī ibn Abī Ṭālib (d. 670 CE), the grandson of the Prophet Muḥammad (Diop 2017).[3]

In her late twenties or early thirties, Mame Diarra, also known as *Boroom Porokhane* (the master of Porokhane), relocated to the village of Porokhane in the central part of Senegal, along with her spouse, Mame Mor Anta Sally (d. 1882). After her death in 1866, Mame Diarra became the patron saint of the town of Porokhane. Ever since her passing, Porokhane has been a major spiritual hub and a favorite site for pilgrimage, especially for Mourid women from Senegal and the diaspora. Today, Porokhane is a semi-urban center that hosts educational, spiritual, and religious institutions, such as the grand mosque (known as "Mame Diarra Mosque"), Mame Diarra's imposing mausoleum; an annual national celebration in her honor, which is attended by thousands of people; and an all-girl boarding school that is dedicated to her memory. These female students, all of whom are named after Mame Diarra, receive free educational and vocational training.

FEMALE AGENCY

Since the dawn of humanity, women across time and space have been victims of misogyny, subjected to patriarchy, or otherwise treated as second-class citizens. In *The Second Sex* (2009), Simone de Beauvoir writes expansively about the plight and predicament of women who kept a very low profile ever since Antiquity, through the Middle Ages and the Renaissance, all the way up to the Enlightenment era. De Beauvoir highlights a few misogynic statements from eminent male scholars and thinkers of these periods: for Pythagoras, "there is a good principle that created order, light and man and a bad principle that created chaos, darkness and woman," (. . .) for Menander, "there are many monsters on the earth and in the sea, but the greatest is still woman" (De Beauvoir 2009, 91 and 102)). De Beauvoir also writes that "among the blessings Plato thanked the gods for was, first, being born free and not a slave, and second, a man and not a woman" (De Beauvoir 2009, 11 and 102). She quotes Aristotle as saying that "the female is female by virtue of a certain lack of qualities" (De Beauvoir 2009, 5), St-Aquinas according to whom "woman is 'an incomplete man'" (De Beauvoir 2009, 5), and St-Augustine who contends that "the wife is an animal neither reliable nor stable" (De Beauvoir 2009, 11). These misogynistic statements show how sexism, androcentrism, and male chauvinism have stifled the female person for centuries by giving her no room and depriving her of any authority and agency in society. In the introduction to her translation of as-Sulami's book titled *Early Sufi Women*, Rkia Cornell critiques the androcentric tendency to veil the woman in the male-dominated Sufi hagiography. For instance, Abu Bakr Kalābādhī's (d. 990 CE) did not reveal 'the identity of the woman who so impressed [the famous Egyptian Sufi] Dhū an-Nūn al-Miṣrī' (d. 859 CE), *ipso facto* making her anonymous despite her immense Sufi scholarship and leadership (as-Sulami 1999, 17).

Female agency is usually addressed against the backdrop of patriarchy, as if it were patriarchy that should determine how much agency or lack thereof women should enjoy. Many criteria should be considered when it comes to determining women's agency, such as power, authority, autonomy, and influence. There are a few anecdotes that have been repeated time and again in the Mourid oral literature on Mame Diarra and that may unintentionally challenge the issue of female agency. However, these biographical accounts are usually distorted or misconstrued, and they often present seeming contradictions for outsiders who may not be conversant with the spiritual and cultural realities in which Mame Diarra's life was embedded.

Roy Bhaskar (1989, 34) argues that "society is both the ever-present condition and the continually reproduced outcome of human agency." Agency is a social construct, and as such it is contingent upon social and cultural processes. In many respects, Mame Diarra was an influential woman who transcended gender barriers by being a transformative agent in the whole Senegalese social fabric, both spiritually and socially. She is also regarded as a role model by both genders. For instance, in the Mourid community, both men and women visit Mame Diarra's mausoleum with the same spiritual fervor and equally regard her as a spiritual master.

FEMALE SAINTHOOD AND SPIRITUALITY: MAME DIARRA AS A SAINT AND A SUFI

Female spirituality is one of the major gender-neutral and equal-treatment issues between the male and the female in Islam. In a conversation about female sainthood and spirituality, Nizamuddin Awliyā (d. 1325 CE), a Sufi master in the Chishti Sufi order, uses a compelling metaphor to underscore gender neutrality in Islamic sainthood. He states: "when a wild lion leaves the jungle and enters an inhabited area, no one asks: 'Is it male or female?'" (as quoted in Schimmel 1997, 78). The importance of equal treatment between men and women in matters bearing upon spirituality, religiosity, and morality is enshrined in Chapter 33, Verse 35 of the Qur'ān. In this lengthy verse, God promises equal reward to both men and women who display spiritual and ethical qualities such as piety, generosity, and endurance. The Andalusian mystic and philosopher Muḥyiddīn Ibn 'Arabī (d. 1240 CE) pushes this spiritual equal-status theory further by stating that "there is no spiritual qualification conferred on men which is denied women" (Shaikh 2012, 82).

Eva Rosander (2015) contends that Sufism is more conducive to female spirituality and gives more room to female religiosity than non-Sufi Islam. In classical as well as in contemporary Islam, there have been eminent Sufi women who were regarded as spiritual leaders in their community (Coulon and Coulon 1990; Smith 2001). According to the Mourid tradition, Mame Diarra was a saintly figure and a great female Sufi. By all oral accounts handed down from generations to generations, this mystical and quasi-mythical female figure devoutly performed all her daily five canonical prayers on time and would always renew her ablutions prior to each prayer. Furthermore, ever since her early childhood, Mame Diarra would embark upon long supererogatory prayers and would fast for days on end (Mbacké 1995).

In terms of early Sufi connections, Mame Diarra drew upon several spiritual traditions, such as those of the Persian Sufi scholar Abu Ḥāmid al Ghazālī (d. 1111 CE); 'Abd al Qādir al-Jīlānī (d. 1166 CE), the founder of the Qādirīyya Sufi order; and Muḥammad ibn Sulaymān al-Jazūlī (d. 1465 CE), the founder of the Jazūliyya Sufi order. According to the Mourid tradition, Mame Diarra would very often be caught reciting *Dalā'il al-Khayrāt wa Shawāriq al-Anwār fī Dhikr al-Salāt 'alā al-Nabī al-Mukhṭār* (Tokens of Blessings and Advents of Illumination in the Invocation of Prayers on Behalf of the Chosen Prophet) by Shaykh al-Jazūlī.

Mame Diarra was not only a theoretician but also a practitioner of Sufi teachings, engaging in the performance of *wird* (litany), *dhikr* (devotional remembrance), asceticism (*zuhd*), and divine love, all of which she inculcated into the young Cheikh Ahmadou Bamba. By virtue of her being considered a female saint, Mame Diarra is believed by both Mourid men and women to be able to perform miracles. For instance, in Senegal and in the Mourid Diasporic communities across the world—especially in the United States, Italy, Spain, and France—hundreds of stores, small businesses, and private religious and secular schools bear the name of Mame Diarra. Through the use of iconographic symbols, female as well as male disciples seek blessings from Mame Diarra, who is believed to have miraculously intervened in favor of their social, educational, and financial matters (Rosander 2015).

There is a strong visual culture in the Sufi tradition writ large. Places that bear the name of an eminent Sufi or a saintly figure are believed to be imbued with special blessings, because the saintly patron infuses the space with his or her mystical powers. Religious symbols such as shrines, holy objects, photos of religious figures, and similar iconographic representations are presumed to have some agency: "Images appear to act as discrete sources of power that affect events or people as a force or agent of change," David Morgan (2005, 68) observes. To emphasize the hierophany of some objects, Morgan (p. 13) gives the example of the Prophet Muḥammad, who used to kiss the Black Stone (a holy rock located in Mecca). This ritual is imitated and perpetuated by Muslims during the annual pilgrimage to Mecca.

Because Mame Diarra is the patron saint of the town of Porokhane, this town has become an important spiritual and Sufi hub. The annual pilgrimage to Porokhane to pay homage to and seek blessings from this female figure is currently one of the greatest events in the Mourid calendar. Interestingly, albeit an event celebrating a woman, the *Porokhane Magal*, as it is called, attracts thousands of men, who equally claim Mame Diarra as their bestower of blessings. The *Porokhane Magal* crosses gender barriers as both men and women are dedicated to the saint of Porokhane. By virtue of being the burial place of Mame Diarra and hosting a big annual pilgrimage, Porokhane has become the second-most sacred space in Mouridism after Touba, the Mourid spiritual capital city.

Visitation (*ziyāra*) to the burial sites (mausoleums) of eminent Sufis such as Mame Diarra is a significant and symbolic practice in the Sufi tradition. It is one among many Sufi rituals that are shared across Sufi communities. In Senegal, Mourid women highly value visitations to the mausoleum of Mame Diarra, which they believe confers a special yet temporary spiritual aura on the visitor. Robert Rozehnal (2007, 2) underscores the importance of tomb visitation among women in South Asia: "In South Asia, the tombs of Sufi saints provide an alternative outlet for piety and pilgrimage, especially for women who are often marginalized from the public, gendered space of the mosque." I concur with Rozehnal about the alternative sacred spaces that Muslim women enjoy in saints' mausoleums (*ziyāra*). Unlike in some gender-specific Islamic rituals, the female Muslim is not discriminated against or marginalized during visitations of spiritual places.

The oral tradition reports that even while Mame Diarra was busy with her domestic chores, she would concomitantly recite the Qur'ān or prayers (*ṣalawāt*) to the Prophet Muḥammad or would perform *dhikr*. Mame Diarra would also spend her days fasting and constantly reading the Qur'ān (Mbacké 1995). Her relentless spiritual life is reminiscent of her namesake, Maryam or Mary, who is regarded as one of the first and most outstanding mystic and ascetic women in both Islamic and Christian traditions.

According to the Islamic tradition, Maryam used to retreat in a temple and live a secluded, ascetic life, shut off from her community (Qur'ān 19:16). Sadiyya Shaikh (2012, 53) argues that the fact that the Persian Sufi poet Farīd ad-Dīn (d. 1221 CE) **Aṭṭār** "placed Mary at the apex of spiritual attainment, even preceding men in Paradise, implies recognition of women's full spiritual capacities." Mame Diarra shared common traits with Maryam, especially regarding the tendency to be secluded and her practice of devotion and asceticism. Following in the footsteps of Maryam, Mame Diarra would engage in intensive and prolonged devotional practices (Mbacké 1995). Mame Diarra's ascetic pursuits did not preclude her reaching out to her folks and engaging in community service.

Mame Diarra was not only regarded as a saint and a Sufi in the Senegalese Muslim community but she was also considered a dedicated social agent, a humble community servant who used to work tirelessly and selflessly for her people. According to the Indian Sufi Niẓāmuddīn Awliyā (d. 1325 CE), devotion to God is of two kinds:

> *lazmī* (obligatory) and *muta'addī* (supererogatory). In the *lazmī* devotion, the benefit which accrues is confined to the devotee alone. This type of devotion includes prayers, fasting, pilgrimage to Mecca, recitation of religious formulae, turning over the beads of the rosary, and the like. The *muta'addī* devotion, by contrast, brings advantage and comfort to others; it is performed by spending money on others, showing affection to people, and by other means through which one strives to help fellow human beings. The reward of *muta'addī* devotion is incalculable. (as quoted in Sijzi 1992, 10)

The social dimension of Mame Diarra's Sufi doctrine is encapsulated in her praxis-oriented activities. Oral tradition has it that Mame Diarra used to combine spiritual activities with a host of social services dedicated to her community, such as cooking and serving free food to the neighbors and to the poor, assisting the needy, fetching water for the children and the elderly, and providing other community-based services. It is worth noting that Mame Diarra's practice-oriented Sufism has had a lasting influence on Mouridism, which is a Sufi order very much informed by praxis as evidenced by the Mourid work ethics. According to Mbacké (1995), it was Mame Diarra's devout and saintly life, her intimate relationship with God, her generosity, and her constant community services that led her contemporaries to nickname her *Jāra Allāh* (God's neighbor). The name "Mame Diarra" is a deformation of the first half of the nickname *Jāra*.

Rkia Cornell (in as-Sulami 1999, 16) emphasizes the all-encompassing nature of Sufi devotion. She asserts that "the Sufi is the best of Muslims: if a woman, she is a person who differs from her fellow believers mainly to the extent that her devotion to God is an all-consuming vocation." A woman's devotion is an "all-consuming vocation" insofar as it involves all her everyday activities, including her devotional practices and her social actions. Emile Durkheim (1995, 466) made a compelling argument about the social dimension of religion by emphasizing the sacredness of society: "The idea of society is the soul of religion," he writes. The significance of the social dimension of religion has not been underscored enough across religious traditions.

MAME DIARRA AS THE SPIRITUAL MOTHER: THE INFLUENCE OF THE FEMALE OVER THE MALE

An oft-quoted Hadith reported by Ahmad and Nasā'i places the mother on a high pedestal in terms of a Muslim's salvation, by locating Paradise inside the female body: "Paradise lies beneath mothers' feet" (Sunan An-Nasa'i, Book 25, No. 3104). A famous metaphoric Wolof saying, which posits that a man's success to a large extent rests with his mother, goes: "when a baby's dance is well performed, it is certainly because its mother has held tight its shoulders." This Senegalese proverbial wisdom is consonant with the Nigerian Igbo aphorism, *Nneka* ("mother is supreme") that Uchendu reminded his nephew Okonkwo of in Chinua Achebe's (1958) *Things Fall Apart*. Although she did not live long enough to witness her son's full mystical development and his celebrated spiritual success, Mame Diarra used to tell Cheikh Ahmadou Bamba stories of the *al-Salaf al-Ṣāliḥ* (the Righteous Predecessors), who would spend their nights engaged in prayers and in other acts of devotion. She would offer these stories as spiritual exemplars in hopes that her young son would follow in their footsteps (Mbacké 1995).

Scholars such as Eva Rosander (2015) attribute much of the spiritual success of Cheikh Ahmadou Bamba to the mystical dimension of his mother, by virtue of her laying the social and spiritual foundation for her son's promising future. Such a contention is widely popular among the Senegalese people. A popular statement in Senegal, which is drawn from the Mourid oral tradition, assesses the cause-and-effect relationship between Mame Diarra and Cheikh Ahmadou Bamba in this aphorism: "Mame Diarra's good intention blessed her with Cheikh Ahmadou Bamba." This statement is meant to emphasize the power of intention or *niyya* in Islamic theology. *Niyya* consists of an inner formulation of the desire and will to perform an act, whereas *himma* (spiritual motivation) represents the inner driving force that enables you to perform the act.

The great Persian Sufi master Abū Yazīd al Bisṭāmī (d. 874 CE) was particularly impressed by the spirituality of an outstanding female Sufi, Fāṭima of Nishapur (d. 838 CE). He writes: "In all of my life, I have only seen one true man and one true woman. The woman was Fāṭima of Nishapur. Whenever I informed her about one of the stages of spirituality, she would take the news as if she had experienced it herself" (as quoted in Cornell 1999, 144). The fact that al Bisṭāmī veils the male and foregrounds the female in this Sufi narrative is noteworthy. Medieval mystical stories such as these, in which the female overshadows the male, do not abound in modern Islamic literature. Indeed, patriarchy tends to dominate the discourses and the constructions and interpretations of spirituality.

Furthermore, Abū Yazīd al Bisṭāmī chooses a female Sufi as the epitome of *himma*. He states: "Whoever practices Sufism should do so with the spiritual motivation (*himma*) of Umm 'Alī, the wife of Ahmad ibn Khadrawayh, or with a state similar to hers" (as quoted in Cornell 1999, 168). Mame Diarra was instrumental in enhancing Cheikh Ahmadou Bamba's *himma* and in boosting his morale throughout his exile in central Africa (1895–1902) engineered by the French colonialists. According to the Mourid oral tradition, Mame Diarra's mystical empowerment enabled her to work several miracles in favor of her son. The most popular example among these thaumaturgic performances occurred during Cheikh Ahmadou Bamba's exile:

> When Cheikh Ahmadou Bamba was thrown into a deep pit by the French colonialists, the group of angels known as the *Mala al-a'lā* along with those named *Muqarrabūn* came to his rescue. Cheikh Ahmadou Bamba asked them if they had come to rescue him upon God's order, to which they answered negatively, arguing that they only wanted to help him out, which caused the Shaykh to turn down their offer. Suddenly, an individual grabbed him by his shoulders and dragged him out of the abyss, saying: "go ahead and carry on your mission." On looking back, Cheikh Ahmadou Bamba saw his own mother Mame Diarra. (who had passed away decades before)[4]

The mother–son relationship between Mame Diarra and Cheikh Ahmadou Bamba is similar to that of Maryam/Mary and Prophet 'Isā/Jesus Christ in terms of the mother's spiritual influence upon her prominent son. For instance, Mourids subscribe to the idea that the advent of Cheikh Ahmadou Bamba and his being ushered onto the world stage through the Mourid Sufi order bear witness to the lofty mystical dimension of Mame Diarra. However, although this female–male relationship is celebrated in Mouridism, mainstream Mourids are not conversant with the spiritual history of Mame Diarra.

CONCLUSION

This chapter is the first substantive work devoted exclusively to Mame Diarra. Although many scholarly works have been devoted to her son, Cheikh Ahmadou Bamba, who founded a major Sufi order, Mame Diarra has not until now been given due attention in scholarly or in non-scholarly works. Thus, I examined the spiritual and social life of this ignored African female saint and Sufi and tried to make a case for an Islamic female sainthood and spirituality through Mame Diarra's hagiography. I contend that female spirituality and its contribution to male spirituality are not often enough foregrounded in sacred biographies and sainthood studies.

Mame Diarra exerted a towering influence upon her son Cheikh Ahmadou Bamba, both spiritually and socially. Her praxis-oriented Sufism left a lasting imprint on the Mourid Sufi order. Examples of strong African Muslim women are not common in the Islamic literature. In his foreword to Rkia Cornell's 1999 translation of as-Sulami's *Early Sufi Women*, the American scholar of Sufism Carl Ernst rightly states that the widely assumed image of Muslim women as being oppressed, an image especially popular in the West, "is so commonly asserted, and so rarely questioned, that it passes for general knowledge and is accepted as undisputed fact" (As-Sulami 1999, 11).

A perusal of Mame Diarra's hagiography and biography coupled with an examination of how they have been recounted and popularized points to the uniqueness of female spirituality. Because her life was very short yet spiritually, mystically, and socially rich and because of the absence of any biography about her, Mourids have only a smattering of information about this outstanding African woman. They know that she was the mother of their spiritual leader and have heard a few stories about her social and spiritual activities, including her miracles; aside from that, Mourids do not know much about Mame Diarra. The very little available information on Mame Diarra stems from a few oral sources consisting mostly of fossilized socio-spiritual stories.

The agency underlying the story of Mame Diarra challenges deeply entrenched stereotypes about Muslim women. Mame Diarra's story contributes to the deconstruction of the longstanding prejudices and clichés about female women, sainthood, and spirituality and crosses gender boundaries, given that both Mourid men and women are equally dedicated to this famous female figure. This chapter fills the informational gap by showcasing this iconic African female leader. Mame Diarra's unique story challenges patriarchal conceptions as well as Western assumptions about Muslim women, who are usually depicted only as being subservient to men. It offers a view of Muslim women, especially traditional African female Muslims, that is free from the prejudices so common throughout the West.

NOTES

1. The given name Mame (pronounced *mām*) means grandfather or grandmother in the Wolof language. *Mame Diarra* literally means Grandma Diarra.

2. The *Archives Nationales du Senegal* (the Senegalese National Archives) include accounts about select male Muslim figures, some of whom were contemporaries of Mame Diarra.

3. A popular genealogical tree that traces Mame Diarra's ancestry all the way to the Prophet Muḥammad is available in print edition in Senegal.

4. This story was first publicly reported in a 1979 recorded audio sermon delivered in the Wolof language by Shaykh Abdou Ahad Mbacké, the third supreme leader of the Mouridiyya, during the annual celebration of the *Magal* (the Mourid annual

celebration and pilgrimage to Touba, Senegal, commemorating the seven-year exile of Cheikh Ahmadou Bamba). https://www.youtube.com/watch?v=kRf0Lyg_HPg.

REFERENCES

Achebe, Chinua. 1958. *Things Fall Apart*. London: Heinemann.

Al Khadimiyyah TV. 2013, August 25. "Cheikh Abdoul Ahad MBACKE Appel Magal de Touba Edition 1979." *YouTube video*, 13:38. https://www.youtube.com/watch?v=kRf0Lyg_HPg.

as-Sulami, Abu 'Abd ar-Rahman. 1999. *Early Sufi Women: Dhikr an-Niswa al-Muta'abbdat as-Sufiyyat*. Translated and edited by Rkia E. Cornell. Kentucky: Fons Vitae.

Beauvoir, Simone de. 2009. *The Second Sex*. London: Jonathan Cape.

Bhaskar, Roy. 1989. *The Possibility of Naturalism: A Philosophical Critique of the Contemporary Human Sciences*, 2nd edition. New York: Harvester Weatsheaf.

Cornell, Vincent J. 1998. *Realm of the Saint: Power and Authority in Moroccan Sufism*. Austin: University of Texas Press.

Coulon, Christian and Odile R. Coulon. 1990. *L'Islam au féminin: Sokhna Magat Diop, cheikh de la confrérie mouride, Sénégal*. Bordeaux: CEAN.

Diop, Mouhammadou L. 2017. *Irwā al Nadīm Min 'Azbi Hubb al Khadīm*. Ribat, Morocco: Al Ma'ārif al Jadīda Press.

Durkheim, Emile. 1995. *Elementary Forms of Religious Life*. New York: Free Press.

Gross, Rita M. 1996. *Feminism and Religion: An Introduction*. Boston: Beacon Press.

Mbacké, S. Bassirou. 1995. *Les Bienfaits de l'Eternel ou la biographie de Cheikh Ahmadou Bamba*. Dakar: Imprimerie Saint-Paul.

Morgan, David. 2005. *The Sacred Gaze: Religious Visual Cultural in Theory and Practice*. Berkeley: University of California Press.

Rosander, Eva E. 2015. *In Pursuit of Paradise: Senegalese Women, Muridism and Migration*. Uppsala: The Nordic Africa Institute.

Rozehnal, Robert T. 2007. *Islamic Sufism Unbound: Politics and Piety in Twenty-First Century Pakistan*. New York: Palgrave Macmillan.

Schimmel, Annemarie. 1997. *My Soul Is a Woman: The Feminine in Islam*. Translated by Susan H. Ray. London: Continuum International Publishing Group.

Shaikh, Sadiyya. 2012. *Sufi Narratives of Intimacy: Ibn 'Arabi, Gender and Sexuality*. Chapel Hill, NC: University of North Carolina Press.

Sijzi, Amir Hasan. 1992. *Nizam ad Din Awliya: Morals for the Heart*. Edited by Bruce Lawrence. New York: Paulist Press.

Smith, Margaret. 2001. *Muslim Women Mystics: The Life and Work of Rābi'a and Other Women Mystics in Islam*. Oxford: Oneworld.

Chapter 12

Misogyny, Xenophobia, and Masculinity in the Academy

An Epicenter of Violence, Abuse of Power, and Humiliation

Veronica Fynn Bruey

Oh, sorry to hear that things didn't work out with X. This continent has serious problems dear. No wonder Africa's brightest minds have all abandoned this God forsaken place. Forget any hopes of transforming Africa. This place ain't going nowhere.

In October 2017, en route to Liberia and Ethiopia, a job interview was scheduled in Ghana for a lecturer position at a newly open law school. The interview panel comprised seven males and one female (the secretary, who was not allowed to participate). The presentation to the panelists, "Systematic Violence and the Rule of Law: Indigenous Communities in Australia and Post-War Liberia," was based on my PhD dissertation. Using a complex mixed-methods research design that draws on feminist jurisprudence (Mossman 1987), intersectionality (Crenshaw 1989), decolonization (Fanon 1963), critical legal studies (Tushnet 1990), and social determinants of health (WHO Healthy Cities Project 2003) theoretical concepts, the dissertation questions the legitimacy of the legal maxim—the rule of law (Fynn Bruey 2016).

"Asking the woman questions" (Bartlett 1990), the dissertation assessed whether Indigenous girls and women survivors of colonial violence and armed conflict in Australia and Liberia receive equal treatment before a law that is patriarchal and discriminatory. After the presentation, the male interviewers on the panel started an attack that lasted until the end of the interview session. One asked, "Do you hate men?" Another, "Are you a pro-feminist?" Another, "How would you teach students about the law if you have no confidence in the legal system?" And yet another: "So you are saying that men are responsible for all the violence against women?" In hindsight, that dissenting gut feeling that said "this is not the place for you to grow and flourish" should have been taken seriously.

A second interview was conducted on February 6, 2018, an offer for the lecturer position was made on February 12, 2018, and the offer was accepted on March 3, 2018. The first warning sign came when I asked that my start date be delayed for two weeks in order to maximize post-partum care. Dated on March 13, 2018, the faculty's response to my request was:

> Although you intend to start teaching on 17th September 2018. Per the University's calendar, first Academic semester begins on Monday, 13th August, 2018 (Students Arrival and Registration) and Lecturers begins on Monday 20th August, 2018. In view of this, you are required to be available to prepare and start teaching on the 20th of August, 2018 as indicated.

Barely six weeks after giving birth to our son, as I was still limping on one leg because of a pinched nerve, our belongings were shipped across the oceans to allow me to assume duty on August 9, 2018.

The rationale for going to Ghana was simple. The PhD was done, an adorable baby boy was born, and a doting husband became a stay-at-home father. What could convince us to remain in Trump-ruled America? Moreover, there seems no better way to launch an academic career than by contributing to a community that once believed in a poor refugee girl. Much as I wanted to give back to the continent, the thought of doing so by risking the health of our newborn was inconceivable. The worst part of this experience is the shame, humiliation, and guilt I feel for naively assuming that returning to Ghana would be an escape from racism in the United States of America.

The immediate rejection, apathy, and isolation I experienced, coupled with constant bullying and harassment from the students, faculty, and administration, left me with a deep sense of abandonment from a so-called "God-fearing" colonial society steeped in patriarchy, xenophobia, and misogyny. Since violence begets violence, the natural and immediate reaction that could have brought instant gratification would have been to retaliate and return evil for all the trauma, pain, and suffering. However, the dish of revenge is proverbially best served cold. To this effect, resignation from the post was a thoughtful, quiet resistance and displayed the higher moral compass characteristics of authority, power, and the decency needed to restore dignity and sanity, no matter how long it takes.

In the end, it was necessary to bring a lawsuit because there was no other way of getting reimbursed for the cost of moving a fully furnished two-bedroom apartment from the Pacific Northwest to the Atlantic coastline of

Western Africa. After I had spent months chasing bureaucrats and adminis-trators, when the "D-Day" came on February 14, 2020, the finance director said, "I was told not to sign the check because you have not been coming to work since the semester started." The reimbursement for relocation costs had been due six months earlier (on August 8, 2019) pursuant to paragraph 8 of the appointment letter:

> The University will refund your T&T [travel and transportation] after your period of probation. The refund will cover transport for yourself, spouse and children (up to a maximum of six children) from your hometown/previous place of work to the University to assume your appointment, upon submission of cer-tified bills. For Overseas appointments, the University would refund air tickets of yourself and family on assumption of duty. Other expenses relating to your relocation would be refunded after your probation period.

Thus, it did not matter whether I went to work for the three weeks between the start of the semester (i.e., January 27, 2020) and February 14, 2020, when the finance director refused to sign the check. A clear breach of contract had occurred. Initiating a lawsuit while submitting my resignation letter was the only way to be refunded. The raw emotion of frustration and disgust I still feel is illustrated by the response of a friend, quoted at the beginning of this chapter, after finding out about my departure from Ghana.

THEORETICAL CONCEPTS

With feminism, gender, and sexism at its core, this chapter cuts across sev-eral disciplines, including anticolonial and decolonialization studies, law and legal studies, and male and masculinities studies (to name a few). Feminism in this context is perceived as both "a theory of knowledge and an intellectual practice" for the purpose of deconstructing patriarchal epistemes in contribut-ing to women's freedom to engage intellectually and critically in institutions of higher learning (Mama 2011, 1). Anticolonial feminism is both a theoreti-cal and a political project that challenges colonialist and imperialist practices (Mendoza 2016, 100). The colonial legacy associated with oppressing and subordinating girls and women festers and flourishes deep within the educa-tional system in Ghana.

The anticolonial feminist perspective asserts that the higher education sys-tem in Ghana is notoriously subjected to recolonization tendencies even after girls and women have, for centuries, endured multiple levels of discrimina-tion, exploitation, violence, and abuse by European and African men. Any efforts to decolonize male power and leadership reveal that girls and women must seize every opportunity to speak out/up and become agents of change so as to disrupt hegemonic masculinity. To this end, the three theories most relevant to this lived experience are steeped in a feministic conceptual framework. They are: (a) speaking out, (b) agency, and (c) hegemonic masculinity. Being a young, Black, African, and female foreigner introduces the concept of intersectionality, concentrated in gender, sex, age, class, social status, ethnic, and national discrimination.

Coined by a Black legal feminist, Kimberlé Crenshaw, *intersectionality* is "a metaphor for understanding the ways that multiple forms of inequality or disadvantages sometimes compound themselves." These elements "create obstacles often that are not understood within conventional ways of thinking about anti-racism, feminism, or social justice advocacy structures" (National Association of Independent Schools 2018, 0:11). A principal tactic for feminists in fighting against overlapping social identities related to systems of discrimination against girls and women is to break the silence and fear that prejudice imposes by speaking out/up. Speaking out/up notifies old male oppressors of young women's refusal to be muzzled while alerting the wider society to the injustice, trauma, and abuse suffered as a result of misogyny and male dominance.

Alcoff and Gray argue that survivor of gender violence "speak-outs" are transgressive, in that they challenge conventional arrangements and presume objects antithetical to the dominant discourse (Alcoff and Gray 1993, 260, 267–68). To preclude disempowering girls and women survivors who dare to speak out, Alcoff and Gray suggest a carefully examining where the impetus to speak originates and what power relations and domination exist between the one speaking out and the one to whom the disclosure is directed (Alcoff and Gray 1993, 284). This yearning to speak out/up is about enabling girls and women make the transition from being passive victims of gender discrimination to becoming active advocates of systemic change.

In *Theory as Liberatory Practice*, bell hooks affirms that she desperately came to Black feminist theory with intense emotional pain in search of deeper understanding that would help her to heal and "make the hurt go away" (hooks 1991 1). Although the entire experience of speaking out/up is inherently emancipatory and self-fulfilling for feminists, one challenge is the inevitability of being vulnerable to backlash, especially from male chauvinists. Obviously, this "speak out/up" moment in this chapter is aimed at confronting hegemonic masculinity.

Hegemonic masculinity is a dynamic and diverse character type in gender relations that legitimizes patriarchy to guarantee the dominant position of men by subordinating girls, women, and men (Connell 2005, 76–77; Connell and Messerschmidt 2005, 830–32). Hegemony is a "cultural practice whereby a group claims and sustains a leading position in society" (Connell 2005, 77).

Hegemonic masculinity is apt for explaining the nature, form, and dynamics of male power and dominance in Africa (Morrell et al. 2012, 12). As multiple forms of masculinities, hegemonic masculinity assesses gender politics through the prism of sociocultural hierarchy, ageism, and chauvinism while acknowledging intragroup differences of older males' violent control and abuse of power over younger girls and women (Morrell et al. 2012, 12–13). It is within this context of men's ascendency over girls and women that agency of the oppressed and subordinated must be analyzed.

A major feminist concept, *agency* denotes the ability of individuals to transform their world. Since agency and power are entrenched and intertwined, the former must be evaluated in relation to girls' and women's freedom and constraint. Power, freedom, and transformation are all interrelated feminist struggles as agents of change (McNay 2016, 39). Therefore, inequality existing within and between groups in the academy requires feminist analysis of what girls and women can actually do as agents to be linked to political, social, and cultural emancipation. In a profession, discipline, and institution with very few women in leadership roles, acquiring agency to become agents of change is stifled both by the deliberate lack of representation and by the fear of not being supported by the few tokens socially constructed to internalize women's inferiority to men.

STRUCTURE AND FLOW

It should be emphasized that, given the word limit of the chapter, it is impossible to capture within it the enormity of this experience. The intention of the chapter is to underscore and document a personal account of gender and patriarchy in an African academic institution in real time. The events narrated in this chapter comprise a combination of perspectives, many of which have already been stated in previous chapters. Statements made in the chapter of my own knowledge are believed to be true. All errors and oversights remain mine. Extra care is taken to ensure the anonymity of individuals referred to in the chapter. Because I am protecting the identity of persons mentioned in the chapter and the institutions involved, no names or identities are used to the extent of my knowledge, ability, and academic standards for publishing.

The chapter begins with an introduction and a brief overview of theoretical concepts that underpin the reasoning behind the endemic, entrenched, and staunch nature of discrimination against women, patriarchy, and xenophobia in an African institution of higher learning. A general profile of the academic institution (hereafter, the University) involved is juxtaposed with a summary of my expertise, which will give readers an opportunity to critically assess the legitimacy of the evidence and the claims being made. The Hall of Shame presents a heart-wrenching tirade of insults delivered by six male students, egged on by the then dean of the Faculty of Law (hereafter, the dean) in the presence of the entire law school.

An abridged version of the formal complaint made against the person at the center of this experience, the dean of the Law Faculty, epitomizes a feminist and unflinching defiance that includes to speak up/out against hegemonic masculinity in becoming an agent of change in this recolonized cesspit. As expected, the formal complaint attracted retribution and disdain in the form of complaints to the Ghana Legal Council and the National Accreditation Board, students' refusal to enroll in my classes, shunning by colleagues, the Law Faculty's refusal to assign me courses, and a final petition filed by students to remove me from the classroom permanently. Using hard evidence such as written letters, self-evaluations, e-mail exchanges, assessment grades, and course evaluations, the final part of the chapter deals with various strategies employed to fight against the entrenched system of patriarchy, xenophobia, and misogyny.

After this experience, I am unreservedly convinced that this particular kind of people is chronically hostile and immune to positive change. Shockingly, it is no longer hard to question whether the continent of Africa has "shithole countries" (Woodhouse, 2018). Unless African leaders are intentional, deliberate, and purposeful about investing in the continent's best brains, especially children and young girls, Africa will continue to lag behind the rest of the world in everything. A persistent and nonviolent radical change should be embraced.

A BRIEF OVERVIEW OF LEGAL EDUCATION IN GHANA

Formal legal education in Ghana dates back to the report of the International Advisory Committee on Legal Education, which was appointed by the General Legal Council (GLC) and the Council of the University College of Ghana (now the University of Ghana). The report recommended a system of legal education that would involve an academic and practical component set up at the University and at the Ghana School of Law (GSL), respectively. In 1958, the GLC established the GSL with the mandate to start professional legal training. The function of the GSL is to provide legal education to the Board of Legal Education and to establish courses of instructions deemed expedient, conduct examinations, and publish examination results.

The *Legal Profession Act,* 1960 (Act 32) provides for the organization of legal profession and education in Ghana. The Legal Profession Act establishes the General Legal Council (GLC) with the mandate to be concerned with the legal profession and, in particular, with the organization of education and upholding of the standards of professional conduct.[1] The GLC comprises a chairperson, a deputy chairperson, the two most senior judges of the Supreme Court after the chairperson, the attorney general, the head of Faculty of Law at the University of Ghana, three persons appointed by the attorney-general, and four members elected by the Ghana Bar Association.[2]

To pursue the professional (practical) component of legal education in Ghana, a first degree or its equivalent in a bachelor of laws (LLB) is required. This academic phase of legal training was offered only by the University of Ghana since independence until 2003, when the need to open legal education in Ghana was urgent. The Kwame Nkrumah University of Science and Technology (KNUST) and the Ghana Institutes of Management and Public Administration (GIMPA) began offering a four-year LLB program in 2003 and 2010, respectively. In 2012, the GSL introduced a two-hour entrance exam based on ten law courses to manage the influx of hundreds of students completing some eleven law schools accredited by the National Accreditation Board (NAB) in Ghana.

The minimum entry requirement for pursuing an LLB program in any university in Ghana is an undergraduate degree or its equivalent in an area of study. Some institutions (e.g., KNUST and the University of Cape Coast) admit holders of the West African Senior Secondary School Certificate or General Education (Advance level) into the LLB program. The duration for studying for an LLB in Ghana ranges from two to four years, depending on the structures and modules put in place by the university. Major courses offered by the law faculties include contract, tort, land law, constitutional law, legal research, administrative law, commercial law, company law, legal research and communication, professional development, and the Ghana legal system.

A successful completion of the LLB in any of the recognized or accredited universities is the minimum requirement needed for the professional (practical) phase of legal education in Ghana. The professional/practical component is offered by the Ghana School of Law, which is the professional component of legal education in Ghana. The Ghana School of Law has three campuses: at GIMPA; at KNUST; and in Accra, where the main campus, popularly known as "Makola," is located.[3]

Profile of the Institution's Faculty of Law

The University enrolled an estimated 79,000 students for the academic year 2018–2019. A total of 289 students enrolled in the Faculty of Law, which has 12 faculty members: 8 full-time lecturers (2 women) and 4 part-time instructors, teaching some 27 courses. The student-to-faculty ratio was 36:1. The only PhD holders in the faculty were the two female lecturers. Lecturers are expected to conduct a minimum of two and a maximum of four in-class assessments in addition to administering the end-of-semester exam. A significant percentage of the students are admitted on "protocol" or concession, which implies that many are not qualified for admission but are accepted because of the position of their parent or family members. A notice dated February 4, 2020, reads:

2020/2021 Staff Concession

The University Community is hereby informed that staff who wish to have their biological children/wards admitted into XXX and other sister Universities (XXX) for the 2020–2021 academic year are kindly to note the following:

1) Obtain Staff Concessionary application form at the XXX
2) Attach E-voucher Serial Numbers, E-voucher Receipts and applicants' contact number(s) to their completed Staff Concessionary Application Form for easy referencing and processing.
3) Submit completed Staff Concessionary Application Form together with various attachments to the XXX latest by 31st May, 2020.

Kindly bring this to the notice of all staff in your College/Faculty/School/Ce ntre/Department/Section/Unit/Hall.

Thank you.

Below are examples of assessment grades that are clear indicators regarding the quality of students being admitted into this University. Additional evidence to support the argument that students do not meet the basic admission standards for legal education in Ghana can be seen in the rate at which they consistently fail the GSL entrance exam. For the academic year 2017, only 91 (19 percent) of 474 students passed the GSL entrance exam (Mustapha 2018). In 2018, only 64 (9 percent) of 450 students passed the entrance exam (Serbeth-Boateng 2019; Staff Reporter 2019a). In 2019, of the 1,890 candidates who sat for the GSL entrance exam, only 7 percent (128) passed ("93% of Students Fail" 2019; Staff Reporter 2019b). At this University, it was reported that only four out of some sixty-six students passed in both the academic year 2017–2018 and the year 2018–2019. Although there may be several intersecting factors to explain the GSL entrance exam results, it is not unreasonable to conclude that a major cause of mass failure is the quality of students being admitted into accredited law schools in Ghana.

A SHORT BIO OF MY EXPERTISE

I am a survivor of war, abuse, and all sorts of discrimination, having endured three years of Liberia's civil war that made me a refugee in Ghana for nine years prior to my moving to Canada as a single immigrant. I came to this

University with six world-class university degrees, three of which are law degrees earned on four continents, with over 15 years of academic and professional experiences in teaching, researching, and speaking at conferences. To date, I have authored three academic books, nine book chapters, nine peer-reviewed journal articles, and a long list of other publications, including book reviews, reports, editorials, blog posts, and media commentaries. I founded and manage the *Journal of Internal Displacement* and sit on the editorial board of several academic journals, including the *University of Ibadan Faculty of Law Journal* and the *African Methodist Episcopal University Interdisciplinary Journal.*

When I arrived at the facilities of the Faculty of Law, I instantly observed the following: a cramped classroom space, no internet access, students sitting on slabs to study, because there is no common area, including a toilet, and a space to buy and sell food. Yet this is a fee-paying program. Even more disturbing was the fact that lecturers did not use textbooks to teach, and the PowerPoint slides used for instruction were either out of date or poorly prepared. Students had never heard of citation managers such as Zotero or Mendeley. Thus, since the University had no policy on plagiarism and the law library subscribed only to an electronic database (Heine online), students plagiarized by copying and pasting information from flimsy websites (e.g., "Quora" and "Law Teacher") to complete their assignments.

Regardless, I committed to introducing a world-class standard by giving each student an electronic textbook with assigned readings and a 30-page course guide on the first day of class. The course guide contained all the needed information, including a full instruction and marking scheme of all four class assessments over the semester period. My undoing was in holding students accountable and compelling them to think critically. These students had always been spoon-fed with archaic information and trained to memorize (a technique of instruction referred to locally as "chew and pour"). Students, some of whom were as old as my father, hated me for asking them to read before class and requiring them to conduct legal research in doing their assignments. When they did not get the grades that had been freely given to them in the past, all hell broke loose.

THE HALL OF SHAME

On February 20, 2019, during a consultative meeting with the entire Law School, the dean egged on six male students to attack and rain down insults on me because they had not done well in my courses. During the meeting, the first three students started by saying I was not as intelligent as they were because some of them had two master's degrees. They made demonstrably false claims about my examinations and course preparation. The fourth student wanted to continue repeating the same false claims, when the meeting moderator told the student that the student was providing no new information and should be seated and communicate further issues in private with the faculty. The dean then overrode the moderator and let the remaining three students reiterate the insults and falsehoods.

After witnessing that kind of treatment and the dean's encouragement of it, and given its public nature, I expected that the dean would reach out to me privately in his professional role to debrief and find the truth of the situation, if not simply out of concern for my emotional state as my mentor. However, no attempt to do so was made. I would later learn that the students wrote two letters to the dean voicing concerns about my teaching style and the grades they had received in my class. I was never informed of these concerns. A dean who receives feedback about a teacher outside the channels of systematic evaluation has an obligation to examine that feedback with the teacher, but this obligation was not observed; I was not even informed about the feedback.

As a result, with the stupidest grin on my face, I sat through an hour and a half of students' insults, feeling totally humiliated, singled out, attacked, and betrayed. After the incident, other students confided that they had complained to the dean about my teaching methods and why they were not performing well, and without speaking to me, the dean told them to bring it up during the consultative meeting in front of the entire law school.

A FORMAL COMPLAINT

After the Hall of Shame incident in February, the dean removed me from six committees and continued bullying, intimidating, and isolating me. Although I retracted and avoided being on campus, I fulfilled my teaching, research, and administrative duties until the semester when I was "fired" from the University by virtue of being denied courses to teach. At that point, I filed a formal complaint against the dean, on June 11, 2019, the text of which follows

> As per our phone communication between 22–25 May, I am writing to lodge a formal complaint against the Dean of the Faculty of Law. While my overall experience at the University have been self-fulfilling, encounters with the Dean, who is supposed to be my mentor, and some administrators at the Faculty of Law has grown worse and escalated into a situation whereby I am literally being sacked from the University. I feel the Dean's attitude towards me has been humiliating, disrespectful, demeaning, discriminatory and outright self-destructive. It has been months since the Dean spoke with me personally or

made any effort to communicate with me. Although, my concerns are many, I will attempt to limit my experience to a select few examples in hopes of meeting with you in person after I return to Ghana on 24 June 2019. I have also attached some documents/communications as evidence for your perusal.

I have enormous international networks and affiliations (please see my attached CV). I introduced the Dean to two of these organisations. As a matter of fact (see attached), as an executive and lead member, I am responsible for the Faculty of Law lead collaboration with one of these organisations. Nevertheless, the Dean has chosen to not speak with me about the collaboration even though I am a co-chair of the annual conference planning event of that particular organization. The downward spiral with the Dean began when he asked me to use my credit card to purchase plane tickets for he and I to attend a conference in the US and I refused (please see attached). Furthermore, he asked me to refrain from communicating with him by emails. I refused because whenever I tried to express my concerns, he tended to shut me down without listening to what I have to say.

Thus, immediately after I wrote stating that I am unable to pay for his plane tickets and accommodation (17 December 2018), the Dean called me in his office and "dressed me down" in the presence of two of his administrators. Since, he has "kicked" me out of several committees and literally sidelined me. I strongly believe the Dean is compelled to keep me on two committees because there is no one else with the research and publication skills in the faculty.

More recently, on 20 May the Faculty Coordinator sent an email to all lecturers excluding myself and two others, assigning courses to teach for academic year 2019 and 2020. When I inquired why my name was not on the list, I received a response stating that: "The Faculty is aware of some issues involving your engagement which you have taken up with the Central Administration and are still pending." Therefore, until my probation is over, no courses will be assigned to me. The Dean's assumption is I will have no teaching responsibility unless the University extends my contract as a Lecturer. Furthermore, unlike my colleagues, I will have no ability to prepare to teach until August 2019, which I find unfair, punitive, and discriminatory.

At this juncture, I feel the Dean has no interest in my personal and professional development. I am requesting the following, (1) an investigation be carried out to assess my experience with the Dean; (2) a formal meeting is convened by you, with the Dean and myself present; and (3) re-appoint another person to be my mentor. In the interim, I would appreciate minimizing contact with the Dean.

After filing the complaint, I received an e-mail in July letting me know that the dean had resigned and an ad hoc committee (hereafter, the Committee) was set up to further investigate my claims. I had strong evidence supporting my suspicion that the Committee, comprising six current deans (all male) was biased. During the first and only Committee meeting that I attended, the dean was allowed to scream at me for nearly 45 minutes. I was the only woman and the youngest person in the room. When the Committee members could not control his bullying and intimidation, the chair put on a sermon by a famous Ghanaian bishop using his phone. The message by Bishop Nicholas Duncan-Williams was about how the devil wants to take control of our souls and steal our joy away. After that meeting, I was coerced to withdraw my complaint, which I did on August 18, 2019, using the following words:

> RE: Formal Complaint: Requests Are Addressed
>
> Dear Provost:
>
> I thank you for setting up an ad hoc committee to address my concern. In my formal complaint against the Dean, dated 11 June 2019, I requested the following:
>
> 1) an investigation be carried out to assess my experience with the Dean;
> 2) a formal meeting is convened by you with the Dean and me present;
> 3) an appointment of another person to be my mentor; and
> 4) an expeditious resolution of all issues pertaining to my appointment, so that I can be assigned courses for the 2019/2020 academic year and begin preparations as soon as possible. In the interim, I would appreciate it if any communication regarding my appointment and continuation of my contract come from outside of the Law Faculty, until trust and mutual respect is restored between me and the office of the Dean.
>
> In the interest of returning to a place of mutual respect considering that a new busy academic year is upon us, I feel the committee has addressed my above listed concerns.
>
> Thank you once again for supporting me and I look forward to contributing my best for the progress and development of the Faculty of Law and the University.

Interestingly, the closure of the investigation was not good enough: the College, in support of the dean, asked me to retract my statements. I refused to do this because I believe everything I wrote in the formal complaint is true.

Duress and harassment in the forms of threatened litigation, bullying, and isolation continued until I resigned on February 14, 2020. My appointment was never confirmed after one year (August 2019), and I did not receive the promised reimbursement of approximately USD $11,000, the cost of relocating to Ghana. A lawsuit was brought on February 28, 2020, in an effort to recover my money.

RETRIBUTION, REVENGE, AND BETRAYAL

Faculty, staff, and students loyal to the dean took it upon themselves to fight his battle by attacking me in various ways after I lodged my complaint. First, there was a formal report to the Ghana Legal Council and the National Accreditation Board, followed by a refusal to enroll in my courses, crowned by a final petition to oust me from the University.

Report to the Ghana Legal Council and the National Accreditation Board

On August 19, 2019, a meeting between the National Accreditation Board (hereafter, NAB) and the Faculty of Law was held. Attendees included Supreme Court justices, members of the Ghana Legal Council, and members of the Ghana School of Law. They were all men, and I was the only female faculty present. The first item on the agenda after introduction was: "Veronica Fynn Bruey is not qualified to teach Private International Law because she's not admitted to the Ghana Bar Association, meaning she doesn't have knowledge of the local law." The accusation does not hold water given that the Ghana legal system reflects colonization and is heavily copied from English law with growing influence from the American legal system (Harrington and Manji 2019). Only one textbook has been written on the subject matter, and I was using that textbook.

At the end of the meeting, carefully selected students were called in by the faculty to speak with the NAB. When their closed-door meeting was over, a final debriefing session with all faculty members was held. Just before closing the meeting, the NAB team asked me to stay behind because the students had made some comments about me. Basically, the students reported to the NAB that I was too hard, that I imposed my feminist views on them, and that if they did not tell me what I wanted to hear, they ended up failing my class. I had not taught most of these students, yet they had already formed a view about my teaching method and the impact it would have on them in the future. It is not hard to conclude that I was not only maligned by students who had been emboldened by the dean but that these students were intent on kicking me out of the University.

Refusal to Register for Courses

For the first semester of academic year 2019–2020, I was assigned three courses to teach: two core courses and two electives. One elective class had only three students enrolled and the other, zero. The minimum enrollment in any class, according to the University standard, is five. I would later find out in a faculty–staff meeting that two of the elective courses in which students hastily enrolled, one of the lecturers did not show up for eight weeks, and the other barely attended class. No complaints were leveled against these lecturers, one of whom advised the students to press on with their petition against me.

The Climax: A Petition Protesting High Standards and Feminism

The entire semester was tense, especially in the level 400 core course. These were the same students that had never been taught by me. During the semester, they found ways to humiliate, attack, and harass me, but they did not succeed until after they received their first assessment grade. The assignment, due on September 23, 2020, was a 500-word Think Piece graded on a 10-point scale. The question asked of the students was: *Would it affect the moral argument if the law allowed abortions to be carried out only on victims of rape?* Before the assignment was due, we covered the following topics in class: (1) Introduction (3 September); (2) Legal Theory: General Jurisprudence and Conceptual Analysis (September 10); (3) Natural Law and Morality (September 10); (4) Classical Legal Positivism (September 16); and Individual Theories About the Nature of Law and Modern Legal Positivism: HLA Hart (September 17). Well over half the class (87%) received scores of less than 5 out of 10 on the exercise (*see* table 12.1).

The main reason the students scored so poorly was that they had poor academic writing skills. Even more concerning was their inability to synthesize and apply legal concepts to the broader and everyday issues of society. They had trouble thinking critically—meaning translating complex legal thoughts into an analytical written essay was a serious challenge. They were not able to objectively evaluate online and textual materials. Hence, they had little or no understanding of the importance of distinguishing, say, a primary resource from a secondary or tertiary one.

Table 12.1   A Breakdown of Students' First Assessment Grades

Grade/10 Points	No	%
0	1	2
1	11	18
2	22	35
3	13	21
4	7	11
5	4	6
6	1	2
7	3	5
Total	**62**	**100**

The students' inability to comprehend complex legal ideas, critically assess written materials, and cite research materials properly comes as no surprise. As I stated elsewhere, these students simply could not read, and they had no interest whatsoever in learning to read and write as legal scholars. The aforementioned "chew and pour" method of instruction did not prepare them to read, comprehend, synthesize, and explicate complex legal ideas. No one should ever graduate from law school, let alone be admitted into such a profession, by relying on PowerPoint slides or on plagiarizing information from nonacademic and disreputable sources. The responses of two students who each received a score of 1 out of 10 are below.

Student A:

Moral argument conceives that there are moral laws; not everything is permissible which proves the existence of God. In all honesty, the anti-abortion argument is not about the foetus, it is about power wielded by men over women through religion. Religious fanatics are insanely concerned about a foetus but are major supporters of the death penalty, ironic. To anti-abortionists, a foetus has a brain wave after 6 weeks of gestation[a] making it human and killing a person is morally wrong leading to the conclusion that killing a foetus is morally wrong. However, they forget that by week 8, brain activity is likened to that of a simple insect. If insects are their subjects of defence, then they are all culpable of murder—store bought insecticides, bug zappers, their trusty palms clapping together to squish a mosquito—because insects are killed on an hourly basis.

Abortion is the ending of a pregnancy by removal or expulsion of an embryo or foetus before it can survive outside the uterus, the very nature of the act is seemingly taboo. According to the UN Special Rapporteur on Torture,[b] the effects of total abortion bans can amount to torture and other forms of ill-treatment and are nothing less than institutionalised violence against women and girls. Torture is one of the jus cogens norms and is non derogable, Amnesty International[c] documents that in El Salvador, women who suffer miscarriages receive aggravated homicide charges with a sentence of up to 50 years in prison. It means that a woman who gets raped and aborts is guilty of premeditated murder as one who chose to willingly have the sex that made the foetus, and it should never be the case.

Unnecessary abortion restrictions place a burden on women and make it likely that self-induction will become more common which includes taking herbs and inflicting abdominal trauma and the end result could be death. Countries where abortion is legal, accessible, non-judgmental tend to have lower abortion rates, in France, first trimester abortions is legal as long as the woman seeking the procedure presents a physician's certificate, a counsellor's certificate and her own written consent. Inevitably, there are delays in the processing of the application and this may discourage some women from going through with the abortion.

This conversation is about reproductive choices, and bodily autonomy which invariably includes the health decisions taken by survivors of rape too. Criminalising this type of abortion moves a country from a secular State to being at least a secular theocracy, criminalising abortion requires using certain religion's description of 'human being' rather than a scientific one.[d] Scientific evidence proves that the coordinated brain activity required for consciousness; the thalamus which is responsible for the perception of pain and consciousness do not appear until 24–25 weeks and leads to the logical conclusion that an abortion during the first trimester of pregnancy is safe; does not lead to the killing of a human being and will not affect the moral argument.

Notes

[a] Dr. Tomas Ryan, 'The Moment a Baby's Brain Starts to Function, and Other Scientific Answers on Abortion.' (The Irish Times, Thu May 24, 2018) < https://www.irishtimes.com/opinion/the-moment-a-baby-s-brain-starts-to-function-and-other-scientific-answers-on-abortion-1.3506968%3Fmode%3Damp>

[b] United Nations General Assembly, Report of the Special Rapporteur on torture and other cruel, inhuman or degrading treatment or punishment, Juan E. Mendez.

[c] Amnesty International, El Salvador: Failure to release woman jailed after miscarriage, outrageous step backward for justice, December 13, 2017.

[d] Lee The, Quora. Answered January 26, 2015.

Student B:

Background

Moral standard are those things which are condemnable, whether you do them, or fail to do them. Choosing what is good over bad is a moral duty and obligation for all in every society. This essay discusses the moral question on abortion in the light of the law and how it would affect the moral argument if the law allowed abortions to be carried out only on victims of rape.

Introduction

Abortion is the intentional termination of a pregnancy after conception.[a] During the process the undeveloped fetus is killed by way of terminating the pregnancy. Whether or not abortions should be carried out has always been a very controversial discussion in many societies. The laws in Ghana do not allow would be mothers with healthy pregnancies to get an abortion with the sole reason of not wanting the pregnancy. However, the law permits abortion in certain circumstances which include incest pregnancy, impregnated rape victim, where the fetus may not live a meaningful life or the pregnancy threatens the life of the potential mother.

Analysis

Section 58 of the Criminal Offences Act, 1960[b] criminalizes abortion by stating that a person who intentionally and unlawfully causes abortion or miscarriage commits a second degree felony.

In Ghana, abortion has a negative perception index and evil in our culture. Society frowns on abortion especially the religious groups of which many belongs to. Elsewhere in the world, this is different as many hold the view that whether or not to keep a fetus should be a choice.

To the pro-life, human life begins at conception. The fetus is a potential human being capable of living as any ordinary person and also with a possible future. Thus a fetus is actually a human being and innocent hence killing a human being is wrong making abortion intrinsically evil in itself.

The pro-choice are of the view that it is not always wrong to end the life of a fetus and that abortion is not morally wrong. To them a fetus is only a potential human being and that there is only a possibility of the fetus becoming a human being. A woman has right to decide her own future and also right of ownership over her own body.[c] A pregnant woman also have moral rights. The fetus, in most cases is solely dependent on the survival of the mother. The right of the woman carrying it supersedes the right of the fetus.

In conclusion it would affect the moral argument if the law permits abortion to be carried out on only victims of rape. A child procreated as a result of incest would equally have dire consequence on the mother and society at large. Other conditions with regards to health, emotional and psychological trauma of the mother after birth should also be considered as equally good reason for abortion. Additionally, the choice of carrying a pregnancy or not should be a fundamental freedom and that one may need to live without the burden of guilt.

Notes

[a] <www.thoughtco.com>

[b] Criminal Offences Act, 1960, s 58 (3)

[c] BBC-Ethics-Abortion, www.bbc.co.uk/ethics

Although I employed innovative strategic measures to stay afloat, my ability to persist mentally and physically was arrested by the students' petition to eject me from the University. Barely a week after their papers and grades were released, on October 14, 2019, the students submitted a petition against me to the University and the Ghana Legal Council. It read:

Dear Provost:

PETITION AGAINST VERONICA FYNN BRUEY(PhD)

We the underlisted students of level 400 class of the Faculty of Law, write to bring your attention to the conduct of our Jurisprudence lecturer, Veronica Fynn Bruey (PhD) which is considered to be unacademic and may lead to incessant protest by the class. Our grounds for this petition are as follows:

1. We do not understand the content of what she is teaching as we find it alien and do not fall within the Ghanaian jurisprudence.

2. She has refused to appreciate the fundamentals of the Ghana Legal System which is very fundamental to our learning of jurisprudence.
3. She struggles to relate her knowledge of jurisprudence to the Ghanaian legal context.
4. The lecturer has total disregard for Ghanaian laws. In the first place, she is not conversant with Ghanaian laws. This makes her to question and penalize some factual propositions we make in written and oral presentations. What even makes the situation worrying is that, when her attention is drawn to the laws of Ghana, she questions the basis and rationale for such laws in a very contemptuous manner.
5. There is lack of academic freedom in our class as she does not entertain divergent opinion especially opinions against feminist ideologies.
6. Her everyday language is demotivating, demoralizing and discouraging. She used words like "fuck you," "you are a dummy" "nonsense," "stupid" on us in class.
7. She looks down on all our lecturers in the faculty by stating that she is the most qualified in the school, one of the best on the African continent as such nobody in the school including the Chairman of the National Accreditation Board can bring down her standards.
8. She picks scripts of some students ridicule them, mocks and insult their intelligence. The first time was on 1st October, 2019 where she spent 1 hour and 15 minutes to insult and ridicule the scripts of a student.
9. Conflict of Laws and Human Rights are among the most prestigious elective courses that every law student would love to offer, because of her attitude, no student has registered for Conflict of Laws. Currently, only six students have registered for Human Rights and some indicated their intent of dropping the course.
10. Her materials on Jurisprudence are incongruence with that of our sister schools.
11. On the 8th October, 2019, she made the class assess her. For fear of victimization, some students might have rated her highly. We want to bring to the attention of the faculty and the university authority that any assessment done for that purpose and the university authority that any assessment done for the purpose is attributable to undue influence and hence not a true reflection of our assessment of her teaching.

Based on the aforementioned grounds, we demand that;

1. She should be replaced immediately.
2. In the event that such replacement is not complied with, we shall comply with Section 13 and Section 14 of the Students' Handbook which allow students to hold a press conference, releases and demonstration.

3. We shall also notify the General Legal Council and National Accreditation Board on such threatening matters if the Faculty and the University fail to comply with our request.

4. We hereby give the notice of our intention to boycott jurisprudence lecture from Monday, 21st October, 2019 until we have a new lecturer.

Please find attached her course outline and signatories of petitioners
Yours faithfully,
President and Convenor
CC: Vice Chancellor, Pro Vice Chancellor, Dean of Students' Affair; Director of Academic Affairs

Some forty-four out of sixty-two final year students signed the petition. In response to the petition, the University College sent out two different communications, one to the President of Student Union and the other addressed to me, both dated October 22, 2019. The former:

Dear Sir
PETITION AGAINST VERONICA FYNN BRUEY (PhD)
Your letter captioned above to the Provost, CHLS, dated 14th October 2019 refers.

At an emergency meeting on Tuesday, October 22, 2019, to deliberate on the petition, the Management Committee of the College took the following decisions:

1. A copy of the students' petition be forwarded to Dr. Veronica Fynn Bruey to enable her respond to the allegations stated therein.

2. She is required to submit her response to the Provost by Friday, October 25, 2019 to facilitate further inquiry into the matter.

3. As an immediate measure, the Course on Jurisprudence I be given to a different lecturer to teach.

4. Further inquiry will be carried out on receipt of her response to the petition.

This is submitted for your information and assurance that your concerns will be addressed.
Yours faithfully,
College Registrar. For Provost.

The latter:
Dear Dr. Veronica Fynn Bruey
PETITION AGAINST VERONICA FYNN BRUEY (PhD)
On October 15, 2019, the Law Students Unions submitted a petition captioned as above, stating a number of complaints against you.

At an emergency meeting on Tuesday, October 22, 2019, to deliberate on
the petition, the Management Committee of the College took the following
decisions:

1. You should be given a copy of the students' petition to enable you to
    respond to the allegations stated therein.
2. You should submit her response to the Provost by Friday, October 25, 2019
    to facilitate further inquiry into the matter.

Hence, attached is a copy of the student petition, please.
This is submitted for your information and further necessary action, please.
Yours faithfully,
College Registrar. For Provost.

After the dean had bullied, harassed, and abused me for months, the students
began to do likewise. At that point, the petition was the straw that broke the
camel's back. The harassment, aggression, and violence were not only intentional, targeted, and willful but certainly nonsensical, frustrating, exhausting,
and annoying. As indicated above, at the end of the first semester, during a
faculty meeting, it was reported that one faculty member did not show up
for class for eight weeks and another for almost the entire semester. Others
struggled to give two assessments, and when they did, scripts were not
returned until the end of the semester. Yet not a single complaint or petition
was made against any of these faculty members. The lecturers' responsibility
to provide quality legal education to these so-called fee-paying students of an
institution fully accredited by the GLC was clearly in question, but they were
not deemed worthy of humiliation like that I experienced. In an e-mail dated
October 22, 2019, a response was sent to the provost:

Dear Dr X:
Thank you. Attachments well received. Please consider this email formal.
All claims against me are false with no evidence apart from the detailed
course guides which I have attached—they speak for themselves. I have also
attached past course outlines for Jurisprudence from previous Lecturers of the
University and GIMPA which are generally similar to mine.
I had never taught this cohort of students before they decided not to register
for Conflict of Laws this semester, implying that these 44 out of 62 students had
already decided to undermine me before I even held a single lecture or marked
their first assessment. Therefore, they cannot claim that my teaching style is the
reason they are not registered in the course.
I do not intend to spend precious time providing counter evidence to allegations made without substance, reason, or evidence. Therefore, this letter does
not attempt to refute all claims against me.

I continue to assert that it will require the support of the administration to maintain high standards for our students, to best prepare them for their legal careers and develop their academic skills.

I take the Provost's suggestion today to mean that as of Monday, 28 October 2019, I will not be teaching Jurisprudence.

Thank you.

By the end of the semester, even though the University found that I was qualified to teach this particular course the students had complained about, they still decided to assign a new person to teach these final-year students, and I was dropped with no explanation. Once again, I was humiliated and embarrassed being the most qualified person in this low-grade institution that is not even recognized by the university world ranking nonetheless treated with so much disgust. I was furious and bitter.

EMPTY THREATS, RESIGNATION, AND A LAWSUIT

A bit of back information will help to explain the source and reasoning behind the empty lawsuit threats from the dean. On August 16, 2019, a letter sent to the Provost asked that further investigation of my complaints be closed because most of the concerns leveled against the dean in the formal complaint had been dealt with. Even though the investigation was closed, the University's College and the dean, who is no longer employed by the University, continued with threats, harassment, and bullying. Basically, the dean was furious that I had "fabricated lies" against him. He and the College wrote several letters requesting that all statements made in the June 11, 2019 formal complaint letter be retracted. The first letter came from the College:

October 9, 2019

Dear Madam:

INVESTIGATION INTO "FORMAL COMPLAINT."

We refer to our invitation to a meeting of the College Ad Hoc Committee investigating the above and subsequent reminder on October 8, 2019.

At its sitting on October 8, 2019, the above mentioned Committee after some deliberation and taking cognizance of your statement that you want to bring closure to the issue under investigation, and also not interested in engaging on the matter again, decided that:

1. Due to the gravity of the allegations initially made in your formal complaint against the former Dean, you should write to withdraw and retract same.

2. To bring closure to the investigation and restore peace in the Faculty to facilitate cordial academic work early, you submit the above stated letter of retraction by October 24, 2019.

We anticipate your cooperation and prompt action to restore cordiality among staff and students in the Faculty of Law.
Thank you.
Yours faithfully,
College Secretary

On the same day (October 9, 2019, i.e., a day after I had submitted the level 400 grades and papers), the courier letter from the dean arrived, reproduced below. This letter was still further evidence that the students were joining in attempts to make me look bad and lose my job.

9th October, 2019
FORMAL COMPLAINT: XXX
We act as solicitors for XXX. Our instructions are as follows:

1. That we should initiate the appropriate legal action against you for the lies and fabricated stories you stated in your complaint letter dated 11th June, 2019 and addressed to XXX, which sought to defame the integrity and the reputation of XXX, who served as Dean of the Faculty of Law at the University from August 2017 to July 2019.
2. That the only reason why we have not commenced the said legal action against you is because we are awaiting the report of the committee which was set up by the Provost for the purpose of carrying out your request which you stated in your complaint letter as follows:
    - "An investigation be carried out to assess my experience which XXX;
    - A formal meeting is convened by you with XXX and me present;
    - Expeditious resolution of all issues pertaining to my appointment . . . ."
3. The Provost in accordance with your request established a committee to investigate your complaint.
4. The committee was scheduled to meet on 8th October, 2019 in the conference room of the Faculty of Law.
5. Our client and Mrs. Veronica Fynn Bruey were invited to the said meeting to assist the said committee in its investigative work.
6. Our client travelled all the way from Accra to attend the said meeting.
7. However, you Mrs. Veronica Fynn Bruey, the complainant upon whose request the committee was established failed to attend the meeting.

8. Be informed that we are aware (with the relevant evidence available to us) that you were at the lecture halls of the Faculty of Law and taught some students on the 8th October 2019, which lecture ended officially 12:00pm but informally continued till about 1:15pm.
9. This letter is to assure you that whether you cooperate with the committee or not we will at the appropriate time initiate the necessary legal action against you, to vindicate our client.

Be advised. Thank you.

The third harassment letter, dated February 6, 2020, was received from the Dean; this time it differed slightly from the one dated February 9:

6 February 2020
Dear Veronica Fynn Bruey,
FORMAL COMPLAINT: DEAN XXX
We act as solicitors for XXXX. Our instructions are as follows:

1. That in your complaint letter dated 11th June, 2019 and addressed to XXXX, you told and stated lies and fabricated stories, which sought to defame the integrity and the reputation of XXX, who served as Dean of the Faculty of Law at the University from August 2017 to July 2019.
2. That we have the instructions of our client to take all appropriate legal steps to vindicate his name and reputation.
3. In this regard we are to demand, which we hereby do, that you retract the said lies and fabricated stories and apologize to our client within two (2) weeks upon the receipt of this letter.
4. You are therefore given up to the 20th day of February, 2020 to retract and apologize for the defamatory words and materials you stated in your said complaint letter against our client.
5. Take note that if you fail to retract and apologize by the 20th day of February, 2020 then we have the instructions of our client to commence all appropriate legal actions and processes against you without any further notice to you.

Be advised accordingly.

Because he resigned on July 1, 2019, this dean can no longer be investigated by the University. Students loyal to this Dean were constantly passing on information from the class to him, which is why he had the "relevant evidence" about my whereabouts. To document the initial harassment letter from the dean and his loyal students, on October 17, 2019, I wrote to the vice chancellor of the University, informing him about some concerns I had with the Faculty of Law.

Re: Informing you about some concerns I have at the Faculty of Law
Dear XXX:

I trust you are well.

Firstly, let me take the opportunity to say thank you for following up on my requests by appointing a new mentor for me and ensuring that my resident permit is renewed.

I am writing to inform you that on Tuesday, 15 October 2019, I received a letter from Mr XXX's lawyer stating that he was instructed to advise me that they will be filing a lawsuit against me for "fabrication and lies" I made against Mr XXX.

I have also attached a letter from Dr XXX, the College Registrar, asking me to retract my statements against Mr XXX. In confidence, I have strong reasons to believe that the *Ad Hoc* Committee that was set up to investigate my complaints against Mr XXX is biased. They coerced me to withdraw my complaint, which I did on 18 August 2019 (see attached). Now, to ask me to retract my statements when I strongly believe everything I said in my complaint is true, is absurd. I will never do that whether under duress or being bullied. I am exhausted, frustrated and demotivated at this point.

Legally (pursuant to the Constitution of Ghana, 1992), Mr XXX has no case against me. I filed a private complaint which is not only appropriate and allowed but also that complaint is not made in the public domain. So, his claim of defamation is baseless. Secondly, if the law allows anyone to file a lawsuit against an employee who complains about a behaviour they believe to be true then society will be pervaded with injustice. Thirdly, he is no longer employed by the University , which means the University has no jurisdiction over him to conduct such investigation between he and I. He cannot persuade the *Ad Hoc* Committee to ask me to retract my complaint. Notwithstanding, I have decided to retain a personal lawyer and not engage with the Ad Hoc Committee henceforth.

Speaking of being demotivated, Mr XXX's behaviour last semester wherein he allowed students to rein down insults at me, has incited the students to continuously target and abuse me at the Law Faculty with no recourse. During the National Accreditation Board meeting in August, I (the only female faculty present) was the only person singled out by Justice XXX and attacked for not being qualified to teach Conflict of Laws in Ghana. During the final session of the meeting with the NAB in the library, a select number of students were called to speak to the NAB. These carefully selected students "reported" me to the NAB for being too difficult and having a high standard. Again, I was singled out and queried by the NAB alone, after they asked all other faculty members to leave the room. Yesterday, after receiving Mr XXX's letter, a student told me that the final year students are plotting and writing a petition on behalf of the LSU, asking the University not to allow me to teach them because my standards are too high. Mind you, these are the same students who are flunking the Ghana

Legal Council's exams in record numbers. They also connived and refused to register for my Law 421: Conflict of Laws class. The ongoing attacks and isolation are ridiculous, exhausting and frustrating. What's even more is the lack of support I am feeling from the Faculty.

I am quite disappointed and honestly do regret why I even made the choice to return home. I thought to write you and let you know.

Thank you for your time.

I never received any response to my expressed concerns, and since I was about to resign, leave Ghana, and initiate a lawsuit against the University, I shrugged off the dean's empty threat.

Throughout my employment at the University, I had been concerned that I was underemployed, treated unfairly, and discriminated against. My anxiety grew worse after I had written several letters to secure the confirmation of my employment and receive the refund of my family location cost, as specified in the appointment letter. By January 2020, the University's refusal to refund the cost of shipping our personal effects from the United States to Ghana was six months overdue. I spent precious time between August and December 2019 literally running after the University Administration for both my refund and confirmation of my employment. On January 13, 2020, I wrote to the vice chancellor of the University.

Subject: Confirmation of Employment and Reimbursement of Moving Expenses

Dear XXX:

Happy New Year! And, let me take the opportunity to also formally express my appreciation for your continuous support for me.

I am writing to you in your capacity as the Chair of the Appointment's Committee. When I last met with you in October, re: the stalling of my confirmation of employment, we agreed that by December 2019, the situation would be solved. My confirmation is now six months overdue. Before we left for the holidays, I spent hours at the administration, following up on my confirmation letter. At one instance, I sat in the reception with my baby for nearly four hours waiting for Human Resource to attend to me.

What is becoming unbearable with this delay is the reimbursement for shipping my personal effects from Seattle, WA, USA, to Ghana. As clearly stated in my letter of appointment, the cost of travel and "baggage" was going to be reimbursed one year after my commencement of employment. What was not stated in the appointment letter is that this reimbursement cost was contingent on my confirmation of employment. You will agree with me that the financial sacrifice is enormous as my husband resigned his job in order for me to take up this lecturer position at the University.

As the semester is upon us, I am overwhelmed with marking some 80 exam scripts in addition to preparing to teach two classes. I simply do not have the time and energy to be sent from office to office to search for my confirmation letter and reimbursement of shipping cost.

Professor XXX, could you please assist me? Thank you in advance and I look forward to hearing from you.

Interestingly, on the same day (January 13, 2020) I delivered the above letter to the vice chancellor, I received the letter (below) from the human resource director:

Dear Sir [on a number of occasions I was addressed as "Dear Sir"],

RE: CONFIRMATION OF APPOINTMENT

The Appointments and Promotion Board (Senior Members) at its meeting held on Wednesday, 18th December, 2019 considered among other things, the confirmation of Dr. (Mrs.) Veronica Fynn Bruey.

The Board deferred the consideration of her confirmation and appointment the current Dean of the Faculty of Law, XXX, to mentor Dr. (Mrs.) Bruey for one semester and submit to the Appointments and Promotions Board a confidential report for consideration. The decision was as a result of the resignation of the former mentor XXX which impeded the mentoring process.

We are by a copy of this letter information XXX (mentor) and Dr. (Mrs.) Bruey to act accordingly.

Clearly, the above letter was in breach of the agreement terms set forth in paragraph 3 of the appointment letter, which states:

Your appointment for a probationary period of one (1) year. On confirmation the appointment will continue for a further period of five (5) years, and is renewable subject to satisfactory service and conduct. The appointment is, however, determinable by six months' notice on either side.

Pursuant to the blatant violation of the contractual agreement with University, when efforts to be confirmed and receive the refund did not yield a favorable outcome, I considered one last option—I asked my husband to assist.

As a White man, he was met with much more respect and credence. In barely three weeks, a check written awaited a final signature when on February 14, 2020, the finance director told my husband that he had been instructed to halt the release of the check because I had not been going to work. In fact, the finance officer had been told to address a letter to me requesting the return of my January 2020 salary. The second semester had started barely two weeks earlier; I had submitted my grades on February 6 and was preparing to teach even though three of my four courses had been taken away. With no opportunity left for me to continue working in such a toxic environment, my husband and I immediately packed up all my belongings from my office and closed our local bank account to prevent deposits from the University. On February 14, 2020, the very same day the location check was dangled in front of my husband, I submitted my resignation letter.

> 14 February 2020
> Subject: Resignation
> Dear XXX:
> According to the terms of my appointment, confirmation of my appointment was to be completed at the end of my probationary period in August 2019. The confirmation of my appointment was delayed from August 2019 to December 2019. Then, on 13 January 2020 I received a letter from the Directorate of Human Resources stating that the confirmation of my appointment would be delayed again, to the summer of 2020. Finally, in an e-mail on 24 January 2020, the Faculty of Law, stripped me of my teaching responsibilities without cause or justification, further discriminating against me and undermining my position and opportunity for confirmation.
> At this point, it is clear that the University is either unwilling or unable to meet the terms of the contract embodied in my appointment letter. Therefore, I am resigning my post, effective immediately.
> Sincerely,
> Veronica Fynn Bruey, PhD, LLB (Honours), LLM, MPH, BA, BSc (Honours)
> Lecturer, Faculty of Law

On February 26, 2020, a letter from our lawyers was delivered to the vice chancellor of the University demanding that the following to be paid within fourteen days: (a) Ten thousand, eight hundred and forty-nine United States dollars, eight-three cents (USD$ 10,849.83); and (b) Two thousand nine hundred and fifty Ghana cedis (GHC 2,950.00). With no payment made, a lawsuit was filed against the University and is underway.

Strategy and Resilience

In the wake of these events, it was important that I carefully adopt strategies to vindicate me from the slander of those whose behavior denied my humanity and my expertise. One such strategy so was to allow the students to assess my teaching ability in a way that was free from bias of grades or outside influence. Number 11 of the petition above reads:

On the 8th October, 2019, she made the class assess her. For fear of victimization, some students might have rated her highly. We want to bring to the attention of the faculty and the university authority that any assessment done for that purpose is attributable to undue influence and hence not a true reflection of our assessment of her teaching.

Based on the aforementioned grounds, we demand that; . . .

First, I retyped the same course evaluation the University gives to students at the end of each semester. On October 8, 2019, I called the class president into my office and asked him to distribute the course evaluation to the class while I complete the marking of their assessment scripts. The course evaluation was completed anonymously in my absence. While I waited in my office, the class president was instructed to notify me once the class had completed the evaluations, which took about 10–15 minutes. Herewith are the results (see table 12.2). On a skill of 1 (Excellent) to 5 (Unsatisfactory), students rated the content of the course, my class attendance, and my knowledge of the subject matter. Of the forty-seven students who anonymously completed the course evaluation on the morning of October 8, 2019, 89 percent, 94 percent, and 79 percent rated the course content, attendance, and my knowledge of the subject matter, respectively, as "very good."

Here are some of the comments they made:

- Good but I suggest she gradually transition students from local perspective to international best standards.
- Detailed and well organised, always punctual, satisfactory.
- Very detailed course content, very punctual, very knowledgeable in the course content.
- Impressive, can be more tolerant.
- On point, conscious of her time, good command over communication, command over the subject matter and good at pedagogy.
- Very good, very punctual and always stayed to the end, well organised and very effective.
- Very good, very good, but please we can hardly hear you when you talk in class so if you could please slow it down or speak a bit loud for us.
- Very good, very punctual, informative, comprehensive, and regular, there is still room for improvement, should be a little flexible in marking.
- Keep it up, very good attitude towards work, please we hardly hear you when you speak in class. We would be grateful if you could speak up or slow it down a bit because of your accent.
- Keep it up, good work attitude, good articulation, eloquent, and fluent presentation on topics. Very blunt and straight to point. Quite motivative and resourceful in the areas.

Table 12.2   Students Evaluation of the Course

	Excellent	%	Very Good	%	Good	%	Satisfactory	%	Unsatisfactory
Course Content	0	0	42	89	4	0.1	1	0	0
Attendance	1	0	44	94	2	0	0	0	0
Knowledge of Subject Matter	0	0	37	79	5		4		1

- Excellent, very well to the admiration of the class, very progressive and well delivered.
- Picturesque, demonstrational.
- Impressive so far, excellent, thought provoking, educative, very well on point.
- Good but I still have not found my feet. Very punctual. Very good but the lecturer's voice should be audible enough for us to hear.
- The course content is good and serves as a guideline to students. I have learnt a lot from the lecturer. Due to the largeness of the class, not every student is able to hear what the lecturer says from the back.
- Has very good plan for student, hence she could be encouraged to do so. Very fair and accepts open minded act.
- Detailed lessons, very punctual, very systematic delivery of lectures, quite organised. Grading and assessment are satisfactory generally.
- Course content is very detailed and am pleased with the lessons. I admire her punctuality to class. Her lessons are very systematical, well organised. Great work done. She returns the assessment with expected time or duration.
- Good, excellent, satisfactory but ought to be improved through accepting or appreciating the views of students.
- Very good, excellent, but there is room for improvement.
- I enjoy the fact that we are not compelled to "chew and pour" which is a bane in my studies.

I managed to survive the ordeal for another semester, spending the December–January holiday break marking exam scripts and preparing to teach the next semester. The second semester started on January 27, 2020. Final grades for classes I taught for the first semester were submitted on February 6, 2020.

MOVING FORWARD

This was my worst experience in the sixteen years of my academic career. I hesitate to write a "conclusion" to this chapter, given the raw emotions and trauma I am still going through. Speaking up/out to challenge the subjugated and oppressive powers of patriarchy in one of Africa's entrenched colonial and xenophobic sinkholes is emancipatory in and of itself. It is my hope that young African women facing similar challenges will not be muzzled but will be inspired as agents of change. Notwithstanding the pain and trauma, the unique opportunity to live such an experience while editing a book on the subject matter in real time is priceless. Although I am not sure that I will fully recover from this experience, one thing is sure: despite the racism and other forms of discrimination I constantly endure, Canada/United States is my new home, because the rejection from my own people is worse than racism or other discrimination I experience from White people. Ticked, lessons learned, next . . .?

NOTES

1. Section 1, *Legal Profession Act,* 1960 (Act 32).
2. Schedule 1, *Legal Profession Act,* 1960 (Act 32).
3. Ghana School of Law, 2016.

REFERENCES

"93% of Students Fail Ghana School of Law Entrance Exam." 2019, September 25. *Ghana Web.* https://www.ghanaweb.com/GhanaHomePage/NewsArchive/93 -of-students-fail-Ghana-School-of-Law-entrance-exam-783594#:~:text=Over90p ercentof,representing7percentpassed.

Alcoff, Linda, and Laura Gray. 1993. "Survivor Discourse: Transgression or Recuperation?" *Signs: Journal of Women in Culture and Society* 18 (2): 260–90. https://doi.org/10.1086/494793.

Bartlett, Katharine T. 1990. "Feminist Legal Methods." *Harvard Law Review* 103 (4): 829–88. https://scholarship.law.duke.edu/faculty_scholarship/148/.

Connell, Raewyn W. 2005. *Masculinities*, 2nd edition. California: University of California Press.

Connell, R. W., and James W. Messerschmidt. 2005. "Hegemonic Masculinity: Rethinking the Concept." *Gender & Society* 19 (6): 829–59. https://doi.org/10 .1177/0891243205278639.

Crenshaw, Kimberlé. 1989. "Demarginalising the Intersection of Race and Sex: A Black Feminist Critique of Anti-discrimination Doctrine, Feminist Theory and Antiracist Politics." *University of Chicago Legal Forum* 140: 25–42. https://ch icagounbound.uchicago.edu/uclf/vol1989/iss1/8.

Fanon, Frantz. 1963. *The Wretched of the Earth.* Translated by Constance Farrington. New York: Grove Press.

Fynn Bruey, Veronica. 2016. "Systematic Gender Violence and the Rule of Law: Aboriginal Communities in Australia and Post-War Liberia." PhD thesis, Australian National University). http://hdl.handle.net/1885/159520.

Ghana School of Law. 2016. "Overview." *About Our School.* https://gslaw.edu.gh/about-2/.

Harrington, John, and Ambreena Manji. 2019. "'Africa Needs Many Lawyers Trained for the Need of Their Peoples': Struggles over Legal Education in Kwame Nkurmah's Ghana." *American Journal of Legal History* 59 (2): 149–77. https://doi.org/10.1093/ajlh/njz004.

hooks, bell. 1991. "Theory as Liberatory Practice." *Yale Journal of Law and Feminism* 4 (1): 1–2. https://digitalcommons.law.yale.edu/cgi/viewcontent.cgi?article=1044&context=yjlf.

Mama, Amina. 2011. "The Challenges of Feminism: Gender, Ethics and Responsible Academic Freedom in African Universities." *Journal of Higher Education in Africa* 9 (1–2): 1–23. https://www.jstor.org/stable/jhigheducafri.9.1-2.1.

McNay, Lois. 2016. "Agency." Pp. 39–60 in *The Oxford Handbook of Feminist Theory,* ed. Lisa J. Disch and Mary E. Hawkesworth. Oxford University Press. https://doi.org/10.1093/oxfordhb/9780199328581.001.0001.

Mendoza, Breny. 2016. "Coloniality of Gender and Power: From Postcoloniality to Decoloniality." Pp. 100–121 in *The Oxford Handbook of Feminist Theory,* ed. Lisa J. Disch and Mary E. Hawkesworth. Oxford University Press. https://doi.org/10.1093/oxfordhb/9780199328581.001.0001.

Morrell, Robert, Rachel Jewkes, and Graham Lindegger, G. 2012. "Hegemonic Masculinity/Masculinities in South Africa: Culture, Power, and Gender Politics." *Men and Masculinities* 15 (1): 11–30. https://doi.org/10.1177/1097184X12438001.

Mossman, Mary Jane. 1987. "Feminism and Legal Method: The Difference It Makes." *Wisconsin Women's Law Journal* 3 (147), 147–168. https://digitalcommons.osgoode.yorku.ca/scholarly_works/1558/.

Mustapha, S. 2018, February 21. "Law Students Reject Results after Only 91 out of 474 Students Pass Exams." *Graphic Online.* https://www.graphic.com.gh/news/general-news/law-students-reject-results-after-only-91-out-of-474-students-pass-exams.html.

National Association of Independent Schools. 2018. "Kimberlé Crenshaw: What Is Intersectionality?" June 22, 2018. *YouTube video,* 1:54. https://www.youtube.com/watch?v=ViDtnfQ9FHc.

Serbeth-Boateng, Jude. 2019, October 6. "Opening up Legal Education in Ghana." *GhanaWeb.* https://www.ghanaweb.com/GhanaHomePage/features/Opening-up-legal-education-in-Ghana-786736.

Staff Reporter. 2019a, February 27. "Ghana School of Law Lecturers Lock Horns with GLC over Poor 2018 Results." *My Joy Online.* https://www.myjoyonline.com/news/education/law-school-lecturers-lock-horns-with-glc-over-poor-2018-results/.

Staff Reporter. 2019b, September 25. "Ghana School of Law: 2019 Law School Exams Result Out; Only 128 out of 1,820 Pass." *Ghana Web.* https://www.gha

naweb.com/GhanaHomePage/NewsArchive/Ghana-School-of-Law-2019-law-school-exams-result-out-only-128-out-of-1-820-pass-783473.

Tushnet, Mark. 1990. "A Critical Legal Studies Perspective." *Cleveland State Law Review* 38(1), 137–151. https://dash.harvard.edu/handle/1/13548604.

WHO Healthy Cities Project. 2003. *The Solid Facts: Social Determinants of Health*, 2nd edition. Edited by Richard G. Wilkinson and Michael Marmot. Copenhagen: World Health Organization, Regional Office for Europe.

Woodhouse, Leighton Akio. 2018, June 28. "Trump's 'Shithole Countries' Remark Is at the Center of a Lawsuit to Reinstate Protections for Immigrants." *Intercept.* https ://theintercept.com/2018/06/28/trump-tps-shithole-countries-lawsuit/.

Index

227

About the Contributors

Dr. **Charles Amone** is an Associate Professor of History at Kyambogo University. He is a former Fulbright Scholar of the University of Millersville in Pennsylvania, USA; a former Fellow of the Institute of Languages and Communication of the University of Southern Denmark; a former Fellow of the Institute of Development Policy (IOB) of the University of Antwerp in Belgium; and a former Fellow of the Global Health Institute, Belgium. Dr. Amone specializes in cultural and ethnic studies, in which he has over thirty publications.

Johanna Bond is the Sydney and Frances Lewis Professor of Law at Washington and Lee University School of Law. Professor Bond's teaching and scholarship focuses on international human rights law and gender and the law. In 2001, Professor Bond was selected as a Senior Fulbright Scholar and travelled to Uganda and Tanzania to conduct research that later resulted in her edited book, *Voices of African Women: Women's Rights in Ghana, Uganda, and Tanzania*. Bond has published extensively in the area of women's human rights, with an emphasis on applying intersectionality theory in the context of human rights.

Dr. **Manase Kudzai Chiweshe** is a Senior Lecturer in the sociology department, University of Zimbabwe, and winner of the 2015 Gerti Hessling Award for the best paper in African studies. He is also a research associate in the sociology department, Rhodes University, South Africa. Dr. Chiweshe's work revolves around the sociology of everyday life in African spaces, with special focus on promoting African ways of knowing. His recent work has concentrated on gender, social identities, rural livelihoods, agrarian studies, and youths in agriculture, with a special focus on girls. He has published one single-author book and two co-edited books in addition to articles in journals such as *Critical African Studies, African Identities, Agenda, Agrarian South,* and *Journal of Asian and African Studies.*

Valentina Fusari is currently Post-doc and Adjunct Professor of Population, Development and Migration in the Department of Political and Social Sciences at the University of Pavia, Italy. She was previously Assistant Professor in the Department of Political Science and International Relations at College of Arts and Social Sciences in Adi Keih, Eritrea.

Bernadette Malunga holds an LLB (Honors) from the University of Malawi; a Master's in Women's Law from the University of Zimbabwe; and a Doctorate from the University of Nairobi in Kenya. She is a Lecturer at the University of Malawi, Chancellor College, where she teaches Gender and the Law and the Law of Business Organizations. Bernadette has vast experience in research on women's and children's rights. She has written and researched on a number of issues, such as women in political leadership, the girl child and the right to education, and women and sexual offences, among others.

Dr. **Fatima Mandhu** holds an LLB and LLM from the University of Zambia and PhD from the University Africa. Dr. Mandhu was admitted as an advocate of the High Court of Zambia in 1990. She is participating member of the Southern African Node under the Network of Excellence for Land Governance in Africa. She holds a professional qualification as a Chartered Secretary. She has served as Head of the Private Law Department in the School. As Head of Private Law Department, she was involved in designing programs, coordinating and promoting research supervision and activities. She has taught, *inter alia*, Medical Law and Company Law. Currently, Dr. Mandhu is a Post-doctoral Fellow and Lecturer at the University of Zambia.

Chick Loveline Ayoh Epse Ndi is a PhD student in medical anthropology at the University of Yaounde, Cameroon. She is also an inspector of social welfare, working with the Ministry of Social Welfare. Her professional and working experience is a motivation for her interest in some sensitive societal issues, which has lent support to her research and data collection on the challenges of wedlock children and people living with HIV. She has published two academic articles and a book on the challenges of stigma against people living with HIV in her community.

L. Amede Obiora has been a Professor of Law in the United States since 1992. In 1999, she received an unsolicited offer from the World Bank to manage a program to help advance substantive gender equity in Africa. In

2006, she received another unsolicited appointment to serve as the Minister of Mines and Steel Development for the Federal Republic of Nigeria. She is the recipient of several honors and awards. These include the Coca-Cola World Fund Visiting Faculty at Yale University as well as fellowships from the Center for Advanced Study in the Behavioral Sciences at Stanford, Institute for Advanced Studies at Princeton, Rockefeller Foundation Bellagio Study Center, and the Djerassi Resident Artist Program. She has been the Genest Global Faculty at Osgoode Hall Law School in Toronto and the Visiting Gladstein Human Rights Professor at the University of Connecticut. Dr. Obiora is the Founder of the Institute for Research on African Women, Children and Culture (IRAWCC).

Verena Tandrayen-Ragoobur is an Associate Professor in Economics at the University of Mauritius. Her research is on gender, the labor market, domestic violence, and poverty. She heads a Pole of Applied Socio-Economic Research and Analysis at the University, and this Pole of Research Excellence analyzes economic and social issues relevant to developing economies and produces evidence-based policies. She works closely on different projects locally with ministries and other regional and international institutions. She has published in various journals, including *Community, Work & Family*; *Equality, Diversity and Inclusion: An International Journal*; *Journal of African Business*; and the *Review of Development Economics*.

Venkatanarayanan S. is presently with Christ University, Bangalore, India. He holds a PhD in Political Science, and was earlier teaching and heading the Department of Political Science and International Relations at College of Arts and Social Sciences in Adi Keih, Eritrea.

Cheikh A. Seye obtained his PhD in Religious Studies from the Graduate Division of Religion at Emory University, Atlanta, USA. He earned a Master's in Religious Studies at Arizona State University as a Fulbright scholar. Prior, he earned an MA in English, specialized in African literature, at Gaston Berger University, Saint-Louis, Senegal, and an MPhil in English, specialized in American literature, at Cheikh Anta Diop University, Dakar, Senegal. Before coming to the United States in 2011 to further his education, Seye had served as a high school teacher of English in Senegal for a decade. Currently, he is a Post-Doctoral Fellow at the Department of Theological Studies, St. Louis University in Missouri, USA.

Dr. Ellah TM Siang'andu is a Lecturer and Post-doctoral Fellow at the University of Zambia. She teaches Criminal law and International Law. Her current research interests include Penal Law, Criminal law, African Criminal

Justice, International Law and Gender. Her most recent works include "Introduction: Understanding the Meaning, Context, Role and Importance of African Criminal Justice in Africa" in Sarkin, J. & Siangándu, E. (eds.), *African Criminal Justice* (forthcoming), and "The Use of International Criminal Law in African Countries Including the Incorporation of the Rome Statute Crimes," in Sarkin, J. & Siangándu, E. (eds.), *African Criminal Justice* (forthcoming).

About the Editor

Veronica Fynn Bruey is an award-winning interdisciplinary scholar and author whose expertise spans four continents. She has researched, taught, consulted, and presented at conferences in over twenty-five countries. She is a Module Convener at the University of London's School of Advanced Study, the Director of Flowers School of Global Health Science, a faculty affiliate at Seattle University School of Law, and a research affiliate with the University of London's Refugee Law Initiative. She is the Founder and Editor-in-Chief of the *Journal of Internal Displacement*; the Co-founder and Executive Director of Tuki-Tumarankeh; the Founder of the Law and Society's Collaborative Research Network (CRN) 11: "Displaced Peoples"; the Founder of the Voice of West African Refugees, and the lead organizer of the Law and Society Association's International Research Collaborative: "Disrupting Patriarchy and Masculinity in Africa". She has authored three books, several book chapters, and peer review articles in reputable academic journals. Veronica is a born and bred Liberian war survivor.

www.ingramcontent.com/pod-product-compliance
Lightning Source LLC
Chambersburg PA
CBHW022308280326
41932CB00010B/1026